Sovereign Credit Rating

The current degradation of sovereign balance sheets raises very real concerns about how sovereign creditworthiness is measured by credit rating agencies. Given the disastrous economic and social effects of any downgrade, the book offers an alternative and calls for more transparency about the quantitative measures used in calibrating the rating process and how sovereign ratings are validated. It argues that oversight is required and procedures improved, including subjecting methodologies of assessing default to more standardization and monitoring.

Sovereign Credit Rating explains the process of sovereign creditworthiness assessment and explores the consequences of possible inaccuracies in the process. Developing an innovative new methodology to assess ratings accuracy, it shows that the announcement of each rating action by the major credit rating agencies show alarming inconsistencies.

Written by an internationally recognized author and professor, this unique book will be of interest to researchers and advanced students in corporate governance, accounting, public finance and regulation.

Professor Ahmed Naciri is a Researcher and author at the University of Québec in Montreal. Awarded best researcher of the Administrative Sciences Association of Canada and Fellow of the CPAs Association. Founder of the International Centre for Governance, he advises governments and institutions (including the US Security Exchange Commission) in issues of best practices in public finance and governance.

Routledge Studies in Corporate Governance

1 **Corporate Governance Around the World**
Ahmed Naciri

2 **Behaviour and Rationality in Corporate Governance**
Oliver Marnet

3 **The Value Creating Board**
Corporate Governance and Organizational Behaviour
Edited by Morten Huse

4 **Corporate Governance and Resource Security in China**
The Transformation of China's Global Resources Companies
Xinting Jia and Roman Tomasic

5 **Internal and External Aspects of Corporate Governance**
Ahmed Naciri

6 **Green Business, Green Values, and Sustainability**
Edited by Christos N. Pitelis, Jack Keenan and Vicky Pryce

7 **Credit Rating Governance**
Global Credit Gatekeepers
Ahmed Naciri

8 **Mergers and Acquisitions and Executive Compensation**
Virginia Bodolica and Martin Spraggon

9 **Governance and Governmentality for Projects**
Enablers, Practices, and Consequences
Edited by Ralf Müller

10 **Sovereign Credit Rating**
Questionable Methodologies
Ahmed Naciri

Sovereign Credit Rating

Questionable Methodologies

Ahmed Naciri

LONDON AND NEW YORK

First published 2017 by Routledge

2 Park Square, Milton Park, Abingdon, Oxfordshire OX14 4RN
52 Vanderbilt Avenue, New York, NY 10017

Routledge is an imprint of the Taylor & Francis Group, an informa business

First issued in paperback 2019

British Library Cataloguing in Publication Data
A catalogue record for this book is available from the British Library

Library of Congress Cataloging in Publication Data
A catalog record has been requested

ISBN: 978-1-138-67854-5 (hbk)
ISBN: 978-0-367-87884-9 (pbk)

Typeset in Times New Roman
by Apex CoVantage, LLC

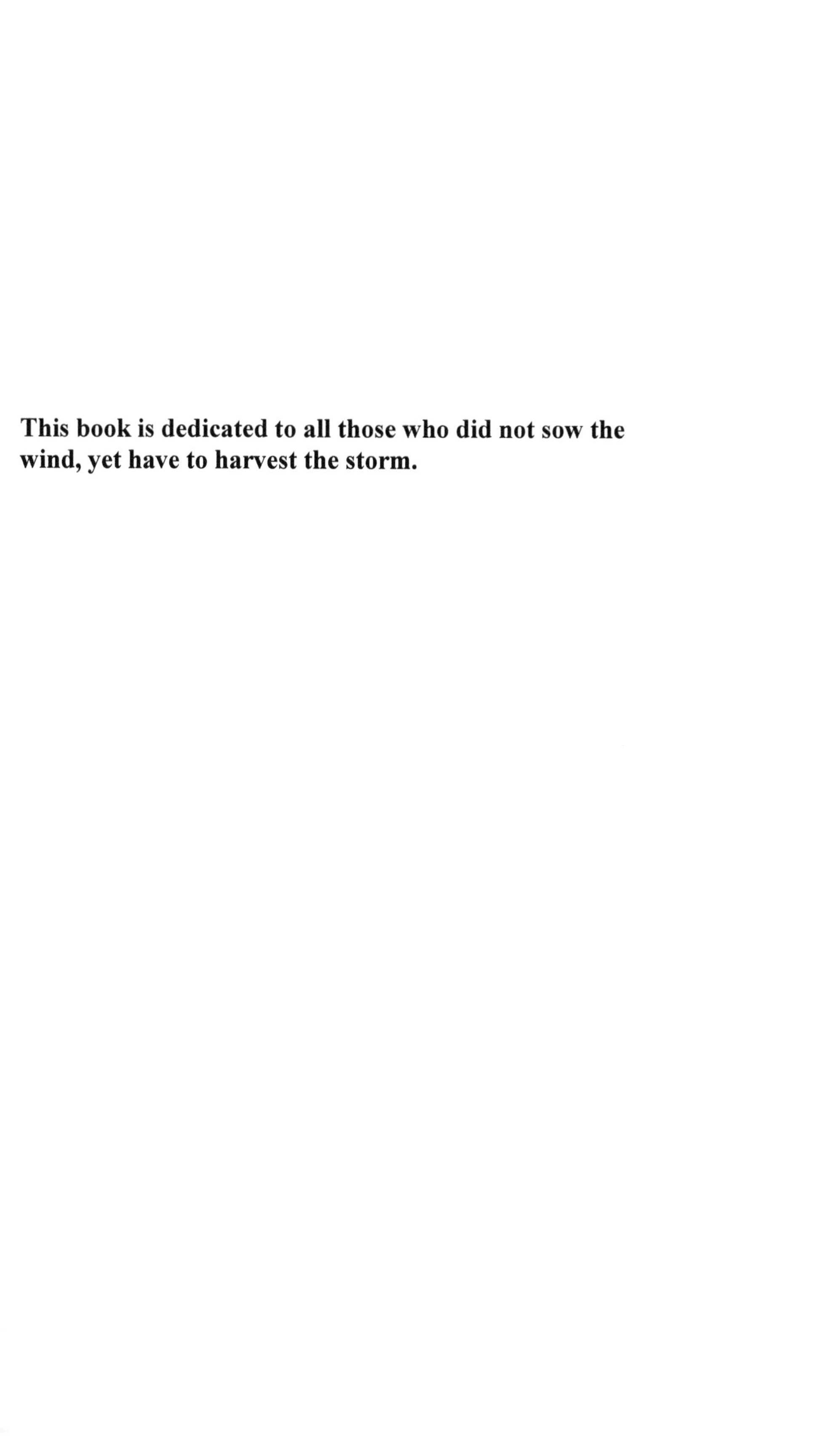

This book is dedicated to all those who did not sow the wind, yet have to harvest the storm.

Contents

Figures

Tables

Appendices

Abbreviations

ABS	Asset-backed securities
AC	Audit committee of the Board
AR	Accuracy ratio
AFS	Australian financial services
APEC	Asia-Pacific Economic Cooperation
ASIC	Australian Securities and investments Commission
A.M. Best	Alfred M. Best Ratings
BCBS	Basel Committee on Banking Supervision
BIS	Bank of International Settlement
BIG 3	Fitch Rating, Moody's and Standard and Poor's
Bill, bn	Billion
Cap	Capacity to service debt
CDO	Collateralised debt obligation
CDS	Credit default swap
CEO	Chief executive of operations
CEREP	Central repository (of the European Securities and Markets Authority, ESMA)
CF	Cash flow
CFR	Council of Foreign Relations
CGFS	Committee on the Global Financial System
CPSS	Committee on Payment and Settlement Systems
CR	Credit Rating
CRA	Credit Rating Agency
CPG	Credit Policy Group CPG
CRP	Credit Rating Provider
CAP	Cumulative accuracy profile
CFR	Council of foreign currency
DAGONG	Chinese Rating Agency
DBRS	Dominion Bond Rating Service
DFATA	Department of Foreign Affairs and Trade, Australia, 2009
EC	European Commission
ECB	European Central Bank
ECORES	Economic resiliency
$_{n}ECORES$	Economic resiliency translated in numerical ranking

$r_nECORES$	Economic resiliency in restated numerical ranking
ECOSTR	Economic strength
$_nECOSTR$	Economic strength translated in numerical ranking
$r_nECOSTR$	Economic strength in restated numerical ranking
EDF	Expected Default Frequency,
EJR	Elgon-Jones Ratings Company
ECB	European Central Bank
EU	European Union
ETF	Exchange traded funds
ESMA	European Securities and Markets Authority
EME	Emerging market economies
EU	European Union
FC	Foreign currency
FIDC	Federal Deposit Insurance Corporation.
FINMA	Swiss Market authority FINMA
FSB	Financial Stability Board
FASB	Financial Accounting Standards Board
FCIC	US Financial Crisis Inquiry Commission
FINSTR	Financial strength
$_nFINSTR_i$	Financial strength translated in numerical ranking
$r_nFINSTR$	Financial strength in restated numerical ranking
FISSTR	Fiscal strength
$_nFISSTR$	Country fiscal strength in translated numerical ranking
$r_nFISSTR$	Country fiscal strength in restated numerical ranking
GDP	Gross National Product
GNI	Gross national income
GNP	Gross national product
G7	Group of seven
IA	Internal Audit
IAIS	International Association of Insurance Supervisors
IAS	International Accounting Standard
IASB	International Accounting Standards Board
IET	Interest equalization tax
ICRA	Investment Information and Credit Rating Agency
IDR	Issuer default rating
IIA	Institute of Internal Auditors
IPMR	Identification, prevention, monitoring and resolution model.
HR Ratings	HR Ratings Mexico
IFRS	International Financial Reporting Standards
IMF	International Monetary Fund
INSSTR	Institustional strength
$_nINSSTR$	Institutional strength translated in numerical ranking
$r_nINSSTR$	Institutional strength in restated numerical ranking
IOSCO	International Organization of Securities Commissions
JCR	Japanese Credit Rating Agency

KBRA	Kroll
MAS	Monetary Authority of Singapore
LC	Local currency
mil	Million
MLI	Multilateral lending institutions
NAIC	National Association of Insurance Commissioners
NFTA	North American Free Trade Agreement
NRSRO	Nationally Recognized Statistical Rating Organization
NTR	Numerically translated ratings
Ob	Objective component
OECD	Organization for Economic Cooperation and Development
OLS	Ordinary least square
PBB	Primary budget balance
PV	Present value
RATRAN	Government bond rating range
$_{n}RATRAN$	Government bond rating range in translated numerical ranking
$r_{n}RATRAN$	Government bond rating range in restated numerical ranking
RMBS	Residential Mortgage-Backed Security
RNTR	Agencies restated numerically translated ratings
R2	R square
SCR	Sovereign credit rating
SCDS	Sovereign credit default swap
SDS	Sovereign debt service
SEC	Securities and Exchange Commission (US)
SIV	Structured investment vehicles
S&P	Standard & Poor's
SPE	Special Purpose Entity
SPV	Special Purpose Vehicle
SRCB	Standing Rating Committee of the Board
SRM	Sovereign rating model
Sub	Subjective component
SUSRIS	Susceptibility to event risk
TRC	Technical rating committee
$_{n}SUSRIS$	Susceptibility to event risk in in translated numerical ranking
$r_{n}SUSRIS$	Susceptibility to event risk in in restated numerical ranking
UK	United Kingdom
UKA	The United Kingdom Authorities
US, USA	United States of America
USD, US$	US dollar
WB	World Bank
Wil	Willingness to service debt

Preface

Indebtness plays a major role in economic development and nations' economic growth. Sovereign countries use sovereign debt to face budgetary constraints, and their solvency is assessed through credit ratings provided by specialised private institutions, called credit rating agencies. Such ratings are supposed to give investors confidence in investing in countries seeking foreign capital and therefore in need of demonstrating credit standing. Three major agencies: Fitch Ratings, Moody's Investors Service and Standard & Poor's (S&P) dominate the global credit scenery and have their say in every dollar of debt allocation throughout the planet. However, they also are suspected of many financial market ills, even for instilling inaccuracy in the ratings. Inaccuracy of the sovereign rating, especially in case of downgrades, can entail disastrous consequences for the issuing sovereign; increases in the cost of indebtedness, refusal to be financed, and social unrest are but few consequences of a credit rating demotion. Besides, the uncertainty produced by shaky credit ratings always creates other types of financing problems, eventually leading to a so-called money market freeze, where, in emergency cases commercial banks might be compelled to seek refinancing from their central bank. It also may lead to an invisible form of financial distress, as private-sector investors may be forced to liquidate potentially risky sovereign bonds, and government institutions may have to absorb the surplus (Sivy, 2011). Finally, as credit ratings convey information to the market about sovereigns' credit quality, a downgrade can lead to a decrease in the potential of indebtedness and to an increase in the certification cost, ultimately supported by borrowers (Faulkender et al., 2006).

In an unprecedented endeavour, this book studies agencies' approach to sovereign credit rating assessment, only to discover many methodological limitations that add up to the important body of classical shortcomings agencies are already blamed for. Two main groups of tests of sovereign rating accuracy are performed in this book: (i) the group of tests aiming to study the soundness of the approach used by agencies and (ii) the group of tests concentrating on the level of accuracy and transparency of the model used by agencies. The book deals with the inaccuracy that may originate from eventual methodological shortcomings within the process of sovereign creditworthiness assessment. Inaccuracies that eventually will be discovered in the book should, therefore, be interpreted in conjunction with the classical limits agencies are already subjected to.

The book replicates agencies' approach to assessing sovereign solvency, using agencies data on the basis, however, of a more defendable theoretical model, and it is surprising to find out how the results deviate from their theoretical stand. Many facets of agencies' approach to sovereign creditworthiness assessment are questioned, the book unearths, for instance, situations where approximation at different stages of agencies' approach may seriously jeopardise rating quality and fairness. It further shows how the scale, opted for by agencies, can neither be summed up nor averaged, without hazardous guesstimates. It shows also how the drivers used by agencies are not uniform across types of rating actions or geographic regions (IMF, 2011), allowing much estimation, susceptible of casting doubt about the rationality of the whole process. The book also challenges the undue complication introduced to the approaches of assessing sovereign solvency, on the basis that excess of variables in any model may decrease its accuracy, while increasing its opacity and favouring information asymmetry. The book concludes that it is currently impossible for anyone to replicate agencies' current process and therefore assess the accuracy of their ratings.

Like for previous critics, agencies response takes in a single argument that sovereign ratings are just opinions whose main objective is clustering countries by defaulting and non-defaulting. Consequently, according to them, the processes are sound, and based on the efficient rating committee system. Unfortunately rating committees were recently seriously challenged for their subjectivity. Further, CRAs are constantly underlining that ratings are not a market's perception of the probability of default and claim that their ratings' sole objective is to express ordinal risk rankings only and do not seek any cardinal classification. Such argument would be acceptable if it were not for the devastating effects any undue downgrade can have on sovereigns, especially when it makes them cross the threshold to the hell of the speculative zone; it also ignores the fact that ratings are used for the evaluation of debt securities on the market and therefore their classification on the risk-return plan. The question of knowing if a rating model that is limited only to an ordinal ranking of sovereign defaulters, while scarifying its cardinal characteristic can still be considered accurate, is raised.

While common sense cannot be dismissed from agencies' sovereign rating process, the finding of the book raises, however, the possibility that the door may find itself wide open to eventual actions that can be of great harm to rated sovereigns and to the fairness of the system. It finally calls for a more efficient monitoring of credit agencies, not in the sense of an increase in the requirements and/or in their volume, but rather by decreasing them, while targeting the most efficient among them, like, for instance, seeking more standardisation of the methodologies and ensuring their real transparency, for the sake of replication. Agencies were recently subjected to legal monitoring from several national authorities, like the United States Securities and Exchange Commission or the European Security Market Authority and others. A rules-based approach to monitoring agencies was privileged, instead of the principles-based despite its higher efficiency. The book indeed argues the rules-based approach monitoring cannot ensure accuracy of the ratings, since it is the kind of system where an agency concedes to disclosure, only to free itself from legal requirements. The principles-based approach to compliance is where agencies will consent to disclosing all the necessary information to allow their users to gain a real understanding of the rating process and to be in a position to replicate them. Agencies seem to have actually initiated a runaway cycle, a sort of a "catch me if you can" system, e.g. constantly creating new needs for their services, the kind of services for which legislation is unable to keep pace with. It is even feared that "the more government has power and is meddling with rating agencies, the more the rating agencies will be browbeaten in to giving a generous rating to the sovereign" (Council on Foreign Relations). For this reason the rules-based approach to monitoring agencies may not work and it may even be enough of requiring agencies through a principles-based approach to be really transparent about their methodology of assessing credit risk. CRAs that love to be generously paid for their credit ratings should take the whole responsibility for their accuracy, instead of constantly disclaiming responsibility.

1 Introduction to the book

Sovereign credit ratings, SCR, are evaluations of the creditworthiness of governments and are determined by specialised private institutions, called credit rating agencies, CRA. The main use of sovereign credit ratings is to orient investors in government bonds investment; to help them assess the likelihood that the sovereign issuer will be able to face its debt financial obligations. Sovereign credit ratings may also play another determining role, especially for emerging and developing countries. They may give investors confidence in investing in emerging and developing environments seeking foreign capital and therefore in need of demonstrating transparency and credit standing. Although sovereign credit ratings may play a major role in global capital allocation and efficiency, they were recently subject of controversies. Three major agencies, Fitch Ratings, Moody's Investors Service and Standard & Poor's (S&P), together called the Big 3, dominate the global credit allocation, but are also blamed for many of its ills. The Big 3 were especially accused of opacity and recently subjected to legal monitoring. Among the Big 3, Moody's seems to have improved more significantly its disclosure procedures and appears to constitute the best bet. For this reason and for simplification purpose, Moody's and the Big 3 will be interchangeably used in this book and Moody's should even be praised for its improved disclosure efforts.

This chapter starts by introducing the reader to the activity of sovereign rating, its history, it role, its definition and principles, its approach and accuracy, and finally the methodology of the book and synopses. It concludes for a need of methodological upgrading and monitoring efficiency improvement, not necessarily an increasing surveillance.

The activity of sovereign rating

Sovereign credit rating seems to have a long history, the first general government bonds is thought to have been issued by the city of Amsterdam around 1517, but the first bond issued by a national government was sold by the Bank of England in 1694, for the purpose of raising money to fund a war against France.[1] Similarly, sovereign defaults have been a fact of life throughout history (Gianviti et al., 2010); in fact, countries like Austria, Greece, Germany, Italy, Portugal, and Spain have each experienced at least one case of sovereign default since 1824

(Zettelmeyer, 2006). Germany alone has defaulted on its sovereign debt three times in the past 100 years (Kratzmann, 1982). Actually, Germany's constitutional court has explicitly recognised the state's right to free itself from an excessive debt burden by means of declaring bankruptcy Looking back to 1929, Poor's Publishing already rated Yankee bonds that were issued by more than twenty-one sovereign governments. A Yankee bond is a bond denominated in U.S. dollars and that was publicly issued in the U.S. by foreign banks and corporations (Bahtia, 2002). According to the Securities Act of 1933, Yankee bonds must first be registered with the Securities and Exchange Commission (SEC) before they can be sold. They are often issued in tranches and each offering can be as large as $1 billion (Investopedia). Table 1.1 gives the repartition of the Yankee bonds by issuer in the year 1929.

Sovereign defaults spiked during the 1930s depression and by 1939 all European sovereign were in the speculative grade, except the United Kingdom and later in the same year most sovereign ratings were suspended during the whole World War II period, with the exception of those on Canada, the United States, and few South American republics. Yankee bonds will be rated again by S&P and Moody's, only after World War II, but the new momentum in the sovereign rating activity will be discouraged again by the introduction of the so called interest equalisation tax (IET), by the United States in 1963. Its withdrawal in 1974 will however give a new start to the sovereign activity and will allow the main agencies to dominate the market, securing themselves a combined market share of about 95 per cent of all ratings revenue (Beers and Chambers, 1999). Although more than 100 credit rating agencies globally issue credit, this book will focus on only the three biggest among them. These are Fitch Ratings, Moody's Investors Service and Standard & Poor's (S&P). The sovereign rating coverage of these three largest agencies dwarfs that of the rest of the agencies around the world, and put them in a position where they count for very little on the global credit market. The Big 3 have a lot in common; they for instance share comparable approaches of ratings and ratings definitions. Table 1.2 gives major rating agency statements on what their ratings are designed to measure.

The three statements are similar and have in common the disclaiming statement of any responsibility regarding the predictive value of ratings of any specific frequency of default or loss that can be used with high confidence in decision

Table 1.1 The repartition of the Yankee bonds by issuer in the year 1929

Region	*Country*
Asia	Australia, China and Japan
Europe	Austria, Belgium, Denmark, Finland, France, Germany, Greece, Hungary, Italy, Norway and the United Kingdom
North America	Canada and the United States
South America	Argentina, Chile, Colombia, Peru and Uruguay

Source: adapted from Bahtia (2002).

Table 1.2 Rating agency statements on what their ratings are designed to measure

Agency	*Statements on what the rating is designed to measure*
Fitch	According to Fitch, credit ratings assess risk in relative rank order (as ordinal measures). They are not predictive of a specific frequency of default or loss. Fitch warns that credit ratings do not directly address any risk other than credit risk and do not deal with the risk of a market value loss on a rated security "due to changes in interest rates, liquidity and other market considerations."
Moody's	Moody's underlines the fact that ratings are intended to convey opinions of the relative creditworthiness of issuers and obligations.
Standard & Poor's	According to Standard & Poor's credit ratings are designed primarily to provide relative rankings among issuers and obligations of overall creditworthiness; the ratings are not measures of absolute default probability. Creditworthiness encompasses likelihood of default and also includes payment priority, recovery, and credit stability.

Source: Fitch, Moody's and Standard & Poor's

making. Such disclaiming appears so strong to the point where one may wonder what is the practical usefulness of ratings, if they cannot be used as predictors of risk of default. Theoretically, however, sovereign credit rating activity is suggested to allow the aggregation of the information about the credit quality of sovereign borrowers and their related debt offerings and further sovereigns seek ratings so that they and their private sector borrowers can access global capital markets and attract foreign investment, thereby adding liquidity to markets that would otherwise be illiquid (IMF, 2010). Previous academic literature has only focused on differences in sovereign rating quality between the major rating agencies; this book aims at a different objective, namely assessing the accuracy of the approach used by agencies in assessing sovereign default.

In theory and potentially CRAs are supposed to provide three kinds of services, basically: an information service, a monitoring service, and a certification service. Indeed, since investors have often less knowledge, compared with issuers, about the factors that determine sovereign credit quality, CRAs consequently are in a position where they can address an important problem of asymmetric information, between sovereign debt issuers and investors. Asymmetric information exists when a sovereign debt issuer has more or superior information compared with investors. CRAs might therefore provide an independent evaluation and assessment of the ability of sovereign issuers to meet their debt obligations. They might actually provide "information services" that aims three distinct objectives (IMF, 2010):

(i) The reduction of information costs
(ii) The increase of the pool of potential borrowers
(iii) The promotion of the liquidity of the markets.

Further, CRAs may also provide valuable "monitoring services" through which they can influence issuers to take corrective actions to avert downgrades via "watch" procedures. This is equivalent to a contractual provision between the issuer and the CRA where the former takes the engagement to undertake specific actions to mitigate the risk of a downgrade (Boot et al., 2006). Accurate sovereign ratings may help strengthen the fundamentals of sovereign balance sheets, especially in those countries facing immediate strains. They may encourage sovereigns to enhance the quality of their balance sheets, by following a credible path to ensure fiscal sustainability (see the October 2010 *World Economic Outlook* and the November 2010 *Fiscal Monitor*).

Finally, a sovereign credit rating can be seen as a certification service, where the CRA insures investors of the capacity and willingness of the issuer to meet its financial commitments regarding interest payments and repayment of principal, on a timely basis. This is supposed to be reached through the measurement of the relative risk that an entity or transaction will fail. "A sovereign is typically deemed to default when it fails to make timely payment of principal or interest on its publicly issued debt, or if it offers a distressed exchange for the original debt (IMF, 2010).

In order to assess sovereign credit ratings, CRAs map the relative risks into discrete rating grades that are usually expressed in terms of alphabetic rankings. For example Moody's rates sovereign issuers from the most creditworthy to the least using Aaa, Aa, A and Baa, Ba, B, Caa, Ca and C. Similarly, Fitch and S&P use AAA, AA, A, BBB, BB, B, CCC, CC, C and D. Modifiers are also added to distinguish and rank ratings within each of the general classifications. In this regard, Moody's uses numbers, e.g., Aa1, Aa2, Aa3; Fitch and S&P use pluses and minuses, e.g., AA+ and AA−. As a general rule, rating symbols above Baa3 for Moody's or BBB− for Fitch and S& P are considered investment grades. These are bonds that are considered by CRAs as likely enough to meet payment obligations. Inversely rating symbols under Ba1 for Moody's and BB+ for both Fitch and S&P included down to Caa/CCC are considered speculative. These are bonds that are judged by the rating agency as unlikely to meet debt payment obligations. CRAs usually signal in advance their intention to consider rating changes, Fitch, Moody's, and S&P, for example, all use negative "review" or "watch" notifications to signal a short term downgrade potential, i.e., a downgrade is likely to happen within the next 90 days. They also use a negative "outlook" notification to signal a medium term downgrade potential, i.e., to point to a potential for a downgrade within the next two years for investment-grade credit and one year in the case of speculative-grade. Although agencies' rankings can have different scales for different debt terms, the discussion in this book concentrates solely on long-term debt rating scales.

Fundamental sovereign credit risk analysis

The CRAs determine sovereign ratings using a range of quantitative and qualitative factors, with which they try to measure a country's ability and willingness to face its yearly debt obligations (interest payments and capital reimbursement). Some factors differentiate the rating of sovereigns over and above other instrument ratings. One of them is the concept of "willingness to pay." Such a concept reflects the potential risk that even if a sovereign had the *capacity* to pay, it may not be willing to do so, whenever it judges the social or political costs to be too high. To capture this willingness element, CRAs assess a range of qualitative factors such as institutional strength. Table 1.3 summarises key factors used by CRAs in sovereign credit rating assessments, and extended discussion of the methodology can be found in Chapter 6.

Major CRAs have recently gained remarkable notoriety, equivalent to a market authority and impacting almost as the state itself, by deriving their influence from three sources: (i) the perceived information content of the ratings; (ii) the incorporation of the ratings into financial regulations which used to given the force of law; and (iii) the incorporation of the ratings in private investment rules (Bruner and Abdelal, 2005). There is, however, another more fundamental reason why investors would want to rely on ratings, irrespective of the previously cited reasons; it is, after all, extremely costly for the average investor to undertake the necessary analysis to rate a sovereign debt. Social efficiency may, of course, suggest trusting a third party with this function, as it may prove beneficial for all the parties involved, conditional that the accuracy of the ratings is assured.

Following the recent crisis, along with the US and the European sovereign downgrades, questions are insistently being asked again about the usefulness of CRAs and the accuracy of their sovereign credit risk assessments. Indeed, such questionings can be encountered going back to the 1990s. CRAs have then been accused of mingling with market efficiency. They were also accused, during the 1997 Asian crisis, of being too slow initially to downgrade East Asian sovereigns, and subsequently of downgrading them more than the worsening fundamentals justified. Such concerns become relevant whenever one of the two following condition is met: when ratings actually influence markets and when ratings are inaccurate and/or ill timed. Empirical tests show that sovereign ratings do in fact influence markets, although more via credit warnings ("outlooks," "reviews" and

Table 1.3 Key factors used by CRAs in sovereign credit rating assessments

Agency	*Key factors in sovereign credit rating assessments*
Fitch	Macroeconomic policies, performance, and prospects; structural features of the economy; public finances; external finances
Moody's	Economic strength; institutional strength; financial strength of the government; susceptibility to event risk
Standard & Poor's	Political risk; economic structure; economic growth prospects; fiscal flexibility; general government debt burden; offshore and contingent liabilities; monetary flexibility; external liquidity; external debt burden

Source: Fitch (2010); Moody's (2008); and Standard and Poor's (2008).

"watches") than through actual rating changes and more significantly when the investment-grade threshold is crossed.

Agencies define rating "accuracy" on an ordinal (rank ordered) basis. They often claim that their ratings are supposed to reflect ordinal risk rankings. In fact, they constantly make it clear concerning sovereign rankings that their ratings do not aim for a mapping of default risk measures into rating grades, and in a mood of half-empty/half-full glass, they constantly pretend that their rating processes only involve forming views about the likelihood of obvious scenarios and not forecasting them. Moody's, however, with what might be considered as a contradictory statement, underlines that although ratings typically are not defined as precise default rate estimates, there is an expectation that they will, on average, relate to subsequent default frequency. In any case, empirical analysis shows that CRAs rank sovereign default risk in a way that defaults tend to cluster in the lowest rating grades, particularly over short time horizons. This suggests that in regulatory situations in which cardinal accuracy is important, such as in the Basel II standardised approach, credit ratings need to do more than just produce measures showing that defaults tend to cluster in the lowest rating grades. CRAs' approach to sovereign default assessment seems, however, to exclude any cardinal accuracy and to lack real transparency. "A judgment flawed by a $2 trillion error speaks for itself," argued the U.S. Government Treasury representative, with regard to the S&P downgrade of the U.S. Government credit rating in 2011 (*The Wall Street Journal*, 2011). Given the important role played by CRAs on the global financial market, they ought therefore be subjected to the same rigorous tests that are expected of their users, and an assessment of the quality of their ratings is as legitimate as necessary and so the transparency and the replication of the methods of measurement. For this reason, more analysis of CRAs' methodology is required, and this constitutes an objective of the book.

Methodology of the book

The recent weakening of sovereign solvency, combined with the many sovereign resounding downgrades, has strongly focused attention on credit rating agencies and their rating methodology. Many are wondering whether CRAs' credit risk assessments are accurate and whether they play at all any useful role in global market stability and efficiency (IMF, 2010). Empirical analysis, however, shows that sovereign ratings, despite their questionable accuracy, do have a significant impact on the funding costs of sovereign issuers and on the global credit allocation. They consequently must be considered a financial stability issue, and the situation invites by itself more care in assessing sovereign default. CRAs constantly claim strong accuracy for their ratings, and when evaluating their own performance as proof of such accuracy, they only focus on their discriminatory power and stability, e.g. their power to steadily differentiate ex-ante between potential defaulters and non-defaulters and where the performed tests are only intended to discover if defaults tend to take place among the lowest rating categories. Honestly, a far more simplified and far less costly test can allow reaching such an objective. Moreover, the so highly publicised discriminatory power of sovereign ratings is, to some extent, only partially validated, as 25 per cent of sovereign defaults are among investment-grade (Naciri, 2015). Further, as ratings seem to be relative, e.g. they are ordinal rankings not cardinal, meaning that in order to rate one sovereign nation one must consider the fundamentals of all nations in the world (Vernazza et al., 2014), classifying issuers in defaulters and non-defaulters may not be enough for enhancing market efficiency, since capital allocation on the global market is based on risk classification and not only on partially discriminating between defaulters and non-defaulters. Although agencies seem to show extreme confidence in the quality of their ratings, and even if such confidence can be proven on a macro level (which does not seem to be the case), inaccuracy of sovereign rating may be feared at the micro level, because the model used by CRAs may not be able to cover all the situations allowed/required by their scaling process, e.g. the model used by CRAs may not fit the data and risks therefore not rating adequately individual sovereigns.

This book raises the possibility that agencies' ratings may indeed be flawed. It focuses on how top CRAs assess sovereign default and whether they inadvertently rate sovereign debt inaccurately and concludes that CRAs' methodologies may affect their sovereign ratings quality. Given, however, the limited number of actual sovereign defaults constrains back-testing of any empirical model (IMF, 2010) and having no means of evaluating the work of rating committees, our investigation will be limited to the measurable aspects of agencies' approach, we consequently limit this book investigation to the study of the approach used by agencies for the purpose of determining its accuracy. The data used are CRAs' own, taken from their publications, mainly as summarised in Moody's (2013a). Our hypothesis will therefore be that agencies' model contains impacting limitations preventing accuracy of sovereign ratings.

Book synopsis

The following gives an overview of issues covered in the book, by chapter:

Chapter 1, *Introduction*, summarises the content of the book, concludes with an assessment of a number of weaknesses, argues that, given their use, credit ratings should be subjected to the same rigorous conditions that are expected from any finance ranking of risk, and raises the possibility that agencies' ratings may indeed be inadvertently flawed. It focuses on how top CRAs assess sovereign default and whether they inadvertently rate individual sovereigns inaccurately and concludes that CRAs' methodologies may affect the quality of their individual sovereign ratings.

Chapter 2, *General sample and general methodology*, explains the general sample and the general methodology followed in the book. Given the book's main objective, e.g. the assessment of the accuracy of CRAs' sovereign credit ratings at two levels; at the approach followed by main agencies and at the accuracy of the final output and its transparency; the chapter also exposes different analyses on which different tests are based: regression analysis, constant analysis, residual analysis and gap analysis.

Chapter 3, *Sovereign credit universe*, introduces the world of sovereign credit rating and shows how most countries issue sovereign debt to generate funding for their general operations and development. It underlines that, from a credit rating perspective, a sovereign issuer is a government that has special unique prerogatives that allow it to raise taxes, to set laws and to control the supply of money, and how this makes it more creditworthy. The chapter deals with sovereign activity and rating activity, sovereign issuers, sovereign defaulters, rating agencies, sovereign credit market, sovereign defaulters profile and the trends in credit quality and the distribution of sovereign ratings.

Chapter 4, *Macroeconomic environment of sovereign default*, deepens macroeconomic conditions of sovereign default and indicates that most defaults seem to have happened when, for instance, a sovereign's previous fiscal or monetary policies left it little room for manoeuver, or when economic policy did not support sustained economic growth, leading investors' perception to shift quickly. The chapter also defines sovereign debt and the sovereign global credit market, examines the relationship between debt levels and growth, discusses the link between public default and financial crisis, examines sovereign ratings pro-cyclicality and asymmetry, examines what happens when a sovereign defaults, explains how business risk and financial risk can be entangled into each other and affect each other and examines the place of sovereign ratings and the global sovereign credit market within economic environment.

Chapter 5, *The history of sovereign ratings and the emergence of the three major sovereign credit agencies*, underlines the fact that discussion of the sovereign rating environment will facilitate a greater understanding of the function and evolution of sovereign credit rating and default. It concentrates on those agencies that control the global sovereign credit market and discusses sovereign market history, discusses a short history of major sovereign rating agencies, underlines sovereign debt development, discusses sovereign defaulters' history, introduces three cases of modern sovereign default, analyses the trends in sovereign credit ratings, analyses the credit rating industry business models and discusses the regulation of the rating agencies and the Nationally Recognized Statistical Rating Organizations system.

Chapter 6, *Agencies' methodology to sovereign default assessment*, examines the methodology of establishing sovereign credit ratings used by the Big 3, namely Fitch Ratings, Moody's Investors Service and Standard & Poor's and underlines how they may differ slightly only, in how their information is aggregated into a single rating. Although emphasis is placed on Moody's approach, as it is the one that allows access to more comprehensive information regarding methodology, the chapter briefly describes what sovereign rating assessment means, describes each big agency approach to sovereign trustworthiness assessment and engages in a synthesis discussion of agencies' methodology.

Chapter 7, *Testing the accuracy of agencies approach*, indicates how the limited number of actual sovereign defaults may constrain back-testing of any empirical model when trying to determine a sovereign's creditworthiness. It shows how such a situation has limited the investigation to the study of the internal approach used by agencies, for the sake of determining its rationale and soundness. The chapter discusses some main sovereign rating critics; presents the methodology of assessing the accuracy of CRAs' sovereign rating approach; explains the process of translating agencies' alphabetical data in numerical ranking and the process of restating of the translated agencies' data; and discusses the empirical results of regression analysis, the Constant analysis, the Residuals analysis and Gaps' analysis.

Chapter 8, *Subjectivity and asymmetry, why accuracy in sovereign ratings should not be expected*, explains why inaccuracy in sovereign credit rating can be expected and raises the possibility that excess of information may obscure the real picture of rating and may serve as a means of asymmetry of information, instead of clarifying it. In any case this indeed gives rating committees more latitude in deciding the ratings. The chapter raises the possibility that rating may not translate the real sovereign financial capacity to face its debt. The chapter concludes that the simpler may prove here again to be the better. Using agencies' approach of assessing sovereign rating as an example, the chapter shows how very few variables would be better in explaining CRAs' ratings and sovereign failure and concludes that the simpler may prove, here again, to be the better.

Chapter 9, *Disclosure and transparency, the quest of accuracy in the sovereign ratings*, adds a milestone to the inaccuracy construct of sovereign ratings, by underlying transparency weaknesses of the rating system disclosure. It deals with the principles-based and the rules-based approaches to disclosure, underlines the damaging effect of sovereign ratings approximation, and shows how disclosure does necessarily match transparency or reinforces information asymmetry. It underlines the damaging effect of sovereign ratings approximation and the risk of rating manipulation due to weak disclosure.

Chapter 10, *Concluding remarks*, discusses major limitations found and risks some solutions, underlines how a number of limitations in the rating process can threaten accuracy, discusses CRAs' sovereign disclosure and transparency as the new form of information asymmetry, examines international harmonization of sovereign credit rating, concludes that gains of accuracy are still needed and are possible within sovereign credit rating activity, and argues that oversight of CRAs should include improvement of their procedures, including their methodologies of assessing sovereign default that need to be subjected to an appropriate standardization.

Self-improvement measures taken by the credit rating agencies

Under intense pressure major CRAs have, since the onset of the financial crisis, taken steps to improve the quality of their ratings, their corporate governance, and transparency. They have conducted rating reviews across asset classes, revised ratings where necessary, and updated criteria and models with new factors and assumptions (Moody's, 2013a). Several CRAs have improved staff training and teamed up with ranking academic institutions. There has been also a further emphasis on the publication of the underlying research, as well as revamped external websites to enhance transparency. For example, given the intensification of the global financial crisis, there has been a particular emphasis on publishing better and more accessible research on sovereign creditworthiness. In order to enhance their governance, the major CRAs have revised their codes of conduct to conform to the updated IOSCO code of May 2008, focusing on the quality and integrity of the ratings process and reducing conflicts of interest. Some CRAs have updated their fee policies to ensure a clearer separation between their core rating activities and other business development activities, and clarified the definition of "ancillary business," e.g. what is not included in the core rating business. Also, and in line with the recently approved U.S. financial sector reform bill, several CRAs have implemented "look-back" reviews, e.g. reviews of historical ratings when a rating analyst leaves a CRA to join an organisation that was previously rated by him. Despite efforts so far, conflicts of interest may persist and will require a further fix.

Conclusion

In a philosophy of having its cake and eat it too, CRAs love to be paid generously for their assessment of sovereign creditworthiness and seem to use any restraint, judging by the level of their margins (around 45 per cent, according to the SEC), but at the same time fiercely disclaim any responsibility for any inaccuracy of the rating, Moody's, for instance, stresses the fact that although the ratings process involves forming views about the likelihood of plausible scenarios, or outcomes, it does not forecast them, but instead places some weight on their likely occurrence and on the potential credit consequences, although CRAs seem to be recently fine-tuning their rating methodologies and the sovereign ratings may have been recently performed somewhat better. However, this book unearths many areas of the rating process where it still has scope to capture more effectiveness, for the sake of sovereign ratings accuracy. There seems to be little theoretical or empirical foundation for several components of the sovereign ratings, and subjectivity seems to play a major role (Vazzema et al., 2014). This book tries to uncover some of the shortcomings in agencies' approach to sovereign ratings, and concludes that the way the situation is presenting itself today a country could find itself battling with a speculative status, due only to approximation in the process of sovereign creditworthiness assessment. The chapter also explores some avenues of solution and suggests, as model of sovereign rating standardisation, rules inspired from the provisions of Sarbanes/Oxley regarding external auditing. A welcome contribution of the CRAs would be the standardisation of credit risk metrics that would make the message embedded in a rating more transparent and would also allow more relevant tests of accuracy.

Note

1 https://en.wikipedia.org/wiki/Government_bond.

2 General sample and general methodology

Sovereign debt issuers, like investors and regulators, all over the world, seem to rely heavily on sovereign credit ratings for their investment decision making. Consequently, dozens of trillion of US$ in outstanding sovereign debt are today globally exclusively controlled by credit agencies' assessments of sovereign creditworthiness. More precisely, mutual funds, international financial institutions, and even regulators use sovereign ratings as benchmarks for their credit investment, financial operations, and legal actions. For this reason sovereign solvency can have implications far beyond any apparent direct impact. Such implications can easily be distinguished on the market and are evident from the rating history that is studded with countries over- or underrated by the ratings agencies, with at times, dramatic consequences (Vernazza et al., 2014). The main objective of this book is the assessment of the accuracy of CRAs' sovereign credit ratings at two levels; at the level of the approach followed by main agencies in their assessment of sovereign creditworthiness and at the level of the accuracy of the final output and its transparency.

This chapter discloses the general sample and the general methodology to be used throughout the book, to assess ratings accuracy and methodological particularities will be discussed at the level of each test. In order to do so we present the sample; examine the test of the fit to the data of agencies model, using constant analysis, residual analysis and gap analysis; discuss the test of subjectivity in the sovereign ratings; discuss the test of the overall accuracy and transparency of agencies model; and conclude the chapter.

The general sample

This book only concentrates on the part of inaccuracy in sovereign ratings that may originate from eventual methodological shortcomings, which add to the other shortcomings that have been already mentioned in the literature. The rationality of agencies' methodology is, for instance, tested in Chapter 6; the accuracy of agencies' approach is tested in Chapter 7; the subjectivity in sovereign ratings is dealt with in Chapter 8; and the quality of agencies disclosure and transparency is assessed in Chapter 9. The sample used in empirical tests covers the period 1983–2014, is based on Moody's data and the main sample composed of 116 sovereign issuers and encompasses the whole spectrum of ratings, as listed in Table 2.1. It includes:

Table 2.1 Sovereign composing the sample

Advanced industrial countries	*Developing countries, Aaa to A3*	*Developing countries, Baa1 to Baa3*	*Developing countries, Ba1 to Ba3*	*Developing countries, B1 to C*
Australia	Bermuda	Azerbaijan	Angola	Albania
Austria	Botswana	Bahamas	Armenia	Argentina
Belgium	Cayman Islands	Bahrain	Bangladesh	Belarus
Canada	Chile	Brazil	Barbados	Belize
Cyprus	China	Bulgaria	Bolivia	Bosnia and Herzegovina
Denmark	Czech Republic	Colombia	Croatia	Cambodia
Estonia	Israel	Costa Rica	El Salvador	Cuba
Finland	Korea	Iceland	Georgia	Dominican Republic
France	Kuwait	India	Guatemala	Ecuador
Germany	Macao	Indonesia	Hungary	Egypt
Greece	Malaysia	Kazakhstan	Jordan	Fiji
Hong Kong	Oman	Latvia	Montenegro	Ghana
Ireland	Poland	Lithuania	Morocco	Honduras
Italy	Qatar	Mauritius	Nigeria	Jamaica
Japan	Saudi Arabia	Mexico	Paraguay	Kenya
Luxembourg	Taiwan	Namibia	Philippines	Lebanon
Malta	United Arab Emirates	Panama	Suriname	Moldova
Netherlands		Peru	Tunisia	Mongolia
New Zealand		Romania		Nicaragua
Norway		Russia		Pakistan
Portugal		South Africa		Papua New Guinea
Singapore		St. Maarten		Senegal
Slovakia		Thailand		Sri Lanka
Slovenia		Trinidad & Tobago		St. Vincent and the Grenadines
Spain		Turkey		Ukraine
Switzerland		Uruguay		Venezuela
United Kingdom				Vietnam
United States of America				Zambia
28	16	26	18	28

(i) 28 sovereign countries, belonging to the "Advanced Industrial Countries" group
(ii) 16 sovereigns countries belonging to the "Developing Countries" group, with Aaa to A3 ratings
(iii) 26 sovereigns countries belonging to the "Developing Countries" group, with Baa1 to Baa3
(iv) 18 sovereigns countries belonging to the "Developing Countries" with Ba1 to Ba3

(v) 28 sovereigns countries belonging to the “Developing Countries” group, with B1 to C.

The alphabetical scale Aaa to C will be discussed in the next chapter.

The sample includes sovereign countries that are scattered all over the planet, Africa, Asia, Australia, Europe, North America and South America. Note, however, that due to lack of some information regarding sovereign advanced industrial countries group, this group may find itself occasionally excluded from the analysis. The number of rated sovereigns varies over time; it has, for example, gradually expanded from 13 nations over the period 1949–1985 to 116 nations in 2015. The main sovereign bonds defaulters during that period were Greece with 75 defaults and Argentina with 34 defaults and other sovereigns follow way back: Jamaica 9, Uruguay 6, Ecuador and Pakistan 3, and Russia and Ukraine 2. The complete list of sovereign defaulters also includes Belize, Dominican Republic, Ecuador, Grenada, Moldova, Nicaragua, Pakistan, Suriname and Venezuela.

Figure 2.1 plots cumulative issuer-weighted default rates for the period 1983–2014, for all rated, investment, and speculative grades, with year 1 represented on the *x*-axis, the year 1983, and year 10, 2014. Overall default has increased during this period and an extraordinary shift has occurred in the distribution of issuer defaults. Investment-grade issuers representing 0 per cent of defaulters in 1983 were counting for around 1.947 per cent in 2014, while at the same time. speculative-grade defaulters increased their proportion from 2.720 per cent in 1983 to 17.219 per cent in 2014.

The shift in defaults underlined by Figure 2.1 had also initiated a change in issuer perception of credit rating agencies, to be discussed later. Figure 2.1 confirms other findings; it shows, for instance, that the number of firms downgraded

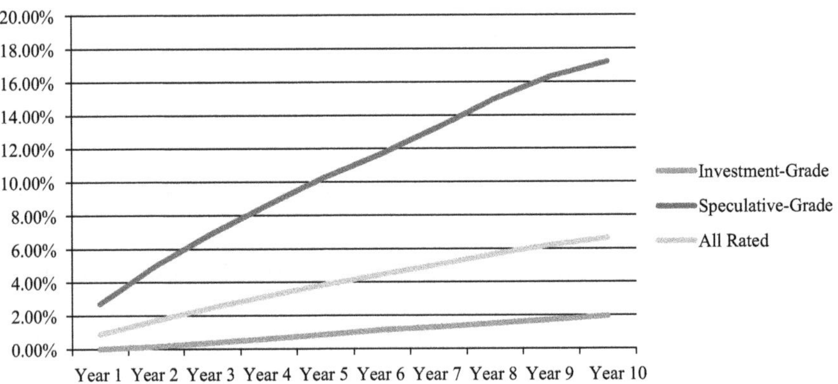

Figure 2.1 Issuer-weighted cumulative default rates, 1983–2014

has increasingly exceeded the number of issuers upgraded over time (Lucas and Lonski, 1992), suggesting that either the quality of issuers declined through time or that rating standards became more rigorous. Credit ratings have, on average, become worse through time, conditional on a set of variables that proxy for the financial and business risks of the rated firm (Blume et al., 1998). The data used in this book originate from different sources, mainly from:

(i) Moody's Statistical Handbook, Country Credit, May 2013
(ii) Moody's, Sovereign Default and Recovery Rates, 1983–2014 (Excel data)
(iii) Moody's, Sovereign Bond Ratings, December 2015
(iv) Bank of Canada Database of Sovereign Defaults, 2015
(v) The International Monetary Fund Guidelines for Public Debt Management.

Methodology

The methodology followed in the book consists first in explaining how CRAs' approach will be evaluated, and second how CRAs' model will be examined. Sovereign rating r can be divided in two different components, an objective component and a subjective one, and can be represented in the following way:

$$r = \text{Ob} + \text{Sub} \qquad \text{E.2.1}$$

where:
r is sovereign rating
Ob represents the objective components of the rating; and
Sub represents the subjective component.

As stated in E2.1, CRAs assess sovereign credit ratings in two successive steps. The first step is wholly based on measurable fundamental variables, such as the general government debt/GDP and the like; we call this step the objective step, Ob. The second step, or subjective step, Sub, is mainly the work of rating committees within CRAs. The rating committee seems to be central to the ratings process and is "designed to nurture a free exchange of views among participants with full consideration of dissenting or controversial views" (Moody's, 2011b). Agencies usually assert, regarding the rating committee, that the selection of committee members is based on competency, expertise and diversity of opinion; they also insure that committee's decisions are based on a majority vote. Opaqueness, however, seems to surround the committee's work and rating methodologies. Instances were even reported where staff members seem to have been sworn to secrecy. Recently however the CRAs' have made some progress en route for more transparency, to be discussed in Chapter 9. It is, however, usually doubted that "the idea that these (self-appointed) committees in each of the CRAs might be able to improve the signal (in terms of default probability) coming from the hard data" is intriguing (Vernazza et al., 2014).

In the case of sovereign default, it may not be enough to make sure that fundamental variables of the sovereign issuer points towards sovereign financial capacity to service its debt, to conclude to its solvency; it is also necessary to make sure that it will be willing to do so when it comes time to pay. For this reason objective component of rating is decomposed in two sub-groups of variables, those only stemming from the sovereign own fundamentals, summarised under the term "capacity to pay", Cap and those submitted to the wish of the sovereign, but that can be also expressed through certain fundamentals and summarised under the term "willingness to pays", Wil. Such dichotomisation is expressed in equation E.2.2:

$$\text{Ob} = \text{Cap} + \text{Wil} \qquad \text{E.2.2}$$

where:
Cap represents the sovereign capacity to face its debt obligations; and
Wil represents the sovereign willingness to service its debt.

The sovereign "willingness to pay" element differentiates the rating of sovereigns from other instruments of credit and debt, as it reflects a subtle potential risk "that even if the sovereign had the *capacity* to pay, it may not be *willing* to do so, if it judges the social or political costs to be too great" (IMF, 2010). Sovereign willingness to pay can be related to a number of fundamentals, such as the sovereign effectiveness, its level of governance, its level of transparency and its track record of default. The use of such category of observations may allow the quantification of the willingness to pay and therefore its inclusion in the models of testing the accuracy of agencies assessment of sovereign creditworthiness.

The book, as mentioned, does not address the overall inaccuracy of the ratings, but only the inaccuracy part that may originate from eventual methodological shortcomings of agencies' approach to sovereign creditworthiness assessment. Therefore the inaccuracies that may be discovered in the book should be interpreted in conjunction with the classical limits for which agencies are traditionally blamed. Three main tests will be performed towards this objective: (i) the test of the fit to the data of the agencies models, using constant analysis, residual analysis and gap analysis; (ii) the test of subjectivity in the sovereign ratings; and (iii) the test of the overall accuracy and transparency of agencies model.

Test of the fit to the data of agencies model

CRAs assert that, by following their approach, one that is based on the 'scorecard' technique (at least for Moody's and S&P), any actual sovereign debt rating can, in most cases, be reached within a three-notch range (Vernazza et al., 2014). Three-notch range, however, can be a devastating error margin for any sovereign that might see erroneously its rating making it a speculative issuer. We will therefore achieve the test of agencies approach, using regression analysis, under different forms, namely constant analysis, residual analysis, and gap analysis. A theoretical model for sovereign creditworthiness assessment will be developed, based on agencies' data, and will serve as a theoretical benchmark for assessing the accuracy of agencies approach, e.g., the test will indicate how agencies are reliable in respecting their own methodology. The theoretical model and agencies model are, however, based on the same original data, e.g., the same agencies data and only the weights used to form combinations of factors toward final ratings distinguish the two. For instance $_nY_i$ agencies' model is formed by computing the weighted average of the translated numerical factors that compose any combination of factors. Once restated using rational weights, $_nY_{i\ \text{becomes}}$ r_nY_i. In fact, it is not clear from agencies approach which weighting is used. The process is thoroughly discussed in Chapter 7. Consequently $_nY_i$ and r_nY_i models should not be expected to diverge significantly at the level of their general significance, as given by the R2, but only at the level of their constants and residuals, taken individually. Consequently, to identify which approach is more accurate, e.g., the one that fits the data better, we will be using three different analyses:

(i) Constant analysis
(ii) Residual analysis and
(iii) Gap analysis

Although intercept can simply be viewed as the value at which the fitted regression line crosses the Y-axis, it can however be used to assess how a regression is fitted to the data. In such case, the constant term can be considered as a corrective element when using particular values of the Xs to predict Y. The constant term serves therefore as the accumulation of bias not accounted for by the terms in the regression model. By absorbing the bias, the constant term insures that the residuals don't have an overall positive or negative bias, and in this regard it can be used to measure how compatible the data are with the null hypothesis (Forest, 2015). Consequently, we use the constant term to see if agencies' approach does not omit important information – in other words, whether such approach is based on a strong theoretical ground. If this is the case, we expect the constant in agencies' numerically translated model $_nY_i$ to equal zero and the same expectation is made for the theoretical or numerically translated and restated model r_nY_i, as will be discussed in Chapter 7.

Agencies conduct their rating process in three steps (see Chapter 6), for this reason we ran a set of two regressions for each of three steps composing agencies' approach:

(i) The step of assessing sovereign economic resiliency,
(ii) The step of assessing sovereign financial strength, and
(iii) The step of assessing government bond rating range.

To proceed with regressions, we must however first convert agencies' alphanumeric ratings into numerically translated ratings (NTRs). We use toward this end, as indicated in Figure 2.2, a linear mapping where the higher the raking, the lower the number assigned more specifically, the top rating or prime is assigned the

Figure 2.2 Numerical linear mapping of sovereign ratings

value 1, the next rating below is assigned the value 2, and so on, till the lowest rating is assigned the value of *n* that can take different values, depending on the scale used by agencies. Indeed agencies use different ranking scales dependent on the stage of the process; sometimes they use a 15-class rating scale, sometimes more, etc. Our numerical translation takes into account such inconsistencies and adjusts accordingly.

Numerical translation can yet play another important role in rating. It allows taking into account whatever weighting is opted for and therefore introducing the lacking "additivity" and "averaging" to the sovereign ratings. Indeed, agencies' current approach seems to exclude the possibility of adding ratings among themselves, or averaging them, except with high approximation. The book relies mainly on Moody's rating symbols where gradations of creditworthiness are indicated by rating symbols. There are nine groups of symbols Aaa, Aa, A, Baa, Ba, B and Caa, "from that used to designate least credit risk to that denoting greatest credit risk" (Moody's, Ratings definitions). Moody's also appends numerical modifiers 1, 2 and 3 to each generic rating classification from Aa through Caa, but not to Aaa.

The tests seek to determine how well numerically translated agency ratings NTR fit their corresponding restated numerically translated agency ratings RNTR, as agency approach does not assign equivalent width to each class of rating. For instance, the width of (Aaa) sovereign class of rating is not the same as the width of the sovereign class (Aa1), etc. We actually assume, as in Naciri (2015) regarding corporate ratings, that sovereign ratings symbols used by agencies should be arithmetically linear, e.g. the difference in credit quality between any two subsequent symbols should be a constant. Therefore, the difference in credit quality between an (Aaa) rated sovereign and an (Aa1) rated sovereign should be the same as between any two subsequent sovereign rating classes and so on. It is therefore assumed that the sovereign rating scale is uniform and each subsequent symbol sees its default increase by the same decrease in credit quality (increase of risk). The model based NTR classification allows the correction of the non-homogeneity problem of the rating scale classes observed in agencies data, and the regression approach also permits the determination of how far agency ratings locate themselves from their corresponding RNTR classification. Therefore, the following regression will be run:

$${}_nY_i = b0 + b1*{}_nX1 + b2*{}_nX2 + \varepsilon_i \quad \text{E. 2.3}$$

$$r_nY_i = b0 + b1*r_nX1 + b2*r_nX2 + \varepsilon_i \quad \text{E. 2.4}$$

where:
${}_{n}Y_{i}$ and $r_{n}Y_{i}$ successively represent numerical ranking translated (NTR) and restated combination (RNTR);
${}_{n}X1$ represents any factor/fundamental or combinations of factors expressed in translated numerical ranking;
$r_{n}X2$ represents any factor or combinations of factors expressed in restated numerical ranking;
b0, b1 and b2 are the intercept and independent variables coefficients, respectively; and
ε_{I} represents residuals.

Depending on the agency, dozens of variables are used to determine the ranking. The value for each sub-factor is assigned a rank on a specific scale. These variables are then aggregated using a set of ad-hoc weights, and the final rating is based on the quantitative assessment and the judgment of the rating committees. An extended discussion of agencies' approach is presented in Chapter 6.

Further, in ordinary regression analysis the model can be validated by analysing residual behaviour. Indeed, randomness and unpredictability are crucial components of any regression model and are requirements for its validity. The regression model can be broken down into constant and two basic components, one objective and the second subjective, therefore E2.1 can be re-written as follows:

$$Y = [b0 + (b1*X1 + b2*X2) + \varepsilon_{i}] \qquad \text{E. 2.5}$$

where:
b0 = Constant;
$(b1*X1 + b2*X2)$ = Objective components, Ob; and
ε_{i} = Subjective components, Sub.

The objective portion of the equation is the part of Y that is explained by predictor variables in the model. All of the explanatory/predictive information of the model should therefore be contained in this portion. While the subjective or error portion is the difference between the expected value and the observed value, none of the explanatory/predictive information should be in the subjective or error portion of the model. The idea is that the prediction portion of the model should be so good at explaining the dependent variable that only the inherent randomness of any real-world phenomenon remains left over for the subjective portion. If we observe explanatory or predictive power in the subjective part, we know that our predictors are missing some of the predictive information. One way to make sure the residuals are consistent with random error is by being insured that residuals themselves are neither systematically high nor systematically low and are centred around zero throughout the range of fitted values – in other words, being sure the model is correct for all fitted values. Our analysis will go deeper than just concentration on the average residual, but rather by also examining residuals individually. Further, in the ordinary least squares context, random errors are assumed to produce residuals that are normally distributed. Therefore, the residuals should fall in a symmetrical pattern and have a constant spread throughout the range. The non-random pattern in the residuals will indicate that the prediction variables portion of the model is not capturing some explanatory information that is "leaking" into the residuals.

Indeed, a significant way of checking whether agencies' model has achieved its goal of explaining, with as much variation as possible, sovereign ratings, while respecting the underlying assumption, is by checking the *residuals* of the regressions used, e.g. by having a detailed look at what is *left over* after explaining the variation in the rating variable using factor independent variables. Ideally all residuals should be small and unstructured; this then would mean that the agencies model is successful in explaining the essential part of the variation of the rating variable. If, however, residuals exhibit a structure or present any special aspect that does not seem random, they will be looked at as shedding a shadow on the model.

Finally, for each of the three steps included in agencies' approach (see Chapter 6) gaps '${}_{n}g_{i}$' between any translated factor and combination of factors (${}_{n}Y_{i}$) and as restated in ranks ($r_{n}Y_{i}$) are unearthed, by subtracting ${}_{n}Y_{i}$ values from their corresponding values $r_{n}Y_{i}$, in the following way:

$$ {}_{n}g_{i} = [r_{n}X_{i} - {}_{n}X_{i}] \qquad \text{E. 2.6} $$

where:
$r_{n}X_{i}$ represents the restated value for any factor/combination of factors;
${}_{n}X_{i}$ represents the translated value of any factor/combination of factors; and
w_{i} is the weight assigned to each factor.

Test of subjectivity in sovereign ratings

To test the accuracy and transparency of the model used by agencies, it should be underlined that in order to measure the 'subjective' component of ratings, all it takes is to estimate the component of ratings that depends only on measurable 'fundamentals' of creditworthiness and compute the 'subjective' component as the residual. Therefore, we will be using regression analysis to isolate subjective components from objective fundamentals. Further a residual analysis will be conducted.

A regression analysis will be used to assess the relationship between sovereign defaults and the sovereign ratings assigned by agencies to defaulted countries for the period 2003–2014. We then estimate the E. 2.7 to E. 2.9 expressions; E. 2.7 for assessing the overall accuracy of the rating and E. 2.8 and E. 2.9 for assessing accuracy, in case of default and in case of non-default respectively:

$$ rating_{i} = \alpha_{i} + \beta' X_{i} + D_{i} + \varepsilon_{i} \; i = 1, \ldots, n \qquad \text{E. 2.7} $$
$$ rating_{d} = \alpha_{i} + \beta' X_{di} + \varepsilon_{i} \; i = 1, \ldots, n \qquad \text{E. 2.8} $$
$$ rating_{nd} = \alpha_{i} + \beta' X_{ndi} + \varepsilon_{i} \; i = 1, \ldots, n \qquad \text{E. 2.9} $$

where:
$rating_i$ is a numeric value for the alphanumeric long-term foreign currency rating of country i during the period 2003–2014;
$rating_d$ indicates a numeric value for the alphanumeric long-term foreign currency rating of a defaulting country i during the period 2003–2014;
$rating_{nd}$ represents a numeric value for the alphanumeric long-term foreign currency rating of a non-defaulting country i during the period 2003–2014.
X_i is the vector of measurable fundamentals, expressing "willingness to pay" and "capacity to pay":
D_i, a dummy variable
β is a vector of coefficients to be estimated.
α_i is a country-specific fixed effect; and
ε_i is an error term.

Expression E2.7 represents the sovereign credit rating and can be divided into two components, as explained in E 2.1 at the beginning of the chapter:

(i) An objective component, Ob
(ii) A subjective component, Sub.

The objective component is the part the sovereign rating assessed through the fundamentals, and it is simply the weighted sum of the fundamentals, e.g. the fitted value. The subjective part of the sovereign rating, on the other hand, is the part that is formed of supplementary adjustment factors used by rating committees. These are supplementary adjustment factors used in "an attempt to capture idiosyncratic country-specific factors which may not be universally available or relevant" (Moody's, 2013a). It can be computed as the difference between the actual rating and the "objective" component (i.e. the residual) (Vernazza et al., 2014). We will therefore be analysing the selected fundamental to assess the rationale of agencies' choices and analysing residuals to assess the rationale of agencies' subjective reactions. The "subjective" component is computed as the difference between the actual rating and the "objective" component, e.g. the residual.

The difference between the observed value of the rating variable and the predicted value of the objective component is called the residual (ε_i). Each data point has one residual, which is the difference between any observed value and its predicted value:

$$\text{Residual } rating_i - [\alpha_i + \beta' X_i + D_i]. \qquad \text{E. 2.10,}$$

where X_i, D_i, β and α_i are as defined previously.

The analysis of the residuals can provide us with a *general approach* to assess the extent of the subjective component in the assessment of sovereign creditworthiness by agencies.

Test of accuracy and transparency of agencies model

In order to test the total extent of the multiple threats facing the sovereign rating process, we express combinations C1 to C3, used by agencies, in mathematical form and set up:

$$C1 = \omega_{F1}X1 + \omega_{F2}X2 \quad (2.11)$$

$$C2 = \omega_{C1}C1 + \omega_{F3}X3 = \omega_{c1}(\omega_{F1}X1 + \omega_{F2}X2) + \omega_{F3}X3 \quad (2.12)$$

And,

$$C3 = \omega_{C2}C2 + \omega_{F4}X4 = \omega_{C2}[\omega_{c1}(\omega_{F1}X1 + \omega_{F2}X2) + \omega_{F3}X3] + \omega_{F4}X4$$

$$= [\omega_{C2}\omega_{c1}(\omega_{C2}\omega_{F1}X1 + \omega_{C2}\omega_{F2}X2) + \omega_{C2}\omega_{F3}X3] + \omega_{F4}X4 \quad (2.13)$$

where:

C1, C2 and C3 are the three successive combinations of economic and political fundamental variables used by agencies in their model of assessing sovereign creditworthiness;

F1, F2, F3 and F4 are the four political variables used by agencies in their model of assessing sovereign creditworthiness; and

ω_{Ci} represents the weight assigned by agencies to the combination of factors;

ω_{Fi} represents the weight assigned by agencies to fundamental factors.

We perform a simulation of sovereign rating, based on E2.13, for different levels of input that are sensitive to the choice of sub-factor weighting to determine the overall sovereign actual rating on the alphanumeric scale and unearth gaps, if any.

Conclusion

This chapter exposes the methodology that will be followed in assessing the accuracy of sovereign credit ratings issued by agencies and will serve as basis to conduct four main tests, e.g. the test of the validity of agencies methodology to sovereign default assessment (Chapter 6), the test of the fit to the data of agencies model, using constant analysis, residual analysis and gap analysis (Chapter 7); the test of subjectivity in the sovereign ratings (Chapter 8); and the test of the overall accuracy and transparency of agencies model (Chapter 9). More explication of methodology is eventually given at the level of each test. All these tests aim to assess the accuracy of the ratings, believed to be so fundamental to economic efficiency, as wrongly valued ratings can misguide trillions in wealth across the planet and have significant unfair impacts on capital flows and asset prices. Further, inaccurate ratings have the extraordinary potential of aggravating sovereign financial situations and fuelling systemic crises, especially if downgrading is reflecting more than the worsening warranted by the concerned sovereign fundamentals, as in the case of the East Asian Crisis (Ferri et al., 1999).

3 Sovereign credit universe

Sovereign governments are the largest borrowers in the vast majority of the world's debt capital markets; they are issued sovereign credit ratings to help investors assess their general creditworthiness, e.g. to demonstrate their capacity to face their debt obligations. Indeed, sovereigns seek ratings so that they and their private sector borrowers can access global capital markets and appeal foreign investment (IMF, 2010) and there are over 100 agencies all over the world whose ratings play a central role in their funding decisions. These credit ratings also provide a benchmark for other important non-sovereign issuers of debt.

This chapter introduces the reader to the sovereign universe and shows how most countries issue debt to generate funding for their general operations and development; it discusses sovereign activity, ratings, security issuers, defaulters, rating agencies, and market. The next section discusses sovereign debt securities and other sovereign market issues, followed by an introduction to the global sovereign debt market, a presentation of the sovereign "raters", a discussion of the sovereign ratings, an analysis of the sovereign the sovereign market, a study of the sovereign defaulters' profile, a discussion of the trends in credit quality and the distribution of sovereign ratings and, finally, the conclusion of the chapter.

The global sovereign debt market

Like many large corporations, a number of governments around the world routinely issue debt instruments to raise capital, either to insure momentary funding during exacting economic times, while running a persistent deficit, or to invest in ways that secure them economic growth. They usually expect the servicing of debt to become easier, mostly by capitalizing on the positive perspective of potential tax revenue improvement, or even by taking advantage of an eventual low trend in interest rate. Government debt securities are issued with a promise to assume periodic interest payments, along with the promise of progressively refunding the face value of the security on the maturity date. Issued debts/bonds are often denominated in the country's own currency, LC, but may also be issued in foreign currencies, FC, to increase their attractiveness in international markets. Sovereign countries typically sell bonds to primary market dealers. This is a market where new securities are first issued. Dealers then turn around and sell them in the secondary market. This is a market where investors purchase second-hand securities or assets from other investors. Government bonds are usually sold to a mix of investors, domestic and international, that find it interesting to invest in government debt securities for both return and security reasons. They can do it in different ways; they can, for instance, buy them from an exchange-traded-fund, and this actually presents the sizable advantage of enabling investors to acquire a basket of international securities under a single traded security and, at the same time, allowing them to attain their sought level of diversification. As many sovereigns directly sell their bonds, investors are also in a position to acquire them directly from issuing countries. In all cases, the conditions imposed to sovereign issuers of these bonds often depend on their solvency, as assessed by ratings agencies. Besides sovereign debt, a sovereign government can have other debt obligations of different types and sources that do not count as sovereign default. Here are some of them (Beers, 2015):

(i) International Monetary Fund lending – these are obligations to pay IMF membership quotas and loans granted to member governments.
(ii) Multilateral lending institutions (MLIs) lending – these are grants to member governments granted by the World Bank and the largest regional development banks.
(iii) Paris Club lending – these are loans extended to other governments by an informal group of bilateral official lenders called the Paris Club.[1]
(iv) Other official creditors lending that covers sovereign loan arrears due to the MLIs and bilateral official creditors, including national export credit and development agencies.

From a credit rating perspective, a sovereign issuer is a government "that de facto exercises primary fiscal authority over a recognized jurisdiction" (IMF, 2011), and the global sovereign universe may exceed 200 governments, to whom it can be added other public policy institutions that are agents of sovereigns, though their debt could be assigned ratings that can differ from those of their sovereign. Sovereign governments have special unique prerogatives that can eventually make them more creditworthy, as they detain the unique power of raising taxes within their territory; they have unique prerogatives of setting laws and controlling the supply of money, and this should actually put sovereigns in a much more creditworthy position than other issuers that are devoid of such authority (S&P, 2011a). The list of sovereign countries composing the main sample of the book, by class of rating for the year 2012 is reproduced in Table 3.1, as published by Wikipedia and listed by Eurostat for the EU and by the CIA's World Factbook 2012 for the rest of the world.

In this book we will be working with a total sample composed of 128 sovereigns, as indicated in Chapter 2; 28 sovereigns come from the environment of advanced Industrial Countries, 18 from developing countries with Aaa to A3 ratings, 26 sovereigns from developing countries with Baa1 to Baa3 ratings, 17 sovereigns from developing countries with Ba1 to Ba3 ratings and 29 sovereigns

Table 3.1 List of sovereign countries, by class of rating

Advanced industrial countries	*Developing countries, Aaa to A3*	*Developing countries, Baa1 to Baa3*	*Developing countries, Ba1 to Ba3*	*Developing countries, B1 to C*
Australia Austria Belgium Canada Cyprus Denmark Estonia Finland France Germany Greece Hong Kong Ireland Italy Japan Luxembourg Malta Netherlands New Zealand Norway Portugal Singapore Slovakia Spain Sweden Switzerland United Kingdom United States of America.	Bermuda Botswana Cayman Islands Chile China Czech Republic Israel Korea Kuwait Macao Malaysia Oman Poland Qatar Saudi Arabia Taiwan United Arab Emirates	Azerbaijan Bahamas Bahrain Brazil Bulgaria Colombia Costa Rica Iceland India Indonesia Kazakhstan Latvia Lithuania Mauritius Mexico Namibia Panama Peru Romania Russia South Africa St. Maarten Thailand Trinidad & Tobago Turkey Uruguay	Angola Armenia Bangladesh Barbados Bolivia Croatia El Salvador Georgia Guatemala Hungary Jordan Montenegro Morocco Nigeria Paraguay Philippines Suriname Tunisia	Albania Argentina Belarus Belize Bosnia and Herzegovina Cambodia Cuba Dominican Republic Ecuador Egypt Fiji Ghana Honduras Jamaica Kenya Lebanon Moldova Mongolia Nicaragua Pakistan Papua New Guinea Senegal Sri Lanka St. Vincent and the Grenadines Ukraine Venezuela Vietnam Zambia
28	18	26	17	29

Source: Adapted from Moody's Investors service (2013), Moody's Statistical Handbook Country Credit May 2013. At: http://alleuropalux.org/fileserver/2013/78/153213.pdf. Accessed January 24, 2016.

from developing countries with B1 to C ratings. Besides sovereign government a number of supranational organisations are also active on the global debt market, Table 3.2 give the list of most popular, as of the year 2015.

Table 3.3, on the other hand, categorises countries by the level of their public debt for the year 2014, based on number of fundamental variables. The figures in column 2 represent the cumulative sum of all government borrowings less repayments that are denominated in a country's home currency. Gross government debt

Table 3.2 List of supranational organisations active on the global debt market

Supranational	*Supranational*	*Supranational*
African Development Bank	Eurasian Development Bank	Int'l Fin. Facil. for Immunisation
African Export-Import Bank	Eurofima	Inter-American Development Bank
Africa Finance Corporation	European Bank for Rec. & Dev.	Inter-American Investment Corp
Arab Petroleum Investments Corp (APICORP)	European Central Bank	International Finance Corp
Asian Development Bank	European Investment Bank	International Investment Bank (IIB)
Black Sea Trade & Develop. Bank	European Investment Fund	Islamic Corporation for the Development of the Private Sector
Caribbean Development Bank	European Stability Mechanism (ESM)	Islamic Development Bank
Central Amer.Bk for Econ. Integr	European Union	Nordic Investment Bank
Corporacion Andina de Fomento	Fondo Latinoamericano de Reservas	North American Development Bank (NADB)
Council of Europe Develop. Bank	GuarantCo	PTA Bank
East African Development Bank (EADB)	Gulf Investment Corporation G.S.C.	Shelter-Afrique (Company for Habitat and Housing in Africa)
EFSF (European Financial Stability Facility)	IBRD (World Bank)	West Africa Development Bank (BOAD)

Source: Adapted from Moody's (2011a).

is among the most pertinent data for the assessment of government default and its borrowing capacity. Gross government debt is different from external debt, which includes foreign currency liabilities of non-government entities. The two, however, are not mutually exclusive. The figures in column 3 indicate the percentages of annual GDP corresponding to gross government debt. The numbers in column 4 give government debt per capita in US$, and column 5 states government debt in percentage of total world sovereign debt.

The global government debt (column 2) reaches 56.31 US$ bil and varies by countries from 17.61 US$ bil for the United States, to 0.283 bil US$ for Pakistan. The weight of government debt does not, however, follow dollar amounts; indeed government debt as per cent of GDP (supposed to give a clear picture of a sovereign capacity to sustain debt) counts only for 64 per cent for the United States despite its 17.607 billion of US$ of public debt, 64.30 per cent for Pakistan with its 0.283 billions of US$ and 231.90 per cent for Japan, with 9.872 billion

Table 3.3 Public debt of countries exceeding 0.5% of world, 2014 estimate (CIA World Factbook 2014)[2] (in billions of US$)

(1) Country	*(2) Public debt (billion USD)*	*(3) Public debt in % of GDP (CIA world factbook 2014)*	*(4) Public debt per capita in USD*	*(5) Public debt in % of world public debt (Wikipedia)*
World	56,308	64%	7,936	100.00%
United States*	17,607	74.40%	55,630	31.27%
Japan	9,872	231.90%	77,577	17.53%
China	3,894	14.90%	2,885	6.91%
Germany	2,592	74.30%	31,945	4.60%
Italy	2,334	132.00%	37,956	4.14%
France	2,105	95.50%	31,915	3.74%
United Kingdom	2,064	88.10%	32,553	3.67%
Brazil	1,324	58.90%	6,588	2.35%
Spain	1,228	97.70%	25,931	2.18%
Canada	1,206	94.80%	34,902	2.14%
India	995	51.70%	830	1.75%
Mexico	629	42.10%	5,416	1.12%
South Korea	535	34.50%	10,919	0.95%
Turkey	489	35.00%	6,060	0.87%
Netherlands	488	69.00%	29,060	0.87%
Egypt	479	93.70%	5,610	0.85%
Greece	436	177.10%	40,486	0.77%
Poland	434	43.70%	11,298	0.77%
Belgium	396	106.30%	37,948	0.70%
Singapore	370	103.20%	67,843	0.66%
Taiwan	323	33.40%	13,860	0.57%
Argentina	323	42.70%	7,571	0.57%
Indonesia	311	25.90%	1,240	0.55%
Russia	308	13.40%	2,159	0.55%
Portugal	297	130.20%	27,531	0.53%
Thailand	292	46.30%	4,330	0.52%
Pakistan	283	64.30%	1,462	0.50%

of US$. Developed countries seem to use debt sparingly, with high government debt per capita. The United States, for instance, has a 55.630 US$ government debt for each American citizen, Japan 77.577, Germany 31.945, the United Kingdom 32.553, but China only 2.885 US$. Only two countries, namely the United States and Japan, with 31.27 per cent and 17.53 per cent of the total world debt, contract almost 50 per cent of the world sovereign debt respectively. The rest of the countries of the world share the remaining 50 per cent, and developing countries count for a very small fraction. The impact of public debt on the GDP seems also to vary among countries: Japan's public debt in 2014, for instance, represents 231.90 per cent of its GDP, while only 13.40 per cent for Russia. The most indebted countries, in percentage of the GDP, seem generally to come from the developed environment.

Overall, in 2012 and on average, the global gross government debt represented over 50 per cent of the world gross domestic product (GDP) and the net government debt embodied 33,6 per cent of the world GDP (IMF, 2012). The famous *debt clock* located at Times Square in New York City reveals by a second the increase in public debt, and as of December 29, 2015, 11:08 AM, we could have read as the global sovereign debt figure the number 57,723,527,705,305 US$, as the global sovereign debt figure in U.S. dollar terms. Times Square's clock is constantly ticking and every second the global debt is increasing (The Economist, 2012). The rise in total debt can be extremely important, as when debt rises faster than economic output, the implication is an increase in the debt burden and in the prospect of more government intervention in the economy and of more future hikes in taxes, inevitably implying rollover of existing debt at regular intervals. Recurring political uncertainty for individual governments should therefore be expected (The Economist, 2012).

The sovereign "raters"

Although there are hundreds of credit rating agencies all over the world, only 10 of them are Nationally Recognized Statistical Rating Organizations (NRSRO),[3] recognised by the Security Exchange of the United States (SEC)[4] and the European Securities and Markets Authority (ESMA), the great majority of the sovereign credit ratings are taken care of by the so-called Big 3: Fitch Ratings, Moody's and Standard and Poor's (S&P), These three large agencies can have impacting effect on issuers and on the global market as whole. The big 3 count for 99.99 per cent of government ratings as of December 2013 (SEC, 2013). One of the reasons ratings are extensively used by investors and previously by regulators is the fact that they are often used to determine the cost indebtedness. Indeed, "the empirical analysis shows that CRA ratings do have an impact on the funding costs of issuers (IMF, 2011). A subjective or imprecise rating may therefore prove to be excessively dangerous to any sovereign issuer, since it can undermine its ability to borrow and to impose on it higher cost and harsher conditions for its borrowing (El Namaki, 2013). Consequently CRA ratings need to be as accurate and fair as possible.

Unfortunately, misconduct seems to have been occasionally discovered in credit rating activity "We've uncovered serious shortcomings at these firms, including a lack of disclosure to investors and the public, a lack of policies and procedures to manage the rating process, and insufficient attention to conflicts of interest. [. . .] When the firms didn't have enough staff to do the job right, they often cut corners" (Cox, 2008). Some agencies were even prosecuted for eventual misbehaviour – S&P, for instance, was fined a record $1.37 billion in 2015 for a settlement with state and the U.S. federal prosecutors, and Moody's is coming under investigation by the U.S. Justice Department (Wall Street Journal, 2015). Consequently, appeals for curbing CRA misconduct and/or "hegemony" were heard all over the world, and they culminate with S&P downgrading the U.S. government. This move seems to have prompted the process of more severely close watching of CRAs and steps were eventually taken by both the United States and European monetary authorities in favour of better monitoring the three main agencies and ensuring more transparency on their behalf, and competitiveness to the rating market. Such oversight actions are especially embodied in the Dodd-Frank Wall Street Reform and Consumer Protection Act of 2010 and the ESMA releases of 2011; both have sought to hold agencies accountable for the sake of protecting investors. As CRAs have accumulated much controversy over the accuracy of their sovereign debt ratings, they have recently been subject to scrutiny of their business practices.

Instead of considering the blame and eventually correcting rating shortcomings, CRAs rather feel wrongly misjudged and argue they do not aim their ratings to default probabilities or expected losses, but rather pursue ordinal rankings of credit risk; they constantly evoke as a proof the fact that "all sovereigns that defaulted since 1975 had noninvestment-grade ratings one year ahead of their default" (IMF, 2011). CRAs also were, till recently, pretending to be protected by the First Amendment (Amendment I) to the United States Constitution of 1791 that "prohibits the making of any law [. . .] impeding the free exercise of religion, abridging the freedom of speech, infringing on the freedom of the press". The applicability of the First Amendment protection to credit ratings was, however, recently seriously rejected by the U.S. Court, which "has ruled that there is no blanket First Amendment protection for published credit ratings" (Baklanova, 2009). The time of regulation has definitely sounded and the wind of change keeps increasing stronger for agencies – the United States, for instance, has recently filled a $5 billion U.S. fraud case against Standard & Poor's. Denounced by S&P, this lawsuit is considered retaliation, intended to punish the agency for "exercising its First Amendment rights". The international community also acts in concert and rarely such homogeneousness was recorded in any international regulatory initiative. The G20, the International Organization of Securities Commissions (IOSCO), the US and the EC, and other countries and jurisdictions all have recently launched regulatory initiatives for monitoring rating agencies.

Nothing should keep CRAs from having an approach to sovereign rating default assessment that can be verifiable by users and not only to be taken as an act of faith. Despite the fundamental questions that were recently asked regarding CRAs' usefulness and the accuracy of their credit ratings (IMF, 2010), they seem to have surmounted this wave of protestation unscratched. It is worth reminding, however, that following the 2008 financial crisis, CRAs seem to constantly fine-tune their rating methodologies, but their control over the rating market seems to remain genuine. The lack of alternatives coupled with the certification role played by CRAs "through their use of 'outlooks,' 'reviews,' and 'watches' (pre-rating change warnings)" (IMF, 2011) may explain such successful survival (Naciri, 2015). Faced with such adaptability of CRAs, it is often suggested that a better way forward in monitoring agencies "is a combination of gradually reducing the regulatory reliance on credit ratings to the extent possible, while at the same time enhancing CRA regulatory oversight" (IMF, 2010).

The sovereign ratings

As indicated in Chapter 1 agencies rate sovereign issuers, using alphabetical rating systems. Table 3.4 reproduces long-term senior debt rating symbols for Fitch, Moody's and S&P. To further distinguish ratings, numbers 1 to 3 are added to letters "Aa" through "Caa" and pluses and minuses are added to letters "Aaa" through "Caa". Ratings are often accompanied by outlook ratings. Symbolised by "NEG," "POS," "STA," "RUR" and "SD," these abbreviations stand for negative, positive, stable, rating under review and selective default, respectively (Investopedia).

Ratings "Aaa/AAA" express the highest credit quality; "Aa /AA" indicate a high credit quality; "A/A" express strong payment capacity; "Baa/ BBB" indicate medium credit quality. Symbols "Baa/ BBB" and higher are considered investment grades. Inversely ratings "Ba/BB" express a certain uncertainty in fulfilling debt obligations; "B/B" express a high-risk in respecting financial obligations; "Caa/CCC" indicate vulnerability to default; "Ca/CC" and lower ratings indicate default. Credit ratings below these designations "Ba/BB" down are considered low credit quality, and are commonly referred to as "junk bonds". Nonrated bonds are also considered speculative grade. Empirical data indicate that around fifty

Table 3.4 Fitch, Moody's and S&P long-term senior debt rating symbols

Fitch and S&P	*Moody's*	*Interpretation*
AAA	Aaa	Highest quality
AA+	Aa1	High quality
AA	Aa2	
AA–	Aa3	
A+	A1	Strong payment capacity
A	A2	
A–	A3	
BBB+	Baa1	Adequate payment capacity
BBB	Baa2	
BBB–	Baa3	
BB+	Ba1	Likely to fulfill obligations on an ongoing uncertainty
BB	Ba2	
BB–	Ba3	
B+	B1	High-risk obligations
B	B2	
B–	B3	
CCC+	Caa1	Vulnerable to default
CCC	Caa2	
CCC–	Caa3	
CC	Ca	Near or in bankruptcy or default
C	C	
D	D	

Source: Fitch; Moody's; Standard & Poor's

countries on the global sovereign debt market have a speculative grade (Moody's, 2011a). For the rest of this book, Moody's symbols "Aaa-Caa" will be indifferently used to express all agencies" symbols.

Sovereign credit ratings are evaluations of the creditworthiness of a sovereign debt issuer, they can be seen as summary evaluation of a sovereigns' ability and willingness to repay, on time, their public debt both in principal and in interest; they can also be regarded as looking toward the future qualitative measures of the probability of default, as estimated by rating agencies. Despite the fact that CRAs have been under a cloud of suspicion, consequence of tarnishing eventual misconduct, following the detection of their role in recent sovereign crisis and the structured credit markets, it should be admitted that in case ratings were performed accurately, they can serve several useful purposes (Afonso et al., 2007):

(i) They can, for instance, contribute to the aggregation of the information about the credit quality of sovereign issuers.
(ii) They may allow sovereign issuers to access more easily the global and domestic financing markets and attract investment funds, thereby "adding liquidity to markets that would otherwise be illiquid" (IMF, 2011).
(iii) They can represent a key determinant of the interest rates a country faces in the international financial market and therefore of its borrowing costs.
(iv) They may have a constraining impact on the ratings assigned to domestic financial institutions.
(v) They can be used as an investment benchmark by institutional investors that are imposed lower bounds for the risk they can assume in their investments.
(vi) They use to be and partially continue to be embedded in many regulations and private contracts, particularly when downgrades cross into non-investment-grade categories.

The architecture of the sovereign credit markets seems to have been transformed tremendously since the second half of the twentieth century; developed sovereign bond markets are no longer the prized safe haven investment, and developing sovereign bond markets are not solely composed of speculative bonds. Excessive sovereign indebtedness over all the spectrum of nations has introduced new risks to traditional bond indices. The latest downgrade of the public debt crisis, for instance, hit hard developed countries like Greece, Ireland and Portugal, and relegated them to "junk" status, implying very high default risk, compared with investment-grade, characterizing debt issues carrying lower risk. It was even argued that such a move has precipitated these countries into crisis. Indeed, a downgrade of rating often constitutes a psychological impairment for a country's economic recovery and may contribute to the increase of investors' lack of faith in a given sovereign country's political system, e.g. rendering investors more anxious about eventual "hidden icebergs" such downgrades may later reveal and the situation can be even worse, when the prompt debt downgrades lead to an increase in the cost of borrowing (Wall Street Journal, 2011).

The sovereign defaulting market

A sovereign defaulter is a country that fails on the service of its debt, for one of the following reasons:

(i) By not servicing its debt on the due date
(ii) By not paying its principal within the time frame specified under a guarantee
(iii) By escaping an outright payment default
(iv) In any circumstances by making creditors suffer material economic losses on the sovereign debt they hold (Investopedia).

Despite the fact that sovereign defaulters are not subject to normal bankruptcy measures and have the potential leeway to escape indebtedness responsibility, often without serious legal consequences, sovereign defaults are, however, relatively rare and, as a general rule, countries are refractory to default on their debts, because they are usually aware of the negative consequences such move may lead to, e.g. the higher cost that may result for future borrowing and the emerging new difficulties of finding future financing. For these reasons, government debt securities are often considered to be the safest investment in the world when rated 'Aaa'. Notwithstanding sovereign credit risk level, a number of key risks should be considered when assessing sovereign creditworthiness (IMF, 2000):

(i) Market risk is the component of uncertainty that encompasses the risks associated with changes in interest rates and exchange rates and that are susceptible of impacting the cost of current and future sovereign's debt servicing.
(ii) Liquidity risk embodies the uncertainty facing investors when they have to support a cost or penalty in trying to exit a position when the number of players has diminished in the market or when a particular market debt has contracted. This is a situation where "the volume of liquid assets can quickly decrease in the face of unanticipated cash flow obligations and/or a possible difficulty in raising cash through borrowing in a short period of time" (IMF, 2000).
(iii) Credit risk refers to the loss on debt resulting from a non-performing sovereign borrowers.
(iv) Inflation risk represents the risk arising from uncertainty over the future real value of the investment in sovereign debt instruments.
(v) Political risk represents the situation where an investment's returns may suffer as a result of political changes or instability in a country.
(vi) Transfer risk is the risk of capital being locked up or frozen by sovereign deliberate action, etc.

The mentioned sovereign default risks are, however, often the direct consequence of a general risk, called economic risk. This is risk that arises each time an investment is made in a foreign country and sovereigns showing stable economic growth assume less economic risk compared with countries whose economic growth fluctuates significantly through time (Business dictionary). Table 3.5 gives summary data of the global sovereign debt in default for the years 1975, 1985, 1995, 2005 and 2014.

From Table 3.5, we can conclude that defaults among sovereign issuers have increased dramatically, from an amount of 1318 US$ mil or 24.56 per cent of all sovereign in 1975 to 128.884 US$ mil or 36.62 per cent of all sovereign, in 2015 with a hike of 52.63 per cent in 1995. Overall sovereign default seems to have decreased since 1995. Table 3.6, on the other hand, states the list of major sovereign defaulters and their cumulative default amounts in US$ mil for the period 1975–2014.

Table 3.5 Summary data, global sovereign debt in default in number of defaulters and in US$ mil

	1975	*1985*	*1995*	*2005*	*2014*
Total number of sovereigns	171	186	209	211	213
Sovereigns in default	42	84	110	99	78
% Sovereigns in default	24.56	45.16	52.63	46.92	36.62
Total debt in default (US$ mil)	1318	164384	219297	339758	128884

Source: Adapted from (Beers and Chambers, 2015) Beers and Nadeau (2015) Database of Sovereign Defaults, 2015. Bank of Canada Technical Report No. 101.

Table 3.6 The major sovereign defaulters for the period 1975–2014

Country	*Cumulative default, in US$ mil*	*Country*	*Cumulative default, in US$ mil*
Iraq (ME)*	794927	Ireland (E) *	88290
Argentina (SA)*	787939	Serbia (E) *	88943
Brazil (SA)*	685334	Philippines (As) *	82903
Greece (E)*	525239	Myanmar (As) *	80509
USSR/Russia (As)*	517325	Tanzania (A) *	77143
Sudan (A) *	418500	Egypt (A) *	76756
Nigeria (A) *	243006	Liberia (A) *	74939
Poland (E) *	195431	Angola (A) *	62754
Venezuela (SA) *	157505	Somalia (A) *	61284
Côte d'Ivoire (A) *	154013	South Africa (A) *	59928
Korea (North) (As)*	134098	Rep. Of Congo (Brazzaville) (A) *	59565
Peru (SA) *	152244	Zambia (A) *	58851
Syria (ME) *	138937	Chile (SA) *	52971
Indonesia (As) *	94662	Portugal (E) *	52712
Nicaragua (CA) *	92794	Ethiopia (A) *	50032

*: A = Africa, As = Asia, CA = Central America, E= Europe, ME = Middle East, SA = South America.
Source: Computed based on the data from (Beers and Chambers, 2015).

Table 3.7 Sovereign defaults in percentages, by categories of debt and for the years 1975, 1985, 1995 and 2014

	1975	*1985*	*1995*	*2005*	*2014*
— IMF	0.00%	2.14%	3.08%	1.39%	3.57%
— World Bank	0.00	0.00	0.00	0.26	0.66
— Paris Club	17.45	10.50	9.49	10.60	29.42
— Other official creditors	49.47	10.15	41.50	45.76	15.45
— Private creditors	23.67	3.50	8.06	3.20	8.93
— FC* Bank Loans	0.00	73.12	37.80	7.71	9.34
— FC Bonds	9.33	0.07	0.05	31.05	32.63
— LC** Debt	0.08	0.52	0.02	0.02	0.00
Total Debt in Default (US$ mil)	100.00	100.00	100.00	100.00	100.00

*: FC: financial currency, **: LC: local currency.
Source: calculated based on data from (Beers and Chambers, 2015).

For the period 1975–2014, Iraq with a cumulative default amounting to 750 US$ bil, is by far the largest sovereign defaulter of the world, followed by Argentina scoring a cumulative amount of 788 US$ bil in default, Brazil with 685 US$ bil, Greece with 525 US$ bil, Russia with 517 US$ bil, down to Ethiopia with cumulative default amounting to 500 US$ mil. Out of the thirty sovereign defaulters in the sample, twelve come from Africa, five from Europe, five from South America, five from Asia, two from the Middle East, and one from Central America.

Table 3.7 on the other hand gives an overview of sovereign defaults in percents, by categories of debt for the years 1975, 1985, 1995 and 2014.

In 2014, we can learn from Table 3.7 that the main subjects of government debt were foreign currency (FC) bank loans and foreign currency bonds, along with the Paris Club. International institutions accounted for little, around 4 per cent. It shows also that the same year and, expressed in US$ mil, foreign currency bonds dominate the sovereign default with 32.63 per cent of all sovereign defaults, followed by the Paris club, scoring 29.42 per cent. The IMF and the World Bank loans have registered a modest rate of default of 3.57 per cent and 0.66 per cent respectively. Further, a shift in default has also occurred during the period 1975–2014. We can see, for instance, that other official creditors and private creditors have lost a lot of ground, to the benefit of the Paris Club and FC bonds. Foreign currency bank loans that were representing the bulk of sovereign default in 1985, with 73.12 per cent, only represented 9.34 per cent in 2014.

Sovereign defaulters profile

A sovereign government is considered a defaulter when it fails servicing its debt obligations, e.g. when it fails to make timely payment of principal or interest on its publicly issued debt, or when it offers a distressed exchange for it. Sovereign default does not cover failures to repay debt owed to the official sector like the International Monetary Fund or the World Bank, as they are not judged sovereign default events. The book considered, however, arrears to official creditors as indicative elements of growing financial distress and/or lack of willingness to pay; it keeps in mind that official creditors usually will seek comparable treatment for private-creditor claims as part of any restructuring of their own claims. Table 3.8 gives a summary view of circumstances surrounding some sovereign

Table 3.8 Circumstances surrounding some sovereign bond defaults during the last three decades

Country and date of foreign currency default	*Circumstances*
Venezuela, 1998	On July 1998 the government of Venezuela failed to pay the coupons on local currency bonds, claiming that the person responsible for signing the checks was not available for the signing. The checks were however signed in following week.
Russia, 1998	Faced with high cost of domestic debt service, because of dramatic decrease of export, the Russian government sped up in 1998 the liberalisation of T-bill market and restrictions on non-resident participation were eliminated. However, the East Asian crisis made non-resident investors to pull out their money from the T-bill market and this has prompted Russia into default.
Ukraine, 1998	Faced with serious macroeconomic difficulties, the government of Ukraine decided in 1998 to declare a moratorium on debt service for anonymous bearers of bonds. Only those among them who were willing to identify and convert to local currency account were eligible to payments. By the beginning of the year 2000, over 90 per cent of non-resident holders of Ukrainian bonds accepted new bonds with a face value of around 50 per cent of the original debt.
Pakistan, 1998	The serious balance of payment crisis Pakistan was facing in 1998 was exacerbated by international sanctions, following Pakistan's nuclear test and consequently foreign currency government bonds were downgraded from B3 to Caa1, reflecting the increased risk of default.
Ivory Coast, 2000	The new Ivory Coast government, resulting from the 2000 "coup d'État", suspended payments on the Ivory Coast's external debt of around $15.6 billion. Although the country resumed payments later, it had to go into technical default.
Argentina, 2001	The significant increase in Argentina's indebtedness, coupled with an international fierce competition, have pushed interest rate ups, resulting in squeezing of private investment out of the Argentinian market and pushing companies' closing and finally resulting in Argentina default on external debt.
Moldova, 1990	As a former USSR republic was significantly affected by the Russian crisis of the end of the 1990, as exports in roubles almost dried up and consequently the country defaulted on its external debt.

defaults during the last three decades. Most sovereign defaults seem, however, to have happened due to the defaulting sovereigns inappropriate past policies and/or unpredictable economic environments.

The statute of sovereign contains determinant benefit for the issuer of sovereign debt but also impacting consequences for investors. Typically the sovereign has the authority to rule and enforce its ruling in the jurisdiction it governs, and such authority may leave creditors with very limited legal or other recourse, in the event the sovereign is prevented from servicing its debt, or it is unwilling to do so. Indeed, given the limitations of international law and its weak enforceability with respect to sovereign nations, assessment of sovereign credit default also includes the willingness to pay of the sovereign issuer.

Trends in credit quality: the distribution of sovereign ratings

Figure 3.1 gives a historical overview of sovereign default in US$ mil for the period 1976–2014. It appears that three major waves of defaults have hit the global sovereign credit market. The first wave of defaults struck during the 1985–1990 and was the consequence of the worsening of global economic conditions, coupled with the unfavourable market sentiment towards Asian sovereign in crisis. The second wave of defaults has taken place during the period 2002–2004, when there have been additional defaults, although less than the previous period. This second wave was led by Argentina's default of 2001 that has extended to other Latin American sovereigns. A third wave of default has materialised during the period 2013–2014, when developed countries like Greece defaulted.

Many countries have indeed defaulted on their debt over the years, but sovereign debts were either renegotiated or restructured during times of adversity. During 1976–2014 the overall sovereign solvency seems to have deteriorated significantly. Table 3.9 shows that by the end of 2010 the share of investment-grade sovereign issuers had declined to slightly over 60 per cent, while in 1983 all rated sovereign issuers were investment grade. Over the same period of time riskier emerging market countries gained access to debt markets and the share of speculative-grade ratings rose.

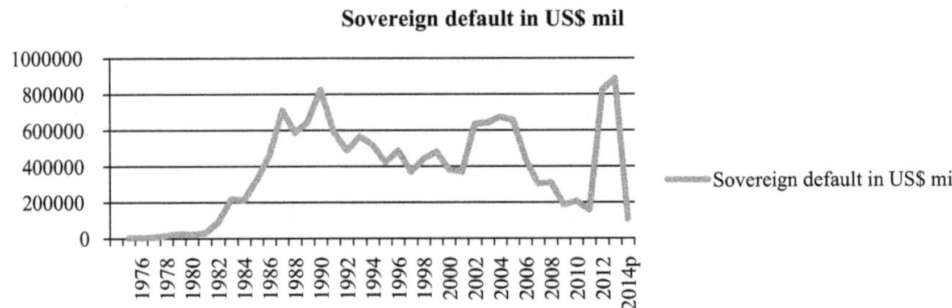

Figure 3.1 Sovereign defaults (1976–2014) in US$ mil

Source: Drawn from Bank of Canada GRAG database, 2015.

Table 3.9 Rating distribution of sovereign issuers on selected dates

	1983	*1990*	*1995*	*2000*	*2005*	*2010*
Aaa	75	40	20	14	20	15
Aa	25	30	26	14	5	15
A	0	17	20	13	24	13
Baa	0	3	13	21	14	19
Ba	0	7	15	17	15	16
B	0	3	7	16	16	22
Caa-C	0	0	0	5	5	1
Investment grade	100	90	78	62	64	61
Speculative grade	0	10	22	38	36	39

Source: Moody's Investors Service (2011), Sovereign Default and Recovery Rates, 1983–2010 (Special Comment).

The share of sovereigns in the Aaa to single-A categories has declined from 100 per cent in 1983 to 41 per cent in 2000, and scaled back to about 50 per cent by the end of 2006, the 2007–09 global financial crisis later eroded all these gains. It has also changed the distribution within the investment-grade category: the proportion of sovereigns rated Aa has increased, both because some advanced economies were downgraded from Aaa and also because of upgrades into the Aa category, for emerging market economies (Moody's, 2011a).

The cost of defaults

When an issuer defaults, this will generally cause investors to lose, in part or totally, their invested capital and/or not to cash the interest earned on it. Such loss is commonly measured using one of two methods:

(i) The average trading price, as expressed by the mean of issuer-weighted trading prices of sovereign's bond, thirty days after its initial missed interest payment and in case of distressed exchange, the average price one day before the closing of the distressed exchange (Moody's, 2011a); or

(ii) The present value ratio of cash flows in percentage (PV ratio of CF in per cent), based on the ratio of the value of the old securities to the value of the new securities received in exchange. This ratio is computed "by discounting the promised cash flows using the yield to maturity implicit in the old securities at the time of the announcement of the exchange offer" (Moody's, 2011a).

The average value-weighted recovery rate for the sovereign sample of both methods is presented in Table 3.10. While there are cases where differences between the two recovery-rate methods are significant, the two approaches to estimating recovery values seem generally to produce similar estimates.

Table 3.10 Average trading prices and PV ratio of CF in %, for a sample of defaulters for the period 1998–2008

Defaulted country	*Year of default*	*Average trading prices*	*PV ratio of CF in %,*
Russia	1998	18	50
Pakistan	1999	52	65
Ecuador	1999	44	60
Ukraine	2000	69	60
Ivory Cost	2000	18	NA
Argentina	2001	27	30
Moldova	2002	60	95
Uruguay	2003	66	85
Nicaragua	2003	NA	50
Grenada	2004	65	NA
Dominican Republic	2005	95	95
Belize	2006	76	NA
Seychelles	2008	30	NA
Ecuador	2008	28	NA
Jamaica	2010	90	80
Issuer-weighted recovery rates		53	67
Value-weighted recovery rates		31	36

Source: Mood Moody's Investors Service (2011), Sovereign Default and Recovery Rates, 1983–2010 (Special Comment).

The material differences in the estimates of recovery rate, Table 3.10, wherever present, seem mainly to be caused by the timing of the recovery estimate (Moody's, 2011a). The two highest recovery rates in the sample are the Dominican Republic at 95 per cent, followed by Jamaica at 90 per cent and Belize at 76 per cent, while the Seychelles, Ecuador and Ivory Coast were low, at 30 per cent, 28 per cent and 18 per cent respectively, and below the average historical sovereign recovery rate (Moody's, 2011a). Russia although scoring 18 per cent average trading prices its PV ratio of CF in per cent, was 50 per cent. The numbers in Table 3.10 also point to the real extent of the sovereign default risk and show that sovereign investors can lose as much as 82 per cent of their original investment, not to count the lost interest payments.

Conclusion

Recent years have witnessed a gain in credit rating agencies crucial task of providing information on which investors base their investment decisions (Alfonso et al., 2014). This chapter aims at a better understanding of the global sovereign rating and default environment. Indeed, CRAs and sovereign ratings have been attracting more interest in recent years than they did in the previous one hundred. The chapter shows how the global sovereign risk universe appears to be important for and inclusive of all the world regions. Such a universe also involves specialised rating agencies, formal ratings, specific defaulted sovereigns, with specific profile and underlines the trend in credit quality, and the distribution of sovereign ratings is evolving, and more developed countries found themselves confronted to default. Indeed, "prior to the financial crisis, sovereign risk conjured up images of such developing countries as Argentina. Now, of course, sovereign risk in developing countries continues to be of interest, but the focus has moved to the larger regional area of Europe" (Altman et al., 2014). As rule, most sovereign defaults seem to have happened because a defaulting sovereign's past permissive policies that make them unprepared to face unexpected events (S&P, 2011a) and this macroeconomic environment of sovereign rating will be discussed in the next chapter.

Notes

1 The Paris Club is an informal group of officials from creditor countries whose role is to find coordinated and sustainable solutions to the payment difficulties experienced by debtor countries. Its permanent members are Australia, Austria, Belgium, Canada, Denmark, Finland, France, Germany, Ireland, Israel, Italy, Japan, the Netherlands, Norway, the Russian Federation, Spain, Sweden, Switzerland, the United Kingdom and the United States of America. (Wikipedia)
2 CIA (2014), "World Factbook 2014". At: https://www.cia.gov/library/publications/the-world-factbook/fields/2186.html. Accessed January 24, 2016
3 A.M. Best, DBRS, EJR, Fitch, HR Ratings, JCR, KBRA, Moody's, Morningstar and S&P. (Adapted from NRSRO annual certifications for the calendar year ended December 31, 2013, Item 7A on Form NRSRO. As reported in SEC Annual Report on Nationally Recognized Statistical Rating Organizations of December 2014.)
4 Most of them also recognised par European Securities and Market authority, ESMA.

4 Macroeconomic environment of sovereign default

It seems, indeed, that most countries have defaulted at least once in their history. As indicated in the previous chapter, most sovereign defaults seem to have happened when a sovereign's previous fiscal or monetary policies left it little room for manoeuver, or when economic policy did not support sustained economic growth. In such cases investors' positive perceptions may tend to quickly shift to a negative, leading to the rise of financing costs, leaving eventually a sovereign with default as the only policy response (Council of Foreign Relations, 2015). Unfortunately, aggregate effects of such happenings can also have a devastating macro effect both nationally and globally.

The chapter discusses some of the macroeconomic effect of sovereign ratings; defines sovereign debt and sovereign global sovereign credit market; checks the relationship between debt levels and growth; discusses the link between public default and financial crisis; considers sovereign ratings pro-cyclicality and asymmetry; underlines what happens when a sovereign defaults; clarifies how business risk and financial risk can be entangled into each other and affects each other; studies the place of sovereign ratings and the global sovereign credit market within economic environment; finally the chapter concludes.

Sovereign debt and sovereign global sovereign credit market

A sovereign issuer, as we know, is a government that issues debt instruments while maintaining a wide range of financial relationships with resident and non-resident entities. One fundamental characteristic that may distinguish sovereign debtors from other debtors is their unique power personified in three supra-capacities:

(i) Their ability to set laws that limit their responsibility to within their own jurisdiction
(ii) Their ability to raise taxes within their jurisdiction, and even beyond
(iii) Their power of controlling the supply of money within their jurisdiction.

Although these abilities should generally make sovereign issuers more creditworthy than other issuers lacking such authority, they are, however, far from keeping them from defaulting on their sovereign debt (S&P, 2014). Actually, because sovereigns are the highest authorities in their environment and have the power to enforce their desire in the jurisdictions they govern; creditors consequently have very limited legal or other recourse in the events of default. Their fate is usually not better when they decide to have recourse to international law either, given the restrictions of such law, or given its weak enforceability, with respect to sovereign nations. The global public debt expressed in US$ has been constantly increasing and recently developing economies, for instance, were more aggressive in sovereign indebtedness than countries with high-income economies status. Table 4.1 gives the extent of the world external debt stock in percentage of gross national income (GNI) that expresses the total debt owed to non-residents and repayable in currency, goods or services. External debt stock is also expressed in proportion of a country's gross domestic product, which represents, for its part, the value, in monetary terms, of all the finished goods and services produced within a year inside country's borders. When net property income from abroad is added to the GDP, it is called gross national product, GNP.

For the year 2013 external debt in percentage of GNI of high-income economies represented 142 per cent of their gross national income. The three most heavily indebted high-income countries were France, Greece and Portugal, which had debt-to-GNP ratios locating above 200 percent (World Bank. 2016). Europe and Central Asia represented 58 per cent each. 29.50 per cent for Latin America and Caribbean, and only 24.5 per cent for sub-Saharan Africa. The total external debt stock for high-income economies rose by 2 per cent in 2013, to score US$68 trillion, while the external debt stock of developing countries during the same period increased by only 1 per cent. Contrariwise, the least indebted countries were the Republic of Korea, Israel and the Russian Federation, scoring less than 40 per cent each of its respective gross national incomes (World Bank, 2016). This, however, did not keep Russia from defaulting. World Bank data for the year 2013 also indicate that developing countries government debt-to-GDP ratio ranged from the lowest, 13 per cent for Russia, to the highest, 82 per cent for Hungary, and in most instances, was lower than the comparable ratio for 2008. In 2012 large developing economies like Turkey, Brazil and India saw their government debt stabilizing or falling; stabilizing at 36 per cent, for Turkey and

Table 4.1 External debt stock in percent of gross national income for the year 2014

Region	*Percent of GNI*
High-income economies	(2013) 142.0%
Europe & Central Asia	58.0%
Latin America & Caribbean	29.5%
Sub-Saharan Africa	24.5%
South Asia	23.5%
Middle East & North Africa	15.3%
East Asia & Pacific	14.6%

Source: Adapted from the World Bank data, at : http://data.worldbank.org/indicator/DT.DOD.DECT.GN.ZS. Accessed January 16, 2016.

Table 4.2 G7 Countries external debt stock, 2008–13, in *US$ billions*

	2008	*2009*	*2010*	*2011*	*2012*	*2013*	*2008–13 variation*
Canada	848	1,029	1,144	1,248	1,408	1,390	0.64
France	4,881	5,180	5,161	5,223	5,377	5,549	0.14
Germany	5,220	5,245	5,37	5,494	5,775	5,503	0.05
Italy	2,396	2,561	2,445	2,36	2,526	2,629	0.10
Japan	2,231	2,086	2,589	3,115	3,017	2,803	0.26
United Kingdom	9,003	9,005	9,228	9,667	9,727	9,365	0.04
United States	13,757	13,662	14,516	15,508	15,68	16,488	0.20
Total G7 Countries	38,335	38,769	40,453	42,615	43,511	43,727	0.14

Source: Adapted from World Bank Quarterly External Debt Statistics.

falling from 55 per cent and 68 per cent of GDP, for Brazil and India respectively. Learning, however, from previous financial crisis, developing economies' governments expanded domestic credits, and this has resulted in drastic increase in the size of domestic debt and consequently higher avoidance of the risk of exchange rate fluctuation (World Bank, 2016). External debt stock of the Group of Seven (G7) countries, in US$ billions, for the period 2008–13, as indicated in Table 4.2 accounted for 64 per cent of the total external debt of high-income economies, totalling $43.7 trillion, during the year 2013.

The G7 countries' external contracted debt increased by more than 14 per cent during the period 2008–2013, with a slight increase of only 0.5 per cent from its 2012 level, led by Canada, for which the external debt stock rose by 64 per cent, followed by Japan, the United States and Italy, scoring increases of 26, 20 and 10 per cent respectively. Germany and the United Kingdom recorded only external debt increases of 5 per cent and 4 per cent respectively during the period 2008–2013.

The relationship between debt levels and growth

The relation of public debt level to economic growth is constantly a debated issue and it is commonly feared that very high public debt level may also make sovereign issuer enter the vicious cycle of sovereign indebtedness, where high level of public debt may appeal higher interest rate to be charged to the sovereign and this may undermine its investors' confidence, and consequently may reduce its growth by crippling its public and private sectors spending. Low growth may also dampen tax revenues and force the indebted government to orient to, or even spend more, on things resulting in a worsening of its budget position, like unemployment insurance and the like, and this may in turn require the issuance of more public debt (Cassidy, 2013). It is, however, suggested that the vicious cycle of indebtedness may not be encountered at every level of debt and there must be a certain threshold at which high levels of public debt will surely tend to be associated with very bad economic growth and severe financial crisis, but this should not be expected to be always the case. It was, however, suggested that once debt passes the level of 90 per cent of GDP the risks of a large negative impact on long-term growth will be highly probable (Reinhart and Rogof, 2010). This claim was not, however, commonly shared, and even seriously challenged on the basis of the serious weaknesses discovered in the work leading to it. Weaknesses such as programming errors, data omissions, questionable methodologies of weighting and elementary coding errors all were underlined with regard to this work (Herndon et al., 2013). Further, the other claim that above a ratio of 90 per cent of debt (Reinhart and Rogof, 2010), the average growth rate becomes negative doesn't seem to exist either (Cassidy, 2013). Locating themselves in the middle, Herndon et al. (2013) assert that with debt-to-GDP ratios below 30 per cent countries grew at an annual rate of 4.2 per cent and with debt-to-GDP ratios of between 30 and 60 per cent, countries only grew at an annual rate of 4.2 per cent, but the positive impact of public debt persists. The question remains however, "is there a level of indebtedness at which growth ceases or turns negative?" To our view the relation of indebtedness to growth should be expected to depend, of course, on level of debt, but also on the use of debt and the conditions of indebtedness, therefore such claim of direct/indirect relation of ratio of indebtedness and economic growth, without taking into account the use of the sovereign debt and conditions of indebtedness, appears difficult to justify.

The link between public default and financial crisis

A sovereign default is encountered whenever a sovereign fails to service its debt on time. Governments have a long history of borrowing outside the legal boundaries and not repaying their debts to foreign investors. "The first recorded sovereign default was in the 4th century BC when ten Greek cities failed to honour loans from the temple of Delos" (The Economist, 2014b). Although this may seem as the equivalent of going bankrupt for individuals or corporations, what precisely happens when sovereign countries put an end to the payment of what they owe to their creditor is a quite different story (The Economist, 2014b); It is indeed far more difficult for creditors to repossess a defaulted sovereign entity's assets than to repossess the assets of a private bankrupt entity (The Economist, 2014d) and the situation is exacerbated by the fact that there seems to be no effective international law or court for settling sovereign default litigations. This "impunity" situation may explain why sovereign default litigations are diverse in both their length and severity. New international legal provisions have recently, however, been enacted, but their success ultimately remains up to issuing countries. No provision can indeed be expected to resolve the huge amount of defaulted outstanding bonds and "like any messy divorce, drawn out negotiations around defaults can be costly for all parties involved. Working towards better pre-nuptial terms might not be such a bad idea" (The Economist, 2014d).

Table 4.3 Selected sovereign defaulters by the number of defaults since 1800

Country	*Number of defaults*	*Country*	*Number of defaults*	*Country*	*Number of defaults*
Ecuador	10	Turkey	8	Nigeria	5
Venezuela	10	Greece	7	Russia	5
Uruguay	9	Dominican Republic	7	Bolivia	5
Costa Rica	9	Nicaragua	7	Ghana	5
Brazil	9	Paraguay	7	Tunisia	5
Chile	9	Guatemala	7	El Salvador	5
Argentina	8	Austria	7	Germany	4
Peru	8	Columbia	7	Portugal	4
Mexico	8	Spain	6		

Source: Adapted from The Economist (2014a).

The classification of sovereign defaulters by the number of defaults, since 1800, is given in Table 4.3. It points to two countries as the world's most serial sovereign defaulters and re-defaulters, namely Ecuador and Venezuela. These two sovereigns seem to have both failed to honour their debts ten times since 1800; four other countries have defaulted nine times in total, Uruguay, Costa Rica, Brazil and Chile; four other countries have defaulted eight times, Argentina, Peru, Mexico and Turkey. Nine of the top ten defaulters are from Latin America, although many have shown no trace of the debt-default addiction for decades. "That, alas, is plainly not the case for Argentina" (The Economist, 2014c).

The link between public default and sovereign economic crisis can become more evident from many sovereign default experiences, or even from the last European sovereign crisis and from the fact that since the beginning of the nineteenth century, most sovereign defaults have occurred because of unexpected turn of economic or social events. It is argued, for instance, that starting in 2009, reports of bad news regarding the sustainability of public debt in Greece, Italy and Portugal undermined the banking sectors in these countries (Gennaioli et al., 2015), as national banks were suddenly exposed to their governments' bonds. Logically, sovereigns should have strong incentives to repay their debt, even if only to escape foreign sanctions and/or exclusion from the international global markets. But sanctions are rarely observed and market exclusions can only be of short duration. Therefore, the relatively low frequency of defaults should have other explication, and it is argued, for instance, that the huge cost on the domestic economy that might be imposed by default is perhaps dissuading governments to repay their debts, at least in part (Arellano, 2008). The Russian default of 1998, for instance, caused a lot of harm to the Russian economy, particularly to Russian banks that were heavily investing in public bonds, and the banking crisis ended up precipitating the devaluation of the rouble and the rapid collapse of whole Russian financial sector. As a rule, defaults, however, can be very painful for defaulting countries, in at least two ways, particularly when financial inabilities are occurring unexpectedly and in a disorderly manner:

(i) When investor and local savers, anticipating a decline in the value of the local currency, may strive to withdraw their bank account deposits and move them out of the troubled countries, eventually forcing troubled governments to temporarily shutting down banks and imposing capital controls, as the only way to avoid bank runs and precipitous currency depreciation, as happened in Greece in mid-2015. Often, however, such desperate reactions only exacerbate crisis.
(ii) Whenever sovereign defaulters find themselves submitted to capital market punishment for their default, either by imposition of punitive borrowing conditions or by opposed plea to all their indebtedness demands. Indeed, it seems that on average defaulted sovereign governments remain out of international capital markets for as long as 5.6 years after default and 4.4 years after final default resolution and 45 per cent of defaulters never regained market access during the study period (Moody's, 2015).

Sovereign ratings pro-cyclicality and asymmetry

The financial system is called pro-cyclical when fundamental measures of financial activity such as economic growth tend to behave differently during economic booms and during economic drops, improving more in economic booms. According to agencies credit ratings are not expected to vary in a pro-cyclical manner and are rather intended to distinguish the relatively risky issuers from the relatively safer. In order to be able to do so, CRAs need not reflect an absolute measure of default risk, but rather ordinal rankings of risk across a class of bonds or firms, at a particular point in time. In fact, rating agencies require that their ratings should be interpreted as ordinal rankings of default risk that are valid at all points in time, rather than absolute measures of default probability that are constant through time. Authors, however, show that ratings have been pro-cyclical during the Asian crisis, for instance (Ferri et al., 1999), thereby amplifying the recessions; they also find that rating changes tend to exhibit serial correlation, meaning that a downgrade is more likely to be followed by a subsequent downgrade than by an upgrade (Altman and Kao, 1992) Thus, rating changes are not independent, a finding that has been carefully modelled (Lando and Skodeberg, 2002). It seems also that rating cycles are characterised by their strong asymmetries, as their length and depth seem to show a very different behaviour during upgrade and downgrade phases (Broto and Molina, 2014). As rating increases tend to be slower than decreases, which are more abrupt, downgrade periods actually tend to be shorter than those of upgrades. Consequently, once a country loses its rating level it takes it a long period of time to recover it (Koopman et al., 2009).

What happens when a sovereign defaults?

Whenever a sovereign default occurs, the defaulter usually tries, as a first option and in order to keep sympathy of international markets, to restructure its debt rather than simply refuse to pay anything at all. This is the situation where the original value of a sovereign debt is reduced partially or substantially, a move called a "haircut". This, however, often proves to be even much more painful for the holders of sovereign bonds than a simple refusal to pay, or what is known as the "clip of the scissors" (The Economist, 2014b). Following its $81 billion default in 2001, Argentina, for instance, offered to pay its creditors a third of what it owed them, and ultimately around 93 percent of the debt was exchanged for performing securities maturing in 2005 and 2010. The remainder seems to be currently still in dispute and investors are waiting for $1.3 billion plus interest (The Economist, 2014b). Similarly, when Greece defaulted in 2012, bondholders were forced to take hits as high as 50 percent of their investment (The Economist, 2014b). In less severe cases, countries may choose to restructure their debt by asking for more time to pay, and this has the effect of reducing the present value of the bond. Such an option isn't entirely pain free either for investors and seems to be the right course of action for sovereigns struggling to balance their immediate domestic priorities against their obligations to their bondholders. A notorious case of sovereign restructuring would be the Brady plan initiated in March 1989.

In the 1980s, in the aftermath of default of many countries on their debt, new bonds were issued in order to convert bank loans to mostly Latin American countries, namely Argentina, Brazil, Bulgaria, Costa Rica, Dominican Republic, Ecuador, Mexico, Uruguay and Venezuela, but also Morocco, Nigeria, Philippines and Poland, into a variety of Brady bonds (Gennaioli et al., 2014). Brady bonds were issued for the principal sum and, in some cases also for the unpaid interest, in exchange for commercial bank loans. Given their improved liquidity and the guarantees they came with, Brady bonds were finally more valuable in some situations to the creditors than the original bonds. More importantly conversion transaction allows commercial banks to swap their claims on developing countries into more liquid instruments and to get sovereign debts off their balance sheets, reducing at the same time the concentration of their risk. The Brady plan was performed in two steps (Wikipedia).

In a first step, creditors and debtors negotiate the new terms of the new Brady bonds, containing a combination of two options, an "exit" option and a "new money" option. Exit options were mainly designed for creditors, looking for the reduction at a discount of their exposure to debtor sovereign countries. In such case, instruments principal and "rolling interest guarantees" were generally pledged as collaterals (Wikipedia). The new money options, on the other hand, or the amount of new lending called for, are determined in first round negotiations, which also involved the assessment of the effective magnitude of discount on the exit options. In such case the principal amount was usually, but not always, collateralised by specially issued U.S. Treasury 30-year zero-coupon bonds and were purchased by the debtor sovereign country.

In a second step, creditors converted their existing claims into their choice between the two options agreed upon in the first step. Although, the penalties for creditors' non-compliance with the terms of the deal were never made explicit, nevertheless compliance did not seem to constitute an important issue under the plan. Creditors wishing to put an end to their foreign lending activities tended to choose the exit option under the deal and used towards this aim a combination of International Monetary Fund, World Bank and the country's own foreign currency reserves. Interest payments on Brady bonds were occasionally guaranteed by securities rated at least Aa credit quality and held with the Federal Reserve Bank of New York. By offering such multiple options to the parties involved, the Brady plan permitted credit restructurings to be tailored to the heterogeneous preferences of creditors. The terms achieved under these deals indicate that debtors used the menu approach to minimise the cost of debt restructuring, which furthermore minimises the holdout where some shareholders may have an incentive to not participate in the restructuring, hoping for better deals (Wikipedia).

Default resolution seems to be relatively quick, taking on average slightly over one year and does not seem to be driven by inability to find a solution, but rather by length of time necessary for a sovereign country to rebuild ability and reputation to service debt (Moody's, 2015). During resolution periods CRAs will no doubt issue warning against investing in the country, but historically lenders were often quick to start lending again so long as they are promised, in convincing manner, sufficient reward for the risk they are taking on. Lenders also often use specific protective financial instruments or credit-default swaps as a form of insurance against sovereign defaults, allowing them to hedge their default risk. A sovereign may also choose to avoid default, and it has at its disposal several options towards this aim that are not mutually exclusive (Tyler Durden, 2014).

1 The first option consists of attempting to grow its GDP faster than public debt, in order to reduce the burden of its ratio of public debt to GDP.
2 The second option is to pursue fiscal adjustment until the budget balance without debt interest, or primary balance payments, reaches a surplus.
3 Another option is to restructure debt.
4 A final and more radical option is to fully default on the debt. This usually happens after years of austerity fatigue.

Indeed, some of these options are easy to say than to do, and when a country can achieve a level of control over its destiny, there will be no room for default, anyway.

Sovereign risk and country risk

Although key components of sovereign risk were presented in Chapter 2, this section distinguishes sovereign credit risk from country risk; these are two related but distinct concepts. While sovereign credit risk is more narrowly focused on the possibility of a sovereign government defaulting on its debt obligations, country risk, on the other hand, is the one that can have negative consequences on sovereign creditworthiness, such as weak property rights, unpredictable tax and legal regimes, and precarious operating and political environments.

Actually any risk raising the level of the possibilities of a sovereign government failing to make debt repayments or not honouring loan agreement can be considered a sovereign risk. In times of economic uncertainty or political unrest, failure solutions can easily be opted for and reached by enacting any sovereign law that may cause adverse losses to investors. In 1998, for instance, and as mentioned in Chapter 3, Ukraine decided on a moratorium on its sovereign debt service and only bearers willing to identify and convert to local currency were qualified to payments. Ukraine like other sovereign defaulters was ill prepared to face default crisis and may have recourse to restrictive monetary policy in the hope of offsetting any spill-over effect from sovereign default risk to private funding conditions. This is how, for instance, sovereign risk has risen sharply in several European countries, in the wake of the recent global crisis, notably in the euro area periphery (Corsetti et al., 2012).

Country risk, is a collection of risks linked to investing in a foreign country and incorporates the other elements of risk discussed in Chapter 2, such as the political risk, the exchange rate risk, the economic risk, the transfer risk and the conversion control risk. This book deals only with sovereign default that relates to the probability of failure on debt owed to private creditors (Fitch, 2014). Sovereign risk and country risk are entangled, and the former can be looked at as a consequence of the latter, as sovereign with high country risk would also face more difficulties in servicing its debt obligations and will eventually find itself forced to have recourse to default. Further, sovereign risk can be transmitted in both directions between sovereigns and financial institutions. In one direction, financial institutions are commonly exposed to sovereign risks through their holdings of sovereign bonds and through the influence of the sovereign's funding costs on their own funding. On the other hand, explicit and implicit government guarantees and potential fiscal costs of recapitalisation transmit bank risk to the sovereign. "Such two-way feedback between the sovereign and financial institutions can create a destabilizing spiral if risks arise in one or the other" (IMF, 2013).

Sovereign ratings and the global sovereign credit market

The global sovereign credit market relies on agencies mainly because of their renewed, although sporadic, updating of the credit ratings (Cantor and Packer, 1994). Studies dealing with the impact of sovereign debt ratings on the global credit market can be broadly gathered into two categories. There are, first, the papers that try to uncover the determinants of sovereign debt ratings and concluding that the rating scale is mainly explained by macroeconomic variables like the level of GDP per capita, the real GDP growth, the external debt, the public debt level and the government budget balance (Afonso Gomes and Rother, 2011). There are also studies dealing with the explanatory power of sovereign ratings for the development of government bond spreads and reporting that sovereign rating changes and credit outlooks have a relevant effect on the size and volatility of lending, particularly in emerging markets, notably for the case of ratings' downgrades and negative outlooks (Afonso et al., 2007). It seems, moreover, that a positive credit rating event is even more relevant for emerging markets and that markets generally tend to anticipate negative events, consequently spill-over effects exist across sovereign ratings (Gande and Parsley, 2005). The spill-over effect of sovereign rating has further been examined only to discover that rating downgrades have statistically significant effects across countries and financial markets, and such finding highlights the spill-over effect between different financial markets (Arezki et al., 2011). This happens particularly when an event in a given context is initiated by something else in a seemingly unrelated context. The form of the spill-over effect seems, however, to depend on linkages between countries (Businessdictionary).

Public monitoring institutions use to rely on agencies' ratings for their monitoring requirements, and private fund charts usually contained specific provision limiting investment to instruments bearing investment grades. Money funds, for instance, used to be obliged to invest at least 97 per cent of their assets in securities that received the highest short-term rating. Further, the SEC's Rule 2a-7 used to require money market funds to limit their portfolio investments to securities that are "eligible securities", by reference to credit ratings provided by NRSROs. This situation has allowed credit ratings to monitor securities investment on the global market and to exercise their complete control over the global financing. The situation seems, however, to be changing. The Securities and Exchange Commission of the United States, for instance, on September 16, 2015, adopted amendments to remove credit rating references in its principal rule that governs money market funds and the form that money market funds use to report information to the SEC each month about their portfolio holdings, under current rules Rule 2a-7. The Basel Committee on Banking Supervision, on the other hand, seems to be backing its project of banning banks from relying on rating agencies when they calculate risks in their portfolio. "The U-turn comes after intense lobbying from banks and the rating agencies themselves, which argued that forcing credit ratings out of calculations would mean a cruder measure of credit riskiness – and one that would drive up the amount of capital banks must hold" (Ft.com). Practically the Basel Committee is setting a comeback of rating agencies in global rules for how lenders assess credit risk (Bloomberg, 2015).

Conclusion

Sovereign credit ratings are predominantly insured by three major agencies, Fitch Ratings, Moody's and Standard & Poor's. Notwithstanding the accuracy/inaccuracy of their ratings, they seem to have real effect on credit market and investors' behaviour. Recent severe adjustments of sovereign credit ratings for many economies throughout the world have seriously raised anxiety about the credit rating impact on the macroeconomic level and the efficiency of the global financial system. Sovereign ratings are feared to initiate pro-cyclicality into global capital flows by accelerating capital inflows during the economic expansion and contributing to their collapse in crisis periods (Kräussl, 2003). Pro-cyclicality refers to the tendency of financial variables to fluctuate around a trend during the economic cycle. For instance, rating agencies downgrade moves stemming from unfavourable indicators may have prompted the latest sovereign crisis. We can indeed either imply that rating events have, to some extent, gone awry of fundamentals or that fundamentals are not fully discounted on a permanent basis by market participants. Although, the rapid reaction of EU spreads to credit rating events (within one to two days) can be seen as the proof that good macroeconomic fundamentals and sound fiscal policies are key elements in preventing both rating downgrades and upward movements in debt securities yield[1] spreads.[2,3] It can therefore be concluded that sovereign credit rating structure and functioning can affect the behaviour of the global financial market but doubts exist regarding the accuracy of the ratings. The next chapter will discuss the evolutionary history of credit ratings and the emergence of credit rating oligopoly.

Notes

1 Yield refers to the interest or dividends received from a security and are usually expressed annually as a percentage based on the investment's cost, its current market value or its face value.
2 A credit spread is the spread between Treasury securities and non-Treasury securities that are identical in all respects except for quality rating.
3 The yield spread is the difference between yields on differing debt instruments, calculated by deducting the yield of one instrument from another. The higher the yield spread, the greater the difference between the yields offered by each instrument.

5 The history of sovereign ratings and the emergence of the three major sovereign credit agencies

Sovereign credit ratings seem to have real effect on investor behaviour and market conditions and the rating of government bonds, as a private activity, was, however, introduced only in the beginning of 1900, although well-organised government bond markets existed even before 1600. Such activity was then meant to provide investors with objective analyses and independent assessments of the capacity of issuers of sovereign debt to face their obligations. Historical information and discussion of sovereign credit market and major agencies will facilitate a greater understanding of the function and the evolution of sovereign credit rating.

This chapter, however, will concentrate on those agencies that influence the global sovereign credit market and will: discuss the sovereign market history and major sovereign rating agencies short history; underline sovereign debt development; examine sovereign defaulters history; introduce three cases of modern sovereign default; analyse the trends in sovereign credit ratings; debate the credit rating industry business models; present the regulation of the rating agencies and the Nationally Recognized Statistical Rating Organizations system; then conclude the chapter.

Sovereign market history

The interest in the activity of sovereign creditworthiness assessment must be as old as sovereign indebtedness itself, and as early as 1600 the Dutch were already creating the first structured system for government securities; they had implemented, since then, an organised government bond market as well as a well-functioning banking system. This may have made the Dutch Republic that has existed from 1581 to 1795 (following its separation from Spain) the leading economy of the seventeenth century (Sylla, 2001). In 1688 and by having a Dutch king, the English also secured themselves the importation at home of the most advanced financial system of the time; King William of England and Ireland from 1689 to 1702 brought with him to England many experienced Dutch financiers and in a relatively short period of time England mastered the key components of the then modern financial system (Sylla, 2001). It was, however, in the aftermath of the American independence that the United States put in place a modern financial system, predominantly inspired by Dutch and English practices. In less than a decade, the United States had also in hand strong public finances and well-operating bond and stock markets (Sylla, 2001). It was only at the beginning of the twentieth century that credit rating emerged as a structured business activity insured by independent agencies. Bond ratings came along rather late in the history of public finance. Indeed when John Moody's introduced its innovative bond rating system in 1909, "Dutch investors had been buying sovereign bonds for three centuries, English investors for two and American investors for one century and all the time without the benefit of agency ratings" (Sylla, 2001).

As long as business transactions operated between parties that knew each other, there was actually no strong incentive for a professional appraisal of clients' and/or suppliers' creditworthiness. As, however, the scale and scope of financial business transactions expanded in new larger economic systems, the need for information on transactions and counterparts, of whom no personal knowledge exists, became important. The creditworthiness of clients and suppliers was before mainly established by looking at the religious morality of the issuer and /or by considering his family ranking in society (Naciri, 2015), and progressively parties to the transaction were requiring letters of recommendation from a person known for probity. By mid-1800, however, new specialised credit-reporting institutions emerged, to cope with the expanding scale and scope of business transactions. By then clients were already classified in a system that was close to today's agencies' ranking. Similarly in the aftermath of the 1837 financial crisis, one of the visionaries in the field of credit quality assessment, Louis Tappan, a New York merchant who, in the course of his business, had compiled extensive records on the creditworthiness of his customers, decided to specialise in providing commercial information; he had the brilliant idea of creating his own and probably the first mercantile credit bureau in the world, the Mercantile Agency, which had as an objective the assessment of merchant ability to meet indebtedness obligations. The Mercantile Agency was acquired by Robert Dun to become R.G. Dun and Company in 1859, when it released its first credit rating guide (Gaillard, 2010). At that time the number of the company subscribers amounted already to over 40,000 and included wholesalers, importers, manufacturers, banks and insurance companies, and by 1900 the company reports covered more than a million businesses.

Ten years before and precisely in 1849, John Bradstreet created his own business, similar to a mercantile credit agency, and published its first ranking of debtors in 1857. Nearly a century later, precisely in 1933, Robert Dun and John Bradstreet consolidated their two businesses under the banner of Dun & Bradstreet, to become in 1962 owner of Moody's Investor Services. Despite the fact that Poor's Publishing Company had issued its first ratings in 1916, Standard Statistics Company issued its own in 1922 and Fitch Publishing Company in 1924, the real take-off of credit rating activity seemed to have been launched only in 1928, by the publication of the Moody's Analyses of Railroad Investments manual (Investopedia).

Similarly John Knowles Fitch launched in 1913 in New York the smallest of the three largest agencies, Fitch Ratings, which in 1997 merged with the London-based IBCA Limited. Although Fitch Ratings enjoys a smaller market share than Moody's and S&P, it has grown substantially through acquisitions of smaller agencies; it has for instance acquired both Chicago-based Duff & Phelps Credit Rating Co., Thomson Financial Bank Watch and several other small agencies (investopedia).

The year 1941 marked yet another turning point in the rating industry; this is the year when Standard Statistics and Poor's Publishing Company joined activities to form Standard and Poor's. Since then newcomers to the rating market have become few, although we can notice the Duff & Phelps market entry in 1982, the foundation of McCarthy Crisanti and Maffer, in 1975, subsequently acquired by Xerox Financial Services a while before its fixed income research and rating service was merged in to Duff & Phelps in 1991.

Despite the fact that it has only been since the 1980s that the most developed economies have been rated, the process actually started in the aftermath of the Second World War, when Standard & Poor's and Moody's extended their rating of individual bond issues to rating national government issuers. By 1985, for example, Moody's rated 14 sovereign issuers, and the majority of these received Moody's top "Aaa" rating (Cantor and Packer, 1996). During the 1990s both the number and diversity of sovereign issuers receiving ratings increased steadily and by 2007, Moody's was rating 107 sovereign issuers, and only around 20 per cent of these received an "Aaa" rating (Cantor and Packer, 1996). A similar pattern of growth in the volume of sovereign ratings from all CRAs was driven by the increasingly global nature of their business and the need to provide a sovereign benchmark for corporate issuers in a wide range of locations around the world (CAPCO, 2013).

Major sovereign rating agencies short history

Although there are hundreds of credit agencies in the world today, three global U.S. based agencies – Standard and Poor's (S&P), Moody's and Fitch Ratings, the Big 3 – dominate the global credit market and have complete control over the global sovereign rating activity. A brief review of the history these three major agencies will contribute to a better understanding of the sovereign credit market itself.

The adventure of Fitch Rating,[1] the third largest global rating player, started with the founding on December 24, 1913, by John Knowles Fitch, of Fitch Publishing Company, which specialised in the publication of financial statistics to be used in the investment industry, through two different manuals: the "Fitch Stock and Bond Manual" and "The Fitch Bond Book". The alphanumerical rating system in use today seems to have been actually introduced by Fitch in 1924. Fitch decided early in the nineties to become the full-service global rating agency it is today and strived to take advantage of every arising merging opportunity encountered: it for instance merged in the late 1990s with IBCA of London, a subsidiary of the French holding company Fimalac S.A., and acquired Market Thomson Bank Watch. Beginning in 2004 Fitch also developed operating subsidiaries specializing in enterprise risk management data services and finance industry training with the acquisition of the Algorithmic and the creation of Fitch Solutions and Fitch Training.

Moody's[2] origins can be traced back to the beginning of the 1900s, when John Moody and Company first published its "Moody's Manual", containing basic statistics and general information about stocks and bonds of various industries. "Moody's Manual" was created based on the company's assessment of the market's needs at the time and remained a national publication for four years, e.g. until the stock market crash of 1907. In 1909 Moody's pushed a step further its business information activity, by launching the publication of "Moody's Analysis of Railroad Investments" and, at the same time, adding analytical information about the value of securities to basic statistics. This expansion of the published data led to the creation of Moody's Investors Service in 1914 and in the decade that followed, Moody's Investors Service would provide ratings for nearly all of the government bond markets at the time. By the 1970s Moody's began rating commercial paper and bank deposits and thus became the full-scale rating agency that it is today. Indeed, "From that original manual Moody's expanded and strengthened its position over the next 100+ years as one of the leading providers of credit and risk opinions in the market".[3]

Henry Varnum Poor's can legitimately be declared as the founder of securities analysis and reporting, to be developed over the next century. He inaugurated the saga of Standard and Poor's by being the first to publish in 1860 the "History of Railroads and Canals in the United States", amassing comprehensive information about the financial and operational state of U.S. railroad companies. He also created in 1868, with his son Henry William Poor, the H.V. and H.W. Poor Co., and published two annually updated hardback guide books: *Poor's Manual of the Railroads of the United States* and *Poor's Directory of Railway Officials*. In 1906 Standard Statistics was formed and published corporate bond sovereign debt and municipal bond ratings; it merged with Poor's Publishing in 1941 to form Standard & Poor's corporation, to be acquired by the McGraw-Hill Companies Inc. In 1966, Standard & Poor's became best known by its S&P 500 index, as a market index that is both a tool for investor analysis and decision making.[4]

The Big 3 have become in around a century an essential part of the global capital markets, providing credit ratings research tools and analysis that have surely contributed to an integrated financial system, and can provide a basis for understanding and managing financial risk; they are, however, the subject of much controversy and source of frustration. The U.S. government has fined some of them heavily for lack of accuracy and the EU officials are convinced and argued that agencies sovereign ratings have "accelerated the euro zone's sovereign debt crisis leading to calls for the creation of an independent European rating agency" (Council of Foreign Relations, 2015).

Sovereign debt development

As early as 2000, as global capital flows shifted from the banking sector to capital markets and thanks to what seems to be easygoing regulators and generous globalisation, large CRAs have found themselves to rating debt in financial markets all over the world, in developed, developing and emerging economies alike (Naciri, 2015). Table 5.1 gives country average general government debt in US$

Table 5.1 Country average general government debt in US$ bil for the year 2014, by group of countries

	Average (US$ Bil.)	*Number of countries*	*% of Advanced industrial countries*
Advanced Industrial Countries	1,568.98	29	1
Developing Countries Aaa to A3	282.57	17	5,5
Developing Countries Baa1 to Baa3	197.24	26	7,95
Developing Countries Ba1 to Ba3	33.99	18	46
Developing Countries B1 to C	43.63	28	36
Total		118	

Source: Adapted from Moody's (2013a), Moody's statistical handbook.

bil for the year 2014, by group of countries. It expresses the total direct debt of the general government held by the public at year-end expressed in US$ bill. Note however that these figures include all short- and long-term obligations regardless of the currency of denomination and the residency of the holder, Moody's (2013a).

In 2014 each one of the of the twenty-nine countries that were members of the advanced industrial countries group has on average signed for a total of 1.569 US$ bil, representing more than five times the 282.57 US$ bil amount of debt contracted by each the seventeen members of the developing countries group, with Aaa to A3 rating, and forty-six times the 33.99 US$ bil amount of debt contracted by each the eighteen members of the developing countries group, with Ba1 to Ba3. As we can see, the global indebtedness is far from being homogenous. Table 5.2, on the other hand indicates that external debt stock developing countries has increased by 36% during the period 2008–2013, while G7 country members have increased their external debt stock by only 8% during the same period. For the period 2008–2013, the group of all developing economies accounted only for around 10 per cent of the total external debt stock of the world (all developing countries and G7 combined). Further, the fifty-seven member countries of the developing economies group have less external debt stock than any single member country of the G7, except for Canada and Japan. Indeed, the G7 countries accounted for around 90 per cent of the external debt stock of developing countries and G7 member countries combined, and 64 per cent of the total external debt of high-income economies, for an amount of $43.7 US$ trillion, for the year 2013. The G7 group was led by the United States for which the external debt stock in 2013 reached 16.488 US$ trillion, followed by United Kingdom with 9.365 US$ trillion, France 5.549 US$ trillion and Germany 5.503 US$ trillion (2015 World Bank Quarterly External Debt Statistics).

On average external debt stock of developing countries for the period 2008–2013, totalled 4.362 US$ trillion, compared with 41.235 US$ trillion for the G7 country members. During the period 2008–2013, the total debt outstanding to developing countries rose 31 per cent. It rose from $3.833 US$ trillion in 2008 to $5.5 trillion by the end of 2013. reflecting net debt increase of over 1.0 US$ trillion. During the same period, the total debt outstanding of G7 country rose by

Table 5.2 External debt stock developing countries and G7 member countries, 2008–2013 (in *US$ billion*)

	2008	*2009*	*2010*	*2011*	*2012*	*2013*	*Mean 2008–2013*	*%*	*2008–2013 change*
All developing countries	3324.9	3629.7	4109.4	4571.6	5032.1	5506.4	4362.35	9.57	0.31
Total G7 countries	38335	38769	40453	42615	43511	43727	41235	90.43	0.08
Total developing and G7	43667.9	44407.7	46572.4	49197.6	50555.1	51246.4	45597.35	100	0.04
All developing countries as a % of Total G7 countries	8.67	9.36	10.16	10.73	11.57	12.59	10.58	10.58	

Source: Adapted from 2015 World Bank Quarterly External Debt Statistics.

only 8 per cent, the total debt outstanding of Canada, Japan, France and Germany, the United States and the UK rose by 39 per cent, 18, 7 and 4, respectively and the United Kingdom had the highest external debt to GDP ratio at 371 per cent in 2013, followed by France with above 200 per cent, Germany 151 per cent.

Sovereign defaulters history

Sovereign default occurs whenever a country is unable or unwilling to service its international debt. The development of sovereign default goes hand in hand with sovereign indebtedness. It is believed that Greece was the very first known country to have defaulted on its debt, around 377 BC and only since its independence in 1829, Greece has spent around half its time in default on its sovereign debt. It defaulted, for instance, in 1826, 1843, 1860, 1893 and 1932. Spain also defaulted on its debt six times in the eighteenth century and seven times in the nineteenth century; Spain escaped, however, unscathed from the twentieth century and (still) hasn't defaulted as of today (Bojesen, 2012). Austria defaulted several times, in 1796, 1938, 1940 and 1945; England defaulted in 1340, 1472 and 1594 and hasn't defaulted since then; France defaulted in 1558, 1624, 1648, 1661, 1701, 1715, 1770, 1788 and 1812 and hasn't defaulted since 1812; Germany defaulted in 1683, 1807, 1813, 1932 and 1939; Portugal defaulted in 1560, 1828, 1837, 1841, 1845, 1852 and 1890; Holland defaulted only once, in 1814. Sovereign defaulting profile seems to have changed tremendously in late centuries, the classical default picture of empires battling with huge war spending efforts and unable to cope with it has gone with major wars and has been replaced by the default picture of countries faced with unsolvable budgetary constraints. Table 5.3 gives the list of major defaulters, by region for the period 1983–2014.

We can learn, for stance, from Table 5.3 that the huge amounts involved in sovereign defaults range from 794.930 US$ mil for Iraq to 50.032 US$ mil for Ethiopia. Also most of the thirty countries reported by Moody's as having defaulted during the period 1975–2014, come from developing and emerging economies and only few countries are part of the advanced industrial countries group, like Greece and Portugal. Two countries belonging to the group of developing countries with Aaa to Aa3 ratings have also defaulted, Poland and Chile, and so five countries belong to the group of developing countries with Baa1 to Baa3 ratings.

All together nine countries out of the twenty-one defaulting countries, reported by Moody's, were classified as investment grade debtors and around 30 per cent of defaults do not seem to locate in speculative grade area. Generally speaking, twenty default issuers come, during the period 1983–2014, from emerging and developing countries, except Portugal and Greece, eighteen come from western Europe region, seventeen from both Latin America and Central and Eastern Europe regions, eleven from sub-Saharan Africa, ten from Middle East and North Africa, and ten from the Caribbean (Moody's, 2013a). Defaults have however, ended up in issuer-weighted recovery rates of 63 per cent for the period 1998–2014, corresponding to a value-weighted recovery average rate of 43 per cent (Moody's, 2015). The next section will concentrate on three modern renowned defaulters, to unearth some of characteristics of sovereign default.

Table 5.3 The major sovereign defaulters for the period 1975–2014 in US$ mil

Country	*Rating*	*Cumulative default in US$ mil*	*Country*	*Rating*	*Cumulative default in US$ mil*
Iraq		794.927	Ireland		88.290
Argentina	B1 to C	787.939	Serbia		8.8943
Brazil	Baa1 to Baa3	685.334	Philippines	Ba1 to Ba3	82.903
Greece	Advanced	525.239	Myanmar		80.509
USSR/Russia	Baa1 to Baa3	517.325	Tanzania		77.143
Sudan	B1 to C	418.500	Egypt	B1 to C	76.756
Nigeria	Ba1 to Ba3	243.006	Liberia		74.939
Poland	Aaa to Aa3	195.431	Angola	Ba1 to Ba3	62.754
Venezuela		157.505	Somalia		61.284
Côte d'Ivoire	B1 to C	154.013	South Africa	Baa1 to Baa3	59.928
Korea(North)		134.098	Rep. of Congo (Brazzaville)		59.565
Peru	Baa1 to Baa3	152.244	Zambia	B1 to C	58.851
Syria		138.937	Chile	Aaa to Aa3	52.971
Indonesia	Baa1 to Baa3	94.662	Portugal	Advanced	52.712
Nicaragua	B1 to C	92.794	Ethiopia		50.032

Source: Computed based on the data from Beers and Nadeau (2015), Database of Sovereign Defaults 2015. Bank of Canada Technical Report No. 101.

Three cases of modern sovereign default

This section deals with three well-publicised cases of sovereign default, namely Argentina, Greece and Ukraine. The first sovereign defaulter to be discussed is Argentina, its economy entered severe recession in 1998, resulting in default by the year 2001 on a USD 93 billion of external debt. As expected, several critical consequences resulted from such event. First, foreign investment ended up deserting the country, and second, capital flow toward the country dried almost completely for four years, 2001–2003, and third, the peso, the national currency, suffered quickly and drastically from a severe devaluation, to nearly 4 to 1, producing a sudden rise in inflation of over 40 per cent and a fall in real GDP of 11 per cent (Wikipedia). Although the country has in an urgent and a large-scale debt restructuring, investors' frustration made any refinancing extremely difficult and it is only till 2005 and later in 2010 that economic recovery eventually allowed Argentina to offer large-scale debt exchange; the 2005 swap brought 76 per cent of bonds out of default and the 2010 swap, 91.3 per cent. The terms of these debt swaps were, however, refused by some bondholders and despite debt restructuring efforts, the country ultimately still found itself in a bad position with, as result, a loss of access to international credit markets. As a desperate reaction, Argentina opted for the freeing of the foreign exchange market and removing all price controls. Unfortunately, a sudden price increase has resulted, one that was accompanied by a huge banking crisis, which ultimately led to large-scale bank deposit withdrawals. Argentina's overall debt level, lower than the one of the majority of advanced industrial countries, should have allowed the country to face its sovereign obligations with relatively more ease and it is far for being the case.

The second sovereign default case concerns Greece. The introduction of the euro in 2001, as a common currency in the European economic space, has negatively impacted Greece's current account deficit, as its labour costs increased, making its export less competitive relative to other more efficient European Union member economies. The situation put Greece in a position where its consumption was higher that its production, and requires the country to contract more foreign borrowing. Consequently, in less than a decade, both the Greek trade deficit and budget deficit rose drastically from below 5 per cent of GDP in 1999 to a peak of around 15 per cent of GDP in 2009. The Greek debt crisis had built up on revelations that the country was misreporting data on government economic fundamentals and an additional confidence crisis has added up by 2012 and made Greece's the largest sovereign debt default in history, with an amount of sovereign debt by 2015 of €323 bil. This also made Greece the first developed country to fail to service an IMF loan (Wikipedia).

The third case of sovereign default is Ukraine; the country's financial troubles started in 1992, when the national bank of Ukraine opened a new chapter of financing facilities and began issuing loans to state-owned enterprises and guaranteeing them foreign loans. Unfortunately, the whole process was introduced while transparent mechanisms and appropriate methodologies of analysing such loans were missing in the country. At the time, indeed, assessments of credit projects in Ukraine were exposed to corruption and ineffectiveness procedures (Wikipedia). Borrowings decisions were made without any real assessment or insurance of the ability of the state budget to service contracted debts. In less than a decade, from 1992 to 1999, the state has guaranteed over US$ 2.4 bil loans that most of the borrowers never pay back and eventually declared fictitious bankruptcies. Ukraine sovereign default of the years 1999–2000 seemed to be the result of such doubtful state credit policy. Consequently Ukraine bonds were reissued with payments scheduled in 2001–2004. Although the country seems to have enjoyed a decade of economic recovery and growth, this favourable episode unfortunately ended by the year 2008, only for Ukraine to experience yet another severe economic distress by 2015, with annual economic contraction in double digits and extremely high inflation rates. Although Ukraine's position was tremendously weakened during restructuring negotiations that followed (Popovych, 2015), the country managed to issue a moratorium on debt service for bearer bonds owned by anonymous entities and, as mentioned before, only investors willing to convert their securities to local currency accounts and identify were eligible for debt repayments.

Some key conclusions can be drawn from the three sovereign default cases presented here; it is clear, for instance, that default is often the consequence of doubtful past economic and political policies that weaken the fundamentals of the defaulting country. It seems, however, that the high level of the fundamental debt-to-GDP does not seem to constitute either necessary or sufficient condition for a default (Moody's, 2015). Indeed, the debt/GDP ratios of Argentina and Ukraine are lower than those of advanced industrial countries (37.7 and 71.2 vs. 78), while Greece's ratio is more than twice higher (177.1 vs. 78). It is also obvious that a significant amount of foreign-currency debt can be a major source of vulnerability; further, debt affordability is better correlated with past defaults than debt-to-GDP; a lack of economic strength and weak institutions are decisive factors in sovereign defaults. It seems also that restructurings may provide liquidity relief but often not solvency relief (Moody's, 2015); finally, we can mention a common weakness shared by the three defaulting countries, namely their very low recovery rates that went as low as 24 and 27 per cent, for Greece and Argentina, respectively, although 69 per cent for Ukraine, compared with 100 per cent for most advanced industrial nations (Moody's statistical handbook, 2013).

Trends in sovereign credit ratings

The demand for sovereign ratings has grown rapidly in recent decades, due to the globalisation of financial markets and investors' increasing focus on international diversification. About $US 6000 bil of debt securities that were issued in 2009 were given Aaa rating, of that about $US 3500 bil was sovereign debt, compared with $US 500 bil of the $US 2000 bil has Aaa and was issued by governments (Rayan, 2012). Table 5.4 represents in columns 2, 3 and 4 Moody's rating distribution of sovereign issuers and in columns 5, 6 and 7 issuer-weighted cumulative default rates for the years 1985 and 2014. Column 4 indicates that by end-2014

Table 5.4 Moody's rating distribution of sovereign issuers and issuer-weighted cumulative default rates on selected dates

Rating	*1985*	*2014*	*Variation*	*1985*	*2014*	*Variation*
	Rating distribution			*Weighted cumulative default rates*		
Aaa	77%	11%	−66%	0.00%	0.00%	0.00%
Aa	23%	11%	−12%	0.20%	1.12%	460%
A	0%	10%	10%	0.54%	5.56%	929%
Baa	0%	22%	22%	0.82%	1.92%	134%
Ba	0%	16%	16%	3.10%	12.67%	308%
B	0%	23%	23%	8.49%	20.19%	137%
Caa-C	0%	6%	6%	50.53%	50.53%	0.00%
Investment-grade	100%	54%	−46%	0.36%	1.95%	441%
Speculative-grade	0%	46%	46%	6.95%	17.22%	147%

Source: Adapted from Moody's Rating Services (Excel Data).

the share of investment-grade (Baa and above) had declined to around 54 per cent, from 100 per cent, its 1985 level. By end-2014 also, the share of Aaa and Aa rated sovereigns declined tremendously, and the share of A to Caa rated sovereigns increased significantly. While all rated sovereign issuers in 1985 were investment grade, they recently score 54 per cent only, riskier emerging market countries have entered the sovereign debt markets and a major shift in ratings has occurred.

Columns 5, 6 and 7 in Table 5.4 present one-year through ten-year issuer-weighted average cumulative default rates for sovereign issuers, calculated by "averaging the experiences of issuer cohorts formed at monthly frequencies by forming and tracking such cohorts of all Moody's-rated issuers at the beginning of every month" (Moody's). Sovereign default rates have been on average significantly higher in 2014 than in 1985. The cumulative default on investment-grade has increased by 192 per cent while default in speculative grade has increased by 1722 per cent. Grades Ba and B have registered the highest increase in cumulative defaults, 100 per cent and 12 per cent respectively. Cumulative default of extreme grade classes Aaa and C remained unchanged at 0 per cent and 50.53 per cent respectively. The shift from investment grade to speculative can be more easily grasped from Figure 5.1, highlighting Moody's rating distribution behaviour during the period 1985–2014. Sovereign issuers with investment-grade ratings have given ground to speculative grade and the shift is so decisive and sharp, to the point where sovereign issuers' speculative-grade ratings have jumped from 0 per cent in 1985 to 46 per cent in 2014. Speculative-grade ratings seem, however, to have stabilised since 2000, when they scored 40 per cent of all the ratings.

Losing investment grade status is feared by most sovereign issuers, as a downgrade to speculative grade is different from other downgrade movements along the rating scale, as they are perceived to be linked to a much higher risk and therefore would result in much substantial financing costs and stricter financing conditions for the sovereign. Indeed, speculative-grade status is expected to increase spreads by triggering lower flows from institutional investors and private funds whose covenants prevent them from taking on high risk in their portfolios.

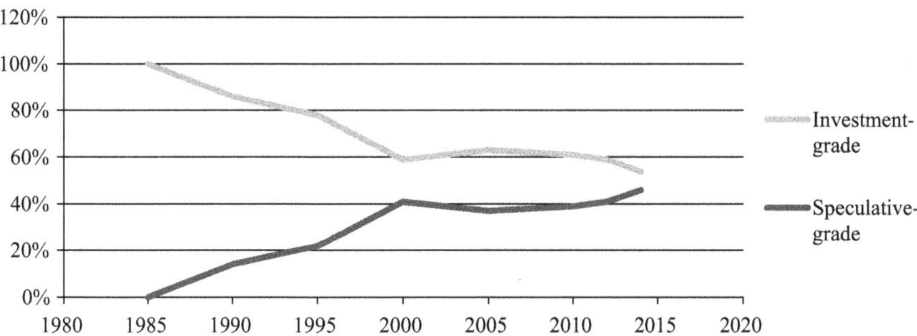

Figure 5.1 Moody's rating distribution of sovereign issuers investment-grade and speculative-grade for the period 1985–2014[5]

Source: Moody's Investors Service Sovereign Default and Recovery Rates 1983–2014 (Excel data).

Overall global sovereign creditworthiness has declined tremendously during the period 1985–2014, the most abrupt decline registered during the period 1985–2000 and a slight respite was scored for the period 2001–2005. The period 2006–14 registered a more modest decline, particularly since the beginning of the global financial crisis in 2008. In the aftermath of the last financial crisis, agencies started to downgrade several advanced economies and even assigned junk status to countries like Ireland, Portugal and Greece. The conclusions withdrawn from Table 5.5 concern mainly Moody's data. Big 3 rating agencies, however, tend to follow each other in their ratings and predominantly in times of crises.

Credit rating industry business models

There always has been vigorous debate around rating agencies business model, the one established by John Moody in 1909 and generalised by the Big 3 in the early 1970s, namely the issuer-pays model, IPM. Accordingly the sovereign that is issuing bonds has also to pay the rating agency for rating them. The IPM is supposed, according to agencies, to present a number of advantages, besides being highly lucrative, like:

(i) Ensuring a standardised quality of ratings
(ii) Giving ratings a wide free-of-charge spread availability through the market and participants
(iii) Keeping ratings in the public domain and maintaining the cost to the system low, allowing their easy access to smaller investors, who otherwise cannot afford paying for them
(iv) Contributing to the enhancement of market efficiency by improving the speed of financial decisions. Indeed an investor can compare the ratings of a wide array of instruments before making an investment decision and can continuously evaluate the relative creditworthiness of a wide range of issuers and borrowers.
(v) Finally, giving rating agencies access to undisclosed information that may enhance the quality of analysis.

The other business model that can be used by CRAs is the "subscriber-pay" model, though it does not seem free from conflicts of interest either. This is a business model where investors, instead of issuers, pay the rating agency a subscription fee to access ratings. Indeed such model is also subject to potential conflicts of interest albeit perhaps to a lesser degree. Other business models were used and/or suggested; see Naciri (2015) for more discussion.

CRAs have come under intense scrutiny and were criticised for their issuer-pays model, especially in the wake of the recent global financial crisis. Meant to provide investors with reliable information on the riskiness of various kinds of debt, agencies have instead been blamed of exacerbating the financial crisis and defrauding investors by offering overly favourable evaluations of insolvent financial institutions and approving extremely risky mortgage-related securities. Although there are alternatives to the issuer-pays model, each has its own disadvantages and the main issue is how well conflicts of interest are managed by each one of them.

Agencies conflicts of interest (SEC, 2014)

Most CRAs, including the largest, operate under the issuer-pays model, discussed in the previous section, and this is a business model that can be extremely sensitive to potential conflicts of interest. It is even thought that the generalisation of such model may have largely opened the door to potential conflicts of interest; it may have put agencies in situations where they may have had serious incentives to push their rating upward so as to keep their issuers continuing to trust their business with them. Issuers in need of a given level of ratings to reach a specific investment decision, may have, for instance, been willing to pay more for these services (OECD report, 2010). In this regard the SEC itself has warned against a number of situations where conflicts of interest are inherent:

(i) In a situation where a CRA in order to retain the obligors or issuers as clients, might accept to be monitored in its credit rating assessment, in favour of more positive than warranted ratings
(ii) In a situation where a given agency might be aware that an influential subscriber holds a securities position (long or short) that could be advantaged if a credit rating upgrade or downgrade causes the market value of the security to increase or decrease, or that the subscriber invests in newly issued bonds and would obtain higher yields if the bonds were to have lower ratings
(iii) In a situation where a CRA may be aware that a subscriber wishes to acquire a particular security but it is prevented from doing so because of the low credit rating of the involved security. Internal investment guidelines or an applicable contract may indeed forbid investing in such security, unless an upgrade of the credit rating of the security by the CRA could remove such impediment.
(iv) CRAs' business model can eventually create an inherent bias towards lower than warranted ratings to secure investors higher yields, "and pressures from investors to avoid rating downgrades would increase considerably since downgrades result in mark-to-market losses on rated securities" (Economic-times, 2010).
(v) The potential for conflicts of interest involving a CRA can be particularly acute in specific situations, such as structured finance products where issuers are created and operated by a relatively concentrated group of sponsors underwriters and managers and rating fees are particularly lucrative.

Big CRAs usually minimise conflict of interest risk, usually arguing that such potential conflicts could be alleviated, as each major CRA has a wide subscriber base and each subscriber has different interests with respect to an upgrade or downgrade of a particular security. CRAs' conflicts of interest can do, however, more harm than it may appear, as the damage extends single transactions to affect entire asset classes. The risk of negatively affecting an entire asset class is high whenever, for instance, a given agency becomes known for issuing higher credit ratings with respect to such class, this may result for such agency in retaining or attracting businesses from most issuers in such class. Recent rules (Dodd-Frank and the like) include new requirements by which CRAs must obey to avoid certain conflicts of interest and have policies and procedures to tackle them and take certain actions to address credit ratings that might be tainted by a conflict of interest. The future will tell if this is enough to curb appetites.

Regulating the rating agencies and the Nationally Recognized Statistical Rating Organizations system (NRSRO)

The 2010 Dodd-Frank Wall Street Reform and Consumer Protection Act and the European Securities and Markets Authority (ESMA) 2011 releases are basic legislations in both the United States and Europe. They both have sought to hold agencies accountable for their ratings and protect investors against their eventually conflicts of interest. Predecessor rules in the United States regulating CRAs were in issue since at least 1975 by the SEC; they create the Nationally Recognized Statistical Rating Organization (NRSRO) system, with Fitch, Moody's and S&P among the first NRSROs. Table 5.5 gives the list of NRSROs as of December 2014 (SEC, 2014).

Although NRSRO designation and registration may seem to only concern transactions under SEC jurisdiction, their effect is far more reaching and can affect financial transactions all over the world. Further agencies included in the NRSROs list are also part of the list of agencies that are registered with the European Securities and Markets Authority. The history of NRSROs registration with the SEC is specifically and intimately related to the SEC's efforts to determine the minimum capital levels required for financial firms to trade certain debt securities depending on their riskiness, but also to allow the selection of which rating agency can be used toward this end. Here again the three major agencies were

Table 5.5 The list of the Nationally Recognized Statistical Rating Organizations (NRSROs) as of December 2014

NRSRO[1]	*Registration date*	*Principal office*
A.M. Best Company Inc. ("A.M. Best")	September 24, 2007	U.S.
DBRS Inc. ("DBRS")	September 24, 2007	U.S.
Egan-Jones Ratings Company ("EJR")	December 21 2007	U.S
Fitch Ratings	September 24, 2007	U.S.
HR Ratings de México S.A. de C.V. ("HR Ratings")	November 5, 201 2	Mexico
Japan Credit Rating Agency Ltd ("JCR")	September 24, 2007	Japan
KBRA	February 11, 2008	U.S.
Moody's	September 24, 2007	U.S.
Morningstar	June 23, 2008	U.S.
S&P	September 24, 2007	U.S.

Source: Adapted from SEC (2014)[2].

[1]SEC (2014) Annual Report on Nationally Recognized Statistical Rating Organizations. At: http://www.sec.gov/ocr/reportspubs/annual-reports/nrsroannrep1214.pdf

[2]SEC (2014) Annual Report on Nationally Recognized Statistical Rating Organizations. At: https://www.sec.gov/ocr/reportspubs/annual-reports/nrsroannrep1214.pdf

initially chosen for the purpose, e.g. S&P, Moody's and Fitch. Though over the years, the SEC has added more rating agencies to its original list of the major three, they manage to maintain their dominance of the global credit without interruption. Since 1975, the SEC added only four additional firms to the NRSROs list, but mergers among the entrants reduced their number again and it was actually felt that NRSRO designation had acted as a significant barrier to entry to the bond-rating business, instead of opening it. Complaints were also voiced about the fact that the SEC had neither established criteria for an NRSRO designation nor provided any justification or explanation as to why it "appointed" some CRAs with the designation and refused to do so for others (White, 2009).

S&P, Moody's and Fitch continue to be the three NRSROs with the highest number of ratings reported to be outstanding as of December 31, 2013. In total these three NRSROs issued about 96.6 per cent of all the ratings that were reported to be outstanding as of December 31, 2013. In 2007, the year when NRSROs began reporting outstanding ratings on Form NRSRO, these NRSROs accounted for about 98.8 per cent of all outstanding ratings. The number of outstanding credit ratings reported by all NRSRO in their annual certification for the calendar year ending December 31, 2013 in sovereign government securities category amounted to 1,868,038 credit ratings and the quasi totality is insured by the Big 3: Fitch 204,303, Moody's 728,627 and S&P 918,800. Among other NRSROs only DBR has insured a modest number of ratings, 16,038 (SEC, 2014b),

Since the NRSRO system implementation, any credit rating that is issued by an agency member of the NRSRO club qualifies a security to be used to satisfy numerous financial requirements, especially by financial institutions to satisfy their capital requirements and by international financial institutions, for their policies for development. Critics of the Big 3 have long voiced concern that the monopolisation of the sector by these agencies has created an uncompetitive environment that leaves investors with very few if any alternatives.

Conclusion

Although CRAs' history is relatively recent, sovereign credit ratings, for their part, have been in the business scenery for a long time. Modern sovereign ratings, by allowing the assessment of eventual losses on sovereign debt, arising from default or debt restructuring, are used by issuers and investors in their decision-making processes, the first to attract investors and the latter to select appropriate issuers. The last few decades have witnessed a serious degradation in sovereign issues quality, but also a serious increase in CRAs' conflicts of interest, mainly motivated by their issuer-pays business model, where the entity that is issuing the bonds also pays the rating agency to rate these bonds, as well as ongoing ratings. The debate about the usefulness of sovereign credit default ratings intensified in the aftermath of the outbreak of sovereign debts stress in the euro area. Agencies are today the subject of serious criticism, especially regarding the tremendous risk of conflict of interest. The NRSRO registration system that was introduced in 1975 to curb CRAs' eventual misconducts and that designated the Big 3 among the first registered agencies seems far from solving the problem, but rather have institutionalised a quasi-monopoly on the global sovereign rating market. New recent rules are, however, calling for the dismantling of such a system starting in 2015, but it is, however, argued that government regulation is unlikely to solve the conflicts inherent to credit rating agencies particularly, when it comes to sovereign debt. Any improvement in agencies' behaviour has to be transcendent to agencies' methodologies, to the assessment of sovereign ratings, to be presented in the next chapter. It is, however, always feared that "the more government has power and is meddling with rating agencies. the more the rating agencies will be browbeaten into giving a generous rating to the sovereign" (Council on Foreign Relations), but let's hope this is not the case.

Notes

1 https://en.wikipedia.org/wiki/Fitch_Ratings
2 https://www.moodys.com/Pages/car002001.aspx
3 https://www.moodys.com/Pages/car002001.aspx
4 http://www.standardandpoors.com/ru_RU/web/guest/home
5 Moody's rating distribution of sovereign issuers investment-grade and speculative-grade for the period 1985–14

Year	*1985*	*1990*	*1995*	*2000*	*2005*	*2010*	*2012*	*2014*
Investment-grade	100%	86%	78%	59%	63%	61%	59%	54%
Speculative-grade	0%	14%	22%	41%	37%	39%	41%	46%

Bartels, B. (2014), Why Rating Agencies Disagree on Sovereign Ratings, Gutenberg School of Management and Economics & Research Unit "Interdisciplinary Public Policy" Discussion Paper Series.

6 Agencies' methodology for sovereign default assessment

The main role and responsibility of credit rating agencies resides in the accurate assessment of sovereign solvency that has developed progressively since the 1800, as described in Chapter 5. To fulfil their role and responsibility, agencies use specific approaches that are based on economic, institutional, fiscal variables and measures of risk, but also use some qualitative factors that may influence the ability and willingness of a given sovereign to honour its financial obligations. Overall agencies seem to use comparable approaches for sovereign creditworthiness assessment. These are measures used by sovereign lenders and investors, to gauge the likelihood of risks they may be facing when lending money to or investing in the securities of a particular sovereign issuer. Given, however, the use made of ratings, their accuracy is a fundamental issue.

This chapter examines the methodology of establishing sovereign credit ratings used by the Big 3, namely Fitch Ratings, Moody's Investors Service and Standard & Poor's, although emphasis is placed on Moody's approach, as it is the one that allows access to more comprehensive information regarding methodology. In this chapter, we: briefly describe what sovereign rating assessment means; describe Moody's approach to sovereign trustworthiness assessment; describe S&P approach; describe Fitch's approach; give a synthesis on agencies' methodology; and conclude.

Sovereign rating assessment

From a risk assessment perspective, a sovereign rating pertains to the evaluation of a sovereign's ability and willingness to service financial obligations to its creditors (S&P, 2011a). A sovereign issuer, on the other hand, can be seen as any government (at any level) that de facto has the power to exercise primary fiscal authority over a recognised jurisdiction. As underlined in previous chapters, sovereign default ratings only relate to the prospect of default on debt owed to private creditors (Fitch, 2014), and this may exclude the probability of default on debt owed to the official sector of international organisations, like the World Bank or the IMF, and public policy institutions like central banks. Although they are agents of the sovereign, their debt may be assigned ratings that differ from those of their sovereign. Therefore different types of default on sovereign debt would typically be reflected in sovereign default (Fitch, 2014), for instance:

(i) The absenting scheduled coupon or principal repayment on a debt security issued in public markets by the sovereign
(ii) The absenting of payment of unrated debt obligations owed to private creditors, e.g. commercial bank loans
(iii) The arrears on payments to suppliers or reported failure to pay out under a government "guaranteed" contract, bilateral loan or similar commitment
(iv) The default by a wholly state-owned and/or controlled issuer, even if it occurs as a direct result of actions by the sovereign
(v) The failure to pay debt owed to other governments and official creditors, excluding multilateral institutions such as the International Monetary Fund (IMF) and the World Bank

Although reported failure to service debt owed to the official sector or multilateral institutions would not be judged a sovereign default event, whenever, however, arrears to such official creditors indicate growing financial distress and/or lack of willingness to pay, the sovereign rating could be adversely affected. Moreover, official creditors may seek comparable treatment for private creditor claims as part of any restructuring of their own claims. As a rule, where investors believe uncertainty or broad information asymmetries exist, they typically insist on being compensated for the risks they are brought to take. They may usually find it more convenient to trust a third party with the task of assessing sovereign issuers' capacity and willingness to honour their debt obligations to them and usually have recourse to CRAs for such endeavour. Credit ratings are actually used for a variety of purposes:

(i) Issuers and sovereign borrowers may rely on opinions issued by CRAs to ease the difficulties they may face in raising capital.
(ii) Investors and lenders typically strive to be compensated for uncertainty they are brought to face and would like issuers to pay for this uncertainty through higher interest rates. They may use ratings to make their point.
(iii) Institutional investors and fiduciary investors, e.g. those with independent authority to invest on behalf of others, such as the managers of trust funds or pensions, likewise use CRA ratings to help them allocate investments in a diversified risk portfolio.
(iv) Till very recently, government regulators tend also to use CRA ratings for a variety of purposes, including setting capital charges for financial institutions according to the risks attendant to the institutions' various investments (IOSCO, 2003).

Fortunately, whenever CRA opinions help reduce uncertainty for investors, they also help reduce the cost of capital for issuers. To assess sovereign ratings, CRAs generally pursue the analysis of current and prospective factors that may affect sovereign credit risk in the future, by researching and analysing information from different sources. As the activities and policy decisions of the sovereign can have a profound impact on and are also influenced by the performance of the economy as a whole, CRAs' approaches to sovereign credit risk analysis are mainly a synthesis of quantitative and qualitative judgements that are supposed to capture the willingness as well as the capacity of the sovereign to meet its debt obligations. Towards this aim, CRAs elaborate and calibrate their sovereign rating criteria based on a general framework they call the "idealized behaviour" of their credit ratings over time through economic cycles (S&P, 2011a).

Before discussing CRAs' approach, let's underline the numerous characteristics that can differentiate sovereign debt issuers from other debtors and that may help identify the appropriate approach for assessing their creditworthiness (Moody's, 2013a). These characteristics include:

(i) The sovereign's ability to curb its expenditures or modify the taxation of its citizenship in order to generate enough revenue, with which it will service its outstanding debt
(ii) The freedom from a higher authority to force debt resolution and dismiss the obligation of collateral
(iii) The high probability of survival even after an event of default, although countries rarely disappear
(iv) The sovereign willingness to pay.

The main element, however, that distinguishes the rating of sovereigns over and above other instruments of credit ratings is the concept of "willingness to pay" – a characteristic that is for sure difficult to measure objectively. It is supposed to reflect the potential risk that even if the sovereign had the *capacity* to pay, it may not be *willing* to do so, if it judges the political and/or social costs to be too high (IMF, 2010). Indeed, because the sovereign is the highest authority in a given jurisdiction and consequently has the power to enforce its will in this jurisdiction, creditors may end up having very diminished legal or other recourses, in the event the sovereign is unwilling (or unable) to service its debt. The situation can be significantly exacerbated by the limitations imposed by international law and its weak enforceability, with respect to defaulting sovereign nations.

Although each CRA may differ slightly in how its information is aggregated into a single rating, the fundamental analysis that nourishes the rating process is comparable across the CRAs (IMF, 2010) and usually takes form in the following environment:

(i) The analysis of sovereign credit risk, which usually takes into account the important factor of "willingness to pay" of the sovereign, as well as its financial capacity
(ii) The information used in assessing the fundamentals to be included in agencies' rating assessment models is generally drawn from a number of international sources, including the International Monetary Fund (IMF), the

Organisation for Economic Cooperation and Development (OECD), the European Commission (EC), the World Bank (WB) and the Bank for International Settlements (BIS).

(iii) CRAs may also use additional information supplied to them by sovereign authorities, and the quality check of such data appears to constitute an important part of countries' risk analysis.

(iv) The rating committee constitutes the core of the rating process used by CRAs, as they usually rely heavily on a process whereby analysts first form an opinion on credit quality, based on quantitative and qualitative indicators and then report this assessment to a rating committee.

(v) The estimation of some indicators by CRAs' analysts may be required, based on data provided by national statistical sources (Moody's, 2013a).

(vi) Analysts being conscious of the sovereign rating will apply to obligations in both local currency and foreign currency, although "currently, rating gaps are only maintained in select cases and subject to certain criteria" (Moody's, 2013a), a distinction between the two ratings had previously been common.

Rating committees, as the essential link in the credit quality assessment chain, are typically composed of a lead analyst, managing directors or supervisors and junior analytical staff. Although rating decisions are made upon a simple majority vote of the committee, they however represent the CRA's opinion regarding the likelihood the issuer will repay to service its sovereign debt (IOSCO, 2003). The next section will discuss major agencies' approaches to the assessment of sovereign credit ratings.

Moody's approach to sovereign rating assessment

Among the Big 3, Moody's is indeed the credit agency that currently gives the most clear and succinct information regarding the methodology it uses in the process of assessing sovereign default and should be praised for such effort. Moody's assessment of sovereign credit risk is usually based on the interplay of four key factors:

(i) Economic strength, *ECOSTR*

(ii) Institutional strength, *INSSTR*

(iii) Fiscal strength, *FISSTR*, and

(iv) Susceptibility to event risk, *SUSRIS*

The sovereign default assessment process is based on a set of relatively standard macroeconomic and political variables and it is performed in steps, as summarised in Figure 6.1.

Figure 6.1 states that once the four fundamental factors are selected, they are combined to form three different and progressive combinations of factors, each shaping a step in Moody's process of assessing sovereign default:

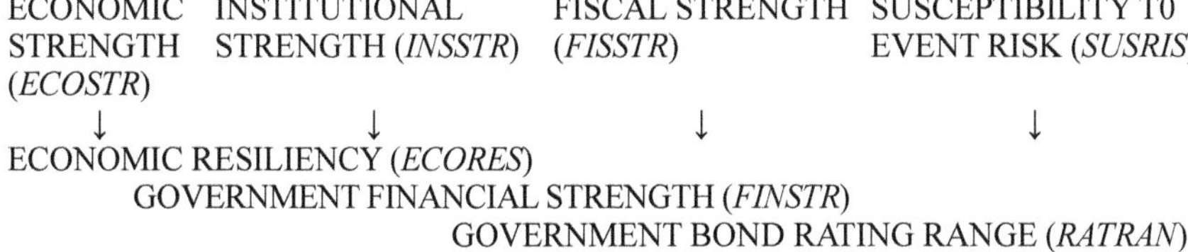

Figure 6.1 CRAs' approach to assigning ratings to sovereigns

Source: Adapted from Moody's 2013, figure 3, p. 4.

(i) The first combination combines the first two key factors, e.g. economic strength *and* institutional strength into economic resiliency (*ECORES* combination).
(ii) The second combination combines the first three key factors, e.g. economic strength, institutional strength and fiscal strength into government financial strength (*FINSTR* combination).
(iii) The third combination combines all the four key factors, e.g. economic strength, institutional strength, fiscal strength and susceptibility to event risk into government bond rating range (*RATRAN* combination).

Key factors comprise in turn sub-factors that provide further detail, as described in Table 6.1.

Additional to highlighting factors and sub-factors used in determining sovereign ratings, Table 6.1 specifies their respective weight and indicators. The sub-factors for each factor are generally calculated or estimated for use in a scorecard and so the weighting for each individual sub-factor. The scorecard is not, however, a methodology, but rather its stylised representation (Moody's, 2013a), with the purpose of facilitating an understanding of the type and range of factors used in assessing sovereign risk. Estimated or calculated sub-factor indicators are mapped to one of fifteen ranking categories, oscillating from very high plus (VH+) to very low minus (VL−); we call this ranking, for the rest of the book, the "VH+ to VL−" scale. Those mappings are then used to determine the score for the relevant sub-factor (using the same scale) and, in turn, the final score for the broad rating factors is based on interval range "Aaa-Aa2 to B2-Caa". We also call this scale the range scale, for the rest of the book.

As indicated, economic strength (*ECOSTR*) (F1) and institutional strength (*INSSTR*) (F2) are combined using an aggregation function, into an equal weight construct, called economic resiliency (*ECORES*) e.g. the 50/50 weighted average of *ECOSTR* and *INSSTR*. The sovereign's economic strength as it focuses on sovereign fundamentals like growth potential, diversification, competitiveness, national income, and scale, is supposed to express the intrinsic strength of a sovereign economy and it is considered important in defining a sovereign's resilience or shock-absorption capacity (Moody's, 2013a). Indeed, the capacity of a sovereign

Table 6.1 Factors and sub-factors used in determining sovereign ratings, their respective weight and indicators

Broad rating factors	*Rating sub-factor*	*Sub-factor weighting (toward factor)*	*Sub-factor indicators*
ECOSTR: Economic strength	*ECOSTR*#1: Growth dynamic	50%	Average Real GDP Growth t–4 to t+5 Volatility in Real GDP Growth, 9 to t WEF Global Competitiveness index
	ECOSTR#2: Scale of the Economy	25%	Nominal GDP (US$) t–1
	ECOSTR#3: National Income	25%	GDP per Capita (PPP, US$) t–1
	ECOSTR# 4: Adjustment Factors	1–6 scores	Diversification Credit Boom
INSSTR: Institutional Strength	*INSSTR#* 1: Institutional Framework and Effectiveness.	75%	World Bank Government Effectiveness Index World Bank Rule of Law Index World Bank Control of Corruption Index
	INSSTR# 2: Policy Credibility and Effectiveness	25%	Inflation Level t–4 to t+5 Inflation Volatility t–9 to t
	INSSTR# 3: Adjustment Factor	1–6 scores	Track Record of Default
FISSTR: Fiscal Strength	*FISSTR#* 1: Debt Burden	50%	General Government Debt/GDP$_t$ General Government Debt/Revenue
	FISSTR# 2: Debt Affordability	50%	Genral Government Interest Payments/ Revenue General Government Interest Payments/ GDPt
	FISSTR# 3: Adjustment Factors	1 to 6 scores	Debt Trend$_{t-4\text{ to }t+1}$ General Government Foreign Currency Debt/General Government Debt Other Public Sector Debt/GDP$_t$ Public Sector Financial Assets or Sovereign Wealth Funds/GDP$_t$

Broad rating factors	*Rating sub-factor*	*Sub-factor weighting (toward factor)*	*Sub-factor indicators*
SUSRIS: Susceptibility to Event Risk	*SUSRIS*#1: Political Risk	Max. Function2	Domestic Political Risk Geopolitical Risk
	SUSRIS#2: Government Liquidity Risk	Max. Function2	Fundamental Metrics Market Funding Stress
	SUSRIS#3: Banking Sector Risk	[] Max. Function2	Strength of Banking System Size of Banking System Funding Vulnerabilities
	SUSRIS#4: External Vulnerability Risk	Max. Function2	(Current Account Balance + FDI) / GDP_t External Vulnerability Indicator $(EVI)_{t+1}$ Net International Investment Position / GDP_t

Source: Adapted from Moody's (2013a).

of nurturing economic growth and prosperity may express its relative ability to generate enough revenue to service its debt over the medium term. Similarly, as institutional strength may express a sovereign capacity to apply sound economic policies that may lead to economic growth, its features may prove to be a strong indicator of the sovereign ability and willingness to service its debt. Table 6.2 reproduces the first three lines and the fifteen columns of the combination of economic strength and institutional strength for a 50/50 weight, as performed by Moody's. Complete data can be found in Moody's (2013a, Figure 4, p. 5).

Each rating in Table 6.2 is the result of combining any level of economic strength with any level of institutional strength. Combining, for instance, 0.5 "VH+" of institutional strength (line 4, column 3) with 0.5 "VH+" of economic strength (line 3, column 4) would result in "VH+" of economic resiliency (line 4, column 4), but resulting also to the same value when 0.5 "VH+" of institutional strength is combined with either 0.5 "VH" or 0.5 "VH–" of economic strength. This kind of unfair score repetitions can be encountered in many instances in Moody's data and raises accuracy problems.

Further, another aggregation function is used to combine economic resiliency (*ECORES*) and fiscal strength (*FISSTR*), into government financial strength (*FINSTR*). The fiscal strength can indeed give an overview of the soundness of sovereign finances. The starting point of the analysis is the assessment of the relative debt burdens, as might be expressed by the ratio debt/GDP, and the assessment of the debt affordability, as expressed by the ratio interest payments relative to revenue and to GDP. Given that countries with high economic resiliency should be less sensitive to fluctuations, in their debt metrics it is expected that the weight of fiscal strength to be usually highest for countries with moderate economic resiliency and the creditworthiness of countries with low economic resiliency should be weak, irrespective of debt metrics (Moody's, 2013a). The combination of economic resiliency, fiscal strength and financial strength results in a preliminary, indicative rating range, and Table 6.3 reproduces the first three lines and the fifteen columns of the combination of economic resiliency with fiscal strength, for an 80/20 weight, as performed by Moody's. Complete results are presented in Moody's (2013a, figure 5, p. 6), they include computations for 70/30, 60/40, 75/25 and 10/90 weight sets, successively.

Each rating in Table 6.3 is supposed to be obtained by combining any level of economic resiliency and any level of fiscal strength. Combining, for instance, 0.80 "VH+" (line 4, column 3) of economic resiliency and 0.20 "VH+" of fiscal strength (line 3, column 4) would result in "VH+" (line 4, column 4) of government financial strength, but resulting also to the same score if 0.80 "VH+"

Table 6.2 Economic resiliency (*ECORES*): combination of economic strength (*ECOSTR*) with institutional strength (*INSSTR*), for a weight set of 50/50 (50% for economic strength and 50% for institutional strength)

INSSTR		*ECOSTR*														
		1	*2*	*3*	*4*	*5*	*6*	*7*	*8*	*9*	*10*	*11*	*12*	*13*	*14*	*15*
		VH+	VH	VH−	H+	H	H−	M+	M	M−	L+	L	L−	VL+	VL	VL−
1	VH+	VH+	VH+	VH+	VH	VH	VH−	VH−	H+	H+	H	H	H−	H−	M+	M
2	VH	VH+	VH	VH	VH−	VH−	H+	H+	H	H	H−	H−	M+	M+	M	M−
3	VH−	VH+	VH	VH−	VH−	H+	H+	H	H	H−	H−	M+	M+	M	M	L+

ECOSTR = economic strength; and *INSSTR* = institutional strength; *ECORES* = economic resiliency combination.

Table 6.3 Government financial strength (*FINSTR*): combination of economic resiliency (*ECORES*) with fiscal strength, 80/20 weight set (80% for economic resiliency and 20% for Government financial strength)

ECORES		*FISSTR*														
		1	*2*	*3*	*4*	*5*	*6*	*7*	*8*	*9*	*10*	*11*	*12*	*13*	*14*	*15*
		VH+	VH	VH−	H+	H	H−	M+	M	M−	L+	L	L−	VL+	VL	VL−
1	VH+	VH+	VH+	VH+	VH+	VH+	VH+	VH+	VH+	VH	VH	VH	VH	VH	VH−	VH+
2	VH	VH	VH	VH	VH−	VH−	VH−	VH−	VH−	H+	H+	H+	H+	H+	H	VH
3	H+	VH	VH−	VH−	VH−	VH−	H+	H+	H+	H+	H+	H	H	H	H	H−

ECOSTR = economic strength; and *INSSTR* = institutional strength; *FISSTR* = fiscal strength; *ECORES* = economic resiliency combination; *FINSTR* = government financial strength combination.

of economic resiliency is combined with either 0.20 "VH", "VH–", "H+", "H", "H–", "M+", and "M" of economic strength. Here again this kind of unjustified score replications is encountered in many instances in Moody's figures.

As a final step, a government bond rating range combination (*RATRAN*) is constructed by combining government financial strength (economic strength, institutional strength and fiscal strength) with sovereign's susceptibility to event risk (*SUSRIS*). The latter denotes the risk that "sudden, extreme events may severely strain a country's public finances, thus sharply increasing the sovereign's probability of default; it is considered as a constraint that can only lower the preliminary rating range. This, however, "will not happen when event risk is scored as 'Very Low', but will happen with increasing severity as the risk is assessed from 'Low' to 'Moderate' to 'High' to 'Very High'" (Moody's, 2013a). Table 6.4 reproduces the first three lines and the fifteen columns of the government bond rating range combination.

The results presented in Table 6.4 are mid-point of three-notch rating ranges that are the final results of the sequential combinations of the rating factors. An "Aaa to Aa2" range of government financial strength, combined with a "VL–" of susceptibility to event risk would result in an Aa1 of rating range, but also when combined to VL+, VL–, VL, L–, L and L+. Such a high level of inconsistencies is very common in Moody's final ratings. The understanding of Moody's approach to sovereign credit rating assessment is fundamental for the understanding of the rest of the book, as Moody's model is used for the tests of rating accuracy, to follow.

Standard and Poor's approach to sovereign ratings (S&P, 2011a)

The process of assessing sovereign's creditworthiness followed by S&P appears similar to Moody's process, although less transparent; it also materialises in several steps: Standard & Poor's analysis starts with the assessment and the scoring of five key factors that form the foundation of sovereign credit, namely (i) Institutional effectiveness and political risks, (ii) economic structure and growth prospects, (iii) External liquidity and international investment position, (iv) Fiscal flexibility and fiscal performance, combined with debt burden, and (v) Monetary flexibility. Here again, like in Moody's, the choice of fundamentals factor is far from been justified rationally. Standard & Poor's analysis of a sovereign's creditworthiness involves several steps as summarised in Table 6.5.

S&P explains the role of the five key factors composing its sovereign rating framework of Table 6.6 as follows: the role of the political score of a given sovereign is to measure how the sovereign institutions and policymaking affect its creditworthiness and this is mainly done by studying sovereign credit fundamentals, by assessing the efficiency of sustainable of its public finances, by measuring its capacity of promoting its economic growth and by gauging its effective response capacity to economic or political shocks. Economic score, on the other hand, has as the main objective the assessment of the adaptability of the sovereign

Table 6.4 Rating range: combination of government financial strength with reversed susceptibility to event risk

Susceptibility to event risk		*Government financial strength*														
		1	2	3	4	5	6	7	8	9	10	11	12	13	14	15
		VH+ Aaa– Aa2	VH Aa1– Aa3	VH– Aa2– A1	H+ Aa3– A2	H A1– A3	H– A2– Baa1	M+ A3– Baa2	M Baa1– Baa2	M– Baa2– Ba1	L+ Baa3– Ba2	L Ba1– Ba3	L– Ba2– B1	VL+ Ba3– B2	VL B1– B3	VL– B2– Caa
1	VL–	Aa1	Aa2	Aa3	A1	A2	A3	Baa1	Baa2	Baa3	Ba1	Ba2	B3	B1	B2	B3
2	VL	Aa1	Aa2	Aa3	A1	A2	A3	Baa1	Baa2	Baa3	Ba1	Ba2	B3	B1	B2	B3
3	VL+	Aa1	Aa2	Aa3	A1	A2	A3	Baa1	Baa2	Baa3	Ba1	Ba2	B3	B1	B2	B3

ECOSTR = economic strength; *INSSTR* = institutional strength; *FISSTR* = fiscal strength; *ECORES* = economic resiliency combination; *FINSTR* = government financial strength combination; *SUSRIS* = sovereign's susceptibility to event risk.

Table 6.5 S&P sovereign rating framework

Political score	*Economic score*	*External score*	*Fiscal score*	*Monetary score*
↓			↓	
Political and economic profile			Flexibility and performance profile	
		Sovereign indicative rating level		
		+		
		Exceptional adjustment factors		
		↓		
		Foreign currency sovereign rating		

Source: Adapted from S&P (2011a), The "Principles of Credit Ratings," published Feb. 16, 2011.

economic structure, and when coupled with positive track record of sustained economic growth, it is supposed to insure a sovereign government with a strong revenue base, susceptible of enhancing its fiscal and monetary policy flexibility and ultimately boosting its debt servicing capacity. The external score, for its part, has a role of reflecting a sovereign's ability to generate foreign receipts. These are the necessary funds to meet sovereign obligations to non-residents; their balance has a direct effect on the sovereign currency exchange rate. The fiscal score objective is to reflect the sustainability of a sovereign's deficits and debt burden, through the consideration of a number of economic fundamentals like the fiscal flexibility, the long-term fiscal trends and vulnerabilities, the debt structure and funding access and potential risks arising from contingent liabilities. Finally, the sovereign's monetary score has as the objective the reflexion of the extent to which sovereign monetary conditions can support sustainable economic growth and attenuate major economic or financial shocks, thereby supporting sovereign creditworthiness (S&P, 2011a).

The first step in Standard & Poor's analysis of sovereign solvency (see Table 6.5) consists of assigning a score to each of the five key fundamentals selected by S&P, on a six-point numerical scale, from 1, the strongest, to 6, the weakest. Each score is based on a series of quantitative factors and qualitative considerations. The political and economic scores are then combined to form the sovereign's "political and economic profile", reflecting S&P view of the economic resilience of a sovereign, the strength and stability of sovereign institutions, and the effectiveness of its policymaking. Similarly, the external, fiscal and monetary scores are combined to form the sovereign "flexibility and performance profile". This profile is meant to reflect S&P's view of the sustainability of a sovereign's fiscal balance and debt burden, in light of the sovereign country's external position, as well as its fiscal and monetary flexibility. This is an average of three scores: the external score, the fiscal score and the monetary score (S&P, 2011a). These two profiles are themselves combined to determine the "sovereign foreign-currency rating", after taking into account exceptional adjustments, whenever applicable. Technically, such combination towards the determination of an indicative rating level is exposed in Table 6.6.

Table 6.6 Determination of indicative rating levels

Flexibility and performance	*Political profile*											
	Category	*Superior*	*Extremely strong*	*Very strong*	*Strong*	*Moderately strong*	*Intermediate*	*Moderately weak*	*Weak*	*Very weak*	*Extremely weak*	*Poor*
Category	Score	1	1.5	2	2.5	3	3.5	4	4.5	5	5.5	6
Extremely strong	1 to 1.7	aaa	aaa	aaa	aa+	aa	a+	a	a–	bbb+	N/A	N/A
Very strong	1.8 to 2.2	aaa	aaa	aa+	aa	aa–	a	a–	bbb+	bbb	bb+	bb–
Strong	2.3 to 2.7	aaa	aa+	aa	aa–	a	a–	bbb+	bbb	bb+	bb	b+
Moderately strong	2.8 to 3.2	Aa+	aa	aa–	a+	a–	bbb	bbb–	bb+	bb	bb–	b+
Intermediate	3.3 to 3.7	aa	aa–	a+	a	bbb+	bbb–	bb+	bb	bb–	b+	b
Moderately weak	3.8 to 4.2	aa–	a+	a	bbb+	bbb	bb+	bb	bb–	b+	b	b
Weak	4.3 to 4.7	a	a–	bbb	bbb	bb+	bb	bb–	b+	b	b–	b–
Very weak	4.8 to 5.2	N/A	bbb	bb+	bb+	bb	bb–	b+	b	b	b–	b–
Extremely weak	5.3 to 6	N/A	bb+	bb	bb–	b+	b	b	b–	b	ccc/c	ccc/c

Source: Standard and Poor's (2011a).

To decide indicative rating levels, S&P first assigns scores to a political profile on a six-point numerical scale from 1, the strongest to 6, the weakest. Similarly, it assigns scores of flexibility and performance also on a six-point numerical scale from "1–1.7", the strongest, to "5.3–6", the weakest. S&P uses, however, different numbers of categories of ratings, eleven categories for the political profile and nine categories for flexibility and performance profile. Further, widths of categories are different, while the width for the political profile contains 0.5 notches, it includes 0.7 notches for flexibility and performance. Second, in order to compute a sovereign indicative rating, Table 6.6 is used in the following way: for instance, a sovereign with a political and economic profile with a superior score of 1 (line 3, column 4) and a flexibility performance profile with an extremely strong score, located between 1 and 1.7 (line 4, column 3) would have an indicative rating of aaa (line 4, column 4),

As in Moody's approach, several methodological shortcomings can be suspected in the S&P approach and can also extremely jeopardise the accuracy of the final credit ratings, as different sovereigns with different scores may end up having the same rating. For example, all sovereigns whose score for flexibility and performance is 1, and with different political profiles, with scores ranging from 1 to 2, would all have the same final rating of aaa. More importantly, similar situations are common in S&P data. On the other hand, it is not clear, for instance, how combinations of factors are formed, nor how weights are determined and allocated. Further, indicative rating levels' determination seems roughly done, although S&P expects rating in most cases to fall within one notch; such notch, if it materialises, can, however, make a big difference for a sovereign whose score is marginally located at the lowest rating level of the investment zone. Such sovereign can see himself shifted to speculative status, because of one, sometimes unjustified, missing notch. One can, however, wonder, if this is the wise way of rating sovereigns, and even if it is fair to declare them in default this way.

Fitch sovereign approach to sovereign ratings (Fitch, 2014)

Fitch uses what it calls the proprietary "Sovereign Rating Model", SRM, a model that incorporates a wider range of factors and generates a score adjusted to the long-term foreign currency, called the debt issuer default rating scale, IDR. Fitch's Sovereign Rating Model for a given year Y_{200x} is estimated by using the ordinary least squares regression, OLS, to the set of economic and financial variables selected in the sovereign rating criteria for all Fitch-rated sovereigns over the period Y_{2000} to Y_{200x} inclusive. Further, variables are included in Fitch's Sovereign Rating Model, based on number of conditions, like the sovereign credit rationale, the consistency of signs (+/–) with economic theory, and the statistical significance. Fitch's Sovereign Rating Model is actually a multiple regression model that is based on nineteen economic/financial variables, presented in Table 6.7.

Fitch believes that economic fundamentals broadly described as "structural features" are the most important factors for sovereign risk measurement, as they incorporate (i) the ease of doing business, (ii) gross national income per

Table 6.7 The 19 economic/financial variables used by Fitch Ratings in the multiple regression model

Structural features	*External finances*	*Public finances, general government*	*Macroeconomic performance*
– Composite governance indicator – GDP per capita – Share in world GDP – Years since default – Money supply	– Gross debt 1. for reserve currency sovereigns 2. for non-reserve currency sovereigns – Budget balance – Public foreign-currency debt – Interest payments	– Reserve currency flexibility – Commodity dependence – Official international reserves for non-reserve currency sovereigns – Sovereign net foreign assets – Current account balance plus net foreign direct investment – External interest service	– Real GDP growth volatility – Consumer price inflation – Real GDP growth
47.4%	16.9%	25.4%	10.3%

capita, (iii) governance indicators, and (iv) money supply/banking sector. Consequently, structural features are allocated a weight of 47.4 per cent, well ahead of before "public finances and general government" factor, which is assigned a weight of 25.4 per cent and encompasses elements as (i) the volatility of government revenue in proportion of the GDP, (ii) the gross general government debt, (iii) the foreign currency debt, and (iv) the general government interest payments. Public finances and general government is believed to affect sovereign creditworthiness directly and indirectly, through its influence on the economy, as it is believed to affect variables such as (i) the availability of credit through taxation and spending, (ii) borrowing level and (iii) the borrowing cost. Further, Fitch assigns a weight of 16.9 per cent to the external finances factor, considered to have an important effect on the sovereign rating assessment, as it includes (i) the quality of the balance of payments, by examining the main components of the current account in the search of identifying strengths and weaknesses, and (ii) the external balance sheet and debt. Finally, Fitch assigns a weight of 10.3 per cent to the macroeconomic performance factor that includes elements such (i) the volatility of gross domestic product and (ii) the consumer price inflation. Although Fitch does not believe past performance can be a good guide to the future, it does, however, believe that country's track factor to be susceptible of reflecting the cohesiveness and robustness of its macroeconomic policy frameworks and the structural strengths and weaknesses that affect sovereign worthiness.

Interestingly, the weight assigned to each set of variables included in Fitch's pillars of analysis is fully determined by the regression model coefficients, and Fitch cautions that there is no subjective judgement involved. The weights indicate, intuitively, how much of the variation in predicted ratings can be explained by variation in a given variable or group of variables. Fitch, however, underlines, at the same time, that there is not a simple linear relationship between sovereign ratings and every metric that it considers in its rating analysis. In part, according to Fitch, this merely reflects the multivariate nature of the analysis such that the relationship between, for example, the government debt burden and the sovereign rating is conditioned on a range of other variables, such as income per head (Fitch, 2014).

The nineteen variables included in Fitch's model are derived from a range of sources, including the sovereign issuer itself, the BIS, the IMF and the World Bank. The data are updated for each rating review but at least quarterly, although the timeliness of availability of certain data can vary across regions and between individual sovereigns. The ability to update the model on a timely basis is therefore dependent on the availability of the relevant input data (Fitch, 2014). The model uses empirical data and does not allow for judgemental analyst input. It aims to provide a transparent and coherent framework for comparing sovereigns across regions and through time. The OLS regression is re-estimated and reviewed annually to incorporate additional data into the estimation period and to test for new variables as appropriate. This ensures that the Sovereign Rating Model evolves in line with Fitch's rating criteria (Fitch, 2014).

Synthesis of agencies' methodology

Table 6.8 summarises main agencies approaches to sovereign solvency; Moody's and Standard & Poor's approaches to sovereign ratings are based on the scorecard technique, a framework that is supposed to combine non-financial considerations and traditional financial metrics, to give a more global view of sovereign creditworthiness. The purpose the scorecard technique, exposed in agencies' official publications, is to facilitate an understanding of the type and range of factors taken into account in assessing sovereign risk. Accordingly, it is warned that rating factors in the scorecard may not in all cases constitute an exhaustive treatment of the considerations that are important for a particular sovereign rating, and further that the rating may differ from the one implied by the scorecard range (Moody's, 2013a). Fitch uses, however, a specific analytical model it calls the Sovereign Rating Model, with the purpose of determining a score that is adjusted to Fitch's long-term rating scale and corresponding linearly to a predicted long-term foreign currency for the sovereign issuer. Such a Fitch move can indeed be considered an important advance in rating methodology refinement. The weights of the nineteen economic/financial variables composing the four pillars of analysis used in the Fitch Sovereign Rating Model are determined by a multiple regression.

As can be seen from Table 6.8, each of the three main credit rating agencies identifies a set of key factors that determine its sovereign credit ratings and for each driver a range of quantitative and/or qualitative criteria is assessed.

The overview of agencies' approaches to sovereign creditworthiness shows that despite the fact that the quantitative and qualitative factors used by CRAs to gauge a country's willingness to repay its debt and its ability to do so are significantly comparable across agencies, differences may still persist, especially in the number of factors used, the relative weightings of factors and/or how the information is aggregated into a single rating, not only between CRAs, but also between types of countries (IMF, 2010).

Regarding differences in the numbers of factors used, Moody's, for instance, bases its sovereign creditworthiness investigation on thirty-one factors, Fitch on nineteen factors and nine factors in the case of S&P. Regarding differences in the

Table 6.8 Comparative presentation of agencies' approaches to sovereign rating assessment

	Fitch Ratings	*Moody's*	*Standard & Poor's*
Key factors	– Economy structural futures – Management of public finances – Public finances – External finances – Macroeconomic performance, policies and prospects	– Economic strength – Institutional strength – Fiscal strength – Susceptibility to event risk	– Institutional effectiveness and political risks – Economic structure and growth prospects – External liquidity and international investment position – Fiscal flexibility and fiscal performance, combined with debt burden – Monetary flexibility
Weights	Weights are fully determined by the coefficients of the regression model, and there is no subjective judgement involved. The weights indicate, intuitively, how much of the variation in predicted ratings can be explained by variation in a given variable or group of variables.	Weights seem to be determined using subjective judgement	Weights seem to be determined using subjective judgement

	Fitch Ratings	*Moody's*	*Standard & Poor's*
Combination of factors	Fitch's sovereign analysts use the Sovereign Rating Model, SRM, as an analytical tool and as one of a range of qualitative and quantitative inputs into the rating process.	– Economic strength and Institutional strength are combined to form economic resiliency combination. – Economic strength, Institutional strength and fiscal strength are combined to form government financial strength combination. – Economic strength, Institutional strength, fiscal strength and Susceptibility to event risk are combined to form government bond rating range combination	– The political and economic scores are combined to form a sovereign's "political and economic profile." The external, fiscal, and monetary scores are combined to form its "flexibility and performance profile." – Those two profiles combine to determine the sovereign foreign-currency rating, after factoring in exceptional adjustments when applicable.

Source: Fitch (2014), Moody's (2013a) and Standard and Poor's (2011a).

relative weightings, for example, Fitch and S&P appear to put relatively more weight on sovereign contingent liabilities, while Moody's appears to put more relative emphasis on event risk. Similarly, both Moody's and S&P appear to consider a broader set of factors when considering the general economic structure, including income discrepancies, competitiveness and protectionist factors (S&P, 2011a), and innovation and investment in human capital (Moody's, 2013a), relative to Fitch. The relevance of each factor also depends on the country under review, for instance, the level of reserves is a much more noticeable factor for countries operating under a fixed or managed exchange rate regime. Certain economic fundamentals are considered key criteria by all of the CRAs, the GDP per capita for instance, but also the level and composition of debt, financial resources of the government, political stability, and the robustness of the financial sector. Regarding differences in how the information is aggregated into a single rating, each CRA differs slightly in its way of reaching this objective. Fitch for example, uses a sovereign rating model that combines the criteria into a single score that is calibrated to derive a long-term issuer default rating. Moody's and S&P use the scoreboard approach. It is not possible to precisely express in the scorecard some important considerations, without making it excessively complex and significantly less transparent. Indeed, ratings may also reflect circumstances in which the weighting of a particular factor will be substantially different from the weighting suggested by the scorecard (Moody's, 2013a). Additionally, rating outcomes may consider additional factors that are difficult to measure or that have a meaningful effect in differentiating credit quality only in some, but not all cases.

Like Moody's, the two other agencies warn that actual ratings can deviate from the chosen model-generated rating, as the model may not include all relevant developments and this is where the rating committee enters in play. This is a body within each CRA that provides additional value to the used model-generated rating. In the case of Moody's, each of the four key factors is rated on a five-point scale and combined in three stages. In the final stage, all factors are merged with peer group information and any missing information considered relevant. In the case of S&P, each of the nine key factors is ranked on a six-point scale, but there is no apparent clear formula for combining the scores. In addition, trends in each of the factors, as well as their absolute level, are taken into account in the final rating. Fitch uses rather the Issuer Default Rating (IDR) discussed previously. The use of supplementary adjustment factors is an attempt "to capture idiosyncratic country-specific factors that may not be universally available or relevant" (Moody's, 2013a). Overall, agencies recognise that no model can fully capture all the relevant influences on sovereign creditworthiness, meaning the actual rating determined by the sovereign rating committee can differ from that implied by the rating model, and reasons are multiple:

(i) Key data and information, for instance, are subject to critical review, such as crosschecking with third-party sources, where available.
(ii) The ratings incorporate expectations around future metrics and risk developments, while the information that is used to determine the scoring is mainly historical. "In some cases, expectations around future credit developments may be informed by confidential information that we cannot publish or otherwise disclose" (Moody's, 2013a).
(iii) All CRAs assign both foreign currency and local currency ratings to each sovereign. While there is often little difference between the two in the case of advanced economies, in the case of emerging and developing economies the local currency rating is generally higher. When determining the foreign currency rating, a country's ability to convert domestic assets into foreign currency is critical to the assessment.
(iv) As rule, agencies rely on the accuracy and reliability of information published by national authorities and international agencies, and the information provided directly by representatives of the sovereign. For some countries, broad economic and financial data that are typically incorporated in sovereign credit and rating analyses have material shortcomings in terms of reliability and coverage. Such data limitations, where judged to be material, are noted and taken into account by the rating committee when assigning sovereign ratings. Agencies, however, do not assign sovereign ratings if they consider that the data limitations are so important as to render any analysis insufficiently robust to support a rating opinion.

Conclusion

Overall CRAs' approaches to sovereign default assessment are quite similar, although Fitch and Moody's classify their indicators under four categories of key factors, while S&P uses five. All CRAs use public information as well as additional information supplied to them by country authorities. The CRAs' methodologies also incorporate a range of refinements to the analytical approach aimed at further enhancing transparency and the forward-looking nature of analysis (Moody's, 2013a). Agencies' rating methodologies evolve over time and continue to be adjusted in response to new legal requirements, information and economic developments. These adjustments tend to be small. However, following the European sovereign crisis, when the CRAs were widely criticised for downgrading many countries, there was a more significant review and change in their sovereign risk methodologies. For example, Fitch adjusted its approach to more closely monitor countries with a high proportion of short-term external debt, even if overall debt levels were modest, while S&P increased its focus on external obligations, including private sector external debt and contingent liabilities (IMF, 2011). Although agencies seem to be confident about the quality of their ratings, and only Fitch seems to use some rationality in its methodology, inaccuracy of sovereign rating may be feared, because the models used by CRAs in assessing sovereign creditworthiness may contain many weaknesses (IMF, Uses and abuses), as unearthed in this chapter, with all the potential damages innocent sovereigns may endure. It seems overall often very difficult, if not impossible, to identify rationally in agencies' models the drivers of sovereign default, the weights assigned to factors, the functional form of factors and even the real significance of final ratings. The described agencies' approaches described in this chapter seem to share several shortcomings that are discussed in the next chapter, which have their impact on rating accuracy tested.

7 Testing the accuracy of agencies' approach to assessing sovereign worthiness

Major credit rating agencies have been recently much criticised and have been accused for having brought many ills to the rating industry, to the point where it is currently wondered whether credit ratings were not flawed. Methodologies of the top three CRAs to sovereign solvency assessment lend themselves to serious critics, as they are very similar. Agencies are, for instance, blamed for a number of shortcomings, particularly their way of assessing and expressing default, as seen in Chapter 6. For their part, CRAs are constantly arguing that ratings are not a market's perception of the probability of default and that their ratings' sole objective is to express ordinal risk rankings only and do not seek any other ranking objective, if only ratings were not used for evaluating debt securities, based on the risk-return rule. This chapter tests the possibility that CRAs may rate sovereign debt inaccurately and concludes that the methodologies used, presented in Chapter 6, may influence their sovereign ratings. This chapter should be read in conjunction of Chapters 2 and 6, and any limit in agencies model, discovered, adds up to agencies ratings classical limits.

Given the similarity of the approaches used by agencies and sometimes the absence of information, Moody's model will be used as a proxy for other agencies' methodologies for the rest of the book. This chapter: discusses some main sovereign rating traditional limits; presents the methodology of assessing the accuracy of the sovereign rating assessment approach; explains the process of translating agencies' alphabetical data to numerical ranking; explains the process of restating the translated agencies' data; discusses the empirical results: regression analysis, constant analysis, residuals analysis and gap analysis; and finally concludes

Sovereign rating shortcomings and critics

Many credit rating inadequacies in the sovereign ratings were commonly uncovered in the literature and made agencies subject to much disapproval regarding their ratings accuracy; the dissatisfaction with agencies has traditionally to do with things like, for instance:

(i) Having often failed to detect financial crisis on time
(ii) Seemingly having contributed to financial crises, "such as tipping Greece into disaster when its sovereign credit rating was downgraded" (Greene, 2014)

(iii) Using the issuer-pays business model, which critics claim has created perverse incentives for the extraordinary power they have built up "that even people who wield it think is too much" (Greene, 2014)
(iv) Distorting the whole financial system by pushing bondholders to substitute their in-depth judgment and analysis to agencies' sovereign credit assessment (Greene, 2014)
(v) Supposedly having no effective contribution to market efficiency and being seen as merely market followers
(vi) Making things worse via their guiding role for fund managers, when, for instance, markets get nervous about a given sovereign credit (Ferri et al., 1999).

Additionally, when we consider agencies' processes, described in Chapter 6, we are quickly faced by several impacting methodological limits on the part of agencies, susceptible of seriously jeopardising rating accuracy. Such processes seem to be implemented in two distinct stages, an objective stage and a subjective stage (see Chapter 2).

The objective stage concerns the choice of fundamentals, their assignment of appropriate weights and their combination to reach an overall rating. The process is therefore based on measurable fundamental variables, such as the general government debt/GDP and the like that are assigned specific ranking. The alphabetical scale "VH+ to VL−" and intervals "Aaa-Aa2 to B2-Caa" are the cornerstones of agencies' models, and their use is central to the process, but can also have determinant implications on sovereign rating accuracy, in agencies' approach, for instance:

(i) The alphabetical scale "VH+ to VL−" or interval scale "Aaa-Aa2 to B2-Caa" adopted by Moody's, and the one adopted by S&P, can neither be summed up nor averaged, without hazardous approximation.
(ii) The resulting model (based on alphabetical scale) risks not describing the data correctly. Indeed, given the high level of approximation induced by the "VH+ to VL−" scale, a substantial part of the information is left over.
(iii) Although there is a list of variables taken into consideration, in the case of S&P, for instance, many of them need justification and further clarification.
(iv) There is little, if any, justification of the chosen weights affected to the variables used in the rating assessment models.
(v) There seems to be no empirical foundation for the cut-offs between classes of the used ranking scale.
(vi) The way combinations are built can be the subject of discussion. In Moody's first combination, for instance, economic strength and institutional strength seems to indicate that different sovereigns, while allocated the same level of financial strength and despite their diverging scores of economic resiliency, can still be scored at the same level of economic resiliency. The same problem occurs in the construction of Moody's combination 2, and the problem is even worse at the level of combination 3, where some sovereign may be allocated better combination scores despite their worse components scores.

In S&P's case, many sovereigns with different sub-factor scores would all end up having the same final rating.

(vii) As a rule, agencies' approach does not allow itself to different levels of weighting as required by the CRAs' chosen approach, except the 50/50 weighting for Moody's. There is, however, no rational justification for always having 50/50 weighting. While CRAs aim to use clear and objective criteria to score country performance under each factor, *ECOSTR* to *SUSRIS*, they however warn that the actual rating is not a mechanical weighting of these factors (Moody's, 2013a), and as with their other ratings, sovereign ratings are determined by a rating committee "that takes into account all the material presented by a relevant analyst and then forms a judgment of where the country stands relative to other credits" (IMF, 2010), meaning leaving an important space for subjectivity.

(viii) Agencies' approach seems to result in the same sovereign rating, for countries with different profiles and such replications are very commonly encountered.

(ix) Agencies expect sovereign ratings to fall, in most cases, within one notch of the indicative rating level. One notch can, however, make a difference between investment and speculative status.

(x) If unfairly allocated, one notch downgrade may mean unjustified economic and financial crisis.

The second step in agencies' approach, the subjective stage, is embodied in the work of rating committees within CRAs. Also very determining, it may constitute a threat to any transparency efforts or standardisation tentative. Agencies constantly claim the soundness of their models, because, they argue, they are based on the efficient system of the rating committees. They underline that such committees are in a position of considering all the relevant material and take into account all the important fundamental factors and then form a judgment of where the sovereign stands, relative to other sovereigns. According to agencies, this also allows the ratings to adapt to the changing environment and issuer conditions (Moody's, 2013a). Dodd-Frank, however, does not seem to see it that way and recently made rating agencies subject to liability for careless behaviours and required regulators to reduce reliance on ratings in their monitoring activities.

At the methodological level, however, critics contend that the ratings of the three largest agencies need to be corrected for enhancement purpose, mainly by decreasing subjective elements of judgment resulting from the committee-based system (Nielsen et al. (2014). Even if people seem commonly to be keen to see personal judgment kept away from mechanistic calculations, the extent of approximation, in the case of the ratings, is making them change their view. Indeed, although rating methodologies evolve over time and continue to be adjusted in response to new legislations, information and economic developments, many believe that the use of committees may actually make the ratings less accurate, rather than more so. They are also intrigued by the fact that "self-appointed committees in each of the CRAs might be able to improve the signal, in terms of default probability" (Vernazza et al., 2014); they even fear committees may overrule the signal from the hard data. A test was conducted of whether ratings are useful in predicting actual default events, including more than one hundred countries, over more than ten years, and it was found that the committees add no value at all for default, one or more years ahead, "it implies that beneath this average zero-value-added 'subjective component' lies multiple sins on both sides" (Nielsen et al., 2014), as a proof that history is littered with countries being over- or under-rated by the CRAs, with dramatic consequences, in downgrades.

To discharge any suggestion of decreasing the role of rating committees, agencies argue that the problem with the research calling for the dismissal of the rating committee resides in its pretension that the impossible task of distinguishing between objective and subjective elements of the ratings can be easily reached (Kraemer, 2014). CRAs give supporting arguments for the use of judgments in the rating process, such as:

(i) Some factors are impossible to quantify.
(ii) Even those that can be quantified are not available for every country at every point in time.
(iii) Some information is even confidential.
(iv) There are factors that are country-specific.
(v) Judgments incorporate forward- looking expectations and risks (Nielsen et al., 2014).

Despite agencies arguments in favour of rating committees, pressure on them has recently significantly intensified, following the shift that has been operated at the level of sovereign rating, and where modern sovereign developed economies are annoyed by the downgrades they have had imposed by agencies; developed countries were not accustomed to see their debt examined under the loop of agencies. For decades, indeed, developed economies' ratings were rather of high quality and stable, and downgrades were known to be the fate of the supposedly "badly managed" emerging economies such as Argentina, Brazil and Russia. The recent degradation of European sovereign balance sheets was the culminating point in igniting very real concerns about CRAs' approaches to assess sovereign solvency and casts doubt on how sovereign ratings are measured. CRAs, however, feel that "when financial market participants are bored or dyspeptic, they frequently turn to credit rating agencies as an always available target of criticism" (Grene, 2014). CRAs constantly insist that their ratings are only measures of the probability of default, not the market's perception of the probability of these defaults. This, however, is to ignore that ratings can have determining effects on issuers, investors and the whole financial system (see Chapter 4).

Overall, it appears often very difficult, if not impossible, to trust agencies' models for the ranking of sovereigns based on their respective solvencies. Indeed, as underlined in Chapter 6, it is difficult to identify in agencies' models the rationality of the choices made regarding a number of the components of their approach to sovereign solvency assessment – for instance and among others:

(i) The choice of the drivers of sovereign default components
(ii) The weights assigned to factors
(iii) The functional form of factors
(iv) The real significance of final ratings.

Major agencies use similar approaches to sovereign creditworthiness assessment, and their results present pairwise correlations in the range of 0.97 to 0.98 (Nielsen et al., 2014); therefore, Moody's model will be used as a proxy for agencies' methodologies and serve for testing their accuracy in this chapter and the two that follow.

Methodology of assessing the accuracy of CRAs' sovereign rating approach

The limited number of actual sovereign defaults prevents empirical testing of any CRA model (IMF, 2010). Our investigation will therefore focus on the measurable aspect of agencies' approach. We also consider sovereign default assessment to be typically based on measurable fundamentals (Nielsen et al., 2014), although almost always a matter of committees' choice. We will limit ourselves to the test of the model used by agencies, for the purpose of determining the level of its accuracy. The data used in the study come from CRA publications, as summarised in Moody's (2013a). This section clarifies how CRAs assess sovereign creditworthiness, using Moody's model as proxy, as thoroughly explained in Chapter 6. The key factors that are used by agencies in their sovereign creditworthiness analysis are:

(i) Economic strength, *ECOSTR*
(ii) Institutional strength, *INSSTR*
(iii) Fiscal strength, *FISSTR*
(iv) Susceptibility to event risk, *SUSRIS*.

These factors are used to form the following combinations:

(i) Economic resiliency, *ECORES*
(ii) Government financial strength, *FINSTR*
(iii) Government bond rating range, *RATRAN*.

Key factors and combination are as defined in previous chapter, and are originally expressed by agencies in alphabetical scales "VH+ to VL−", at the beginning of the process and in range scale "Aaa-Aa2 to B2-Caa", at the end of the process. This way of scaling, as already underlined, does not, however, allow for quantitative computations, like summation or averaging. To overcome such constraint, our methodology of assessing agencies' approach is, therefore, performed in three progressive and cumulative steps:

(i) First, agencies' alphanumerical ranking "VH+ to VL−" will be translated into a corresponding numerical scale of "1 to 15", and similarly, a range scale "Aaa-Aa2 to B2-Caa" will be translated into a corresponding numerical scale of "1 to 15". In order, however, to respect agencies' scale, we may eventually be forced to use, when agencies do, other scales, with more than fifteen classes. For translating purpose, we use a linear mapping where the higher the rating, the lower the number assigned. More specifically, the top rating Aaa is assigned the value 1, the next rating below Aa1 is assigned the value 2, and so on, till Caa, which is assigned the value of 15. See Table 7.2 for the details on the translation process. This will allow expressing agencies' alphabetical combinations, into a corresponding numerical scale. Consequently, a subscript "n" preceding any element (factor or combination of factors) originally expressed in alphabetical scale "VH+ to VL−" or ranges "Aaa-Aa2 to B2-Caa" indicates its translation into an equivalent numerical scale 1 to 15. See the next section for more discussion of the translation process.

(ii) Second, translated combinations in numerical values will be restated, using appropriate weighting. A subscript "r" preceding any translated element (factor or combination of factors) indicates its restatement, using the appropriate weight. For in-depth discussion of the restatement process, see the section "Restatement of the translated agencies' data" below.

(iii) Third, multi-regression analysis will be performed to assess how the agencies' model fits agencies' data.

(iv) Fourth, a regression analysis will be achieved in order to highlight differences between translated and restated data.

The regression analysis will include constant analysis, residual analysis and gap analysis. The chapter uses for the first time constant analysis and gap analysis, to evaluate the fit of agencies' model to agencies' data.

Translating agencies' alphabetical data into numerical ranking

Agencies use three different scales in their assessment of countries default, as indicated in Table 7.1. As a first step, they use the scale "VH+ to VL−" (Table 7.1, line 1) for assessing sovereign economic resiliency and sovereign financial strength (Table 7.1, line 1). This is an alphabetically based fifteen-category scale, where each element receives a score using a fifteen-point scale, ranking from "VH+" (the strongest) to "VL−" (the weakest).

Second, agencies also use range or interval scale "Aaa-Aa2 to B2-Caa" (Table 7.1, line 2) to assess sovereign bond rating ranks. This scale is also

Table 7.1 Different scales used by agencies in their assessment of countries' default

VH+ to VL–	VH+	VH	VH–	H+	H	H–	M+	M	M–	L+	L	L–	VL+	VL	VL–			
"Aaa-Aa2 to B2-Caa"	Aaa-Aa2	Aa1-Aa3	Aa2-A1	Aa3-A2	A1-A3	A2-Baa1	A3-Baa2	Baa1-Baa2	Baa2-Ba1	Baa3-Ba2	Ba1-Ba3	Ba2-B1	Ba3-B2	B1-B3	B2-Caa			
"Aa1 to Caa3"	Aa1	Aa2	Aa3	A1	A2	A3	Baa1	Baa2	Baa3	Ba1	Ba2	B3	B1	B2	B3	Caa1	Caa2	Caa3

composed of fifteen-interval categories, the “Aaa-Aa2” interval as the strongest and “B2-Caa” as the weakest. Such a scale is also characterised by the overlapping of its classes; ratings are mid-point of three-notch rating ranges, and the highest rating can either be “Aaa”, “Aa1” or “Aa2”; Aa1 seems to represent the mid-point notch in the highest class of rating and one of the three-notch rating range of the second highest class of rating and the same with the rest of the scale. This actually comes to choosing as mid-points the scale Aa1, Aa2, Aa3, A, etc. to B3. Third, although, ranges “Aaa-Aa2 to B2-Caa” are translated in numerical values using fifteen ranks, agencies seem, however, to use a numbering eighteen-point scale for computing individual rating within rating ranges (Table 7.1, line 3). We therefore have recourse to a linear mapping method of replacing each alphabetical value of factor, or combination of factors ranges, by their corresponding numerically translated ratings, NTR, while respecting agencies’ different classifications, as indicated by equation 1

$$X_i = {}_{n}X_i \tag{E7.1}$$

where:
X_i represents any level of the alphabetical scale (“VH+ to VL−” or of the intervals “Aaa-Aa2 to B2-Caa”) assigned by agencies to any factor or combination of factors (*ECOSTR, INSSTR, FISSTR, SUSRI, FINSTR, ECORES* and *RATRAN*); and ${}_{n}X_i$ represents the position on a the numerical scale of 1 to 15 (1 to n, depending on the scale used by agencies) of any component of the alphabetical scales, assigned by agencies to any factor, combination of factors or interval.

Equation 1 allows the translation of alphabetical ranking categories (VH+ to VL−, or intervals “Aaa-Aa2 to B2-Caa”) used by CRAs, into corresponding numerically translated ratings. VH+ grade, for instance, corresponds to a rank of 1, VH to a rank of 2, and so on, in ascending order, till VL−, which corresponds to the rank 15. The translation of alphabetical scale into NTR scale allows to take into account the weighting system chosen by CRAs and the introduction of “additivity”, e.g. meaning weighted data can be added and “averaged” to the agencies’ data. For the rest of the paper and as mentioned before, a subscript “n” preceding any factor or combination will indicate their translation in numerical scale 1 to 15 (1 to 18 for final rate computation). For susceptibility to even risk, the ranking is reversed: “VL−” is assigned the rank “1” and “VL” the rank “2” and so on, till “VH+”, which is assigned the rank “15”.

To compute the final result of the sequential combination of the rating factors (*RATRAN*), CRAs use, however, the interval alphabetical scale “Aaa-Aa2 to B2-Caa”, instead of the “VH+ to VL−” scale. We therefore translate in the same way the interval alphabetical scale “Aaa-Aa2 to B2-Caa” into the ranking scale 1 to 15: “1” for the interval “Aaa-Aa2” to “15” for interval “B2-Caa”. According to Moody’s (2013a) the susceptibility to event risk is considered a constraint, which can only lower the preliminary rating range, given by combining the first three factors. Note, however, that although Moody’s asserts using a fifteen-class scale, the real scale used contains eighteen classes. We will therefore be basing our analysis on the fifteen-class scale for studying economic resiliency and sovereign financial strength and eighteen-class scale for the study of the sovereign bond rating range.

The results of the translation of alphabetical scale into corresponding numerical ranking scales of actual data published by CRAs are presented in *A* appendixes:

(i) Appendix *A1*: Agencies' actual economic resiliency, translated into numerical ranking scale ($_n$*ECORES*): Combination of Economic Strength in numerical scale, $_n$*ECOSTR* & Institutional Strength in numerical scale, $_n$*INSSTR* for a weight of 50/50
(ii) Appendix *A2*: Agencies' actual government financial strength, translated in numerical ranking ($_n$*FINSTR*): Combination of Economic Resiliency ($_n$*ECOSTR* and $_n$*INSSTR*) and Fiscal Strength in numerical scale, $_n$*FISSTR*, based on the following weights: 80/20, 70/30, 60/40, 75/25 and 10/90, successively.
(iii) Appendix *A3*: Agencies' actual rating range, translated in numerical ranking ($_n$*RATRAN*): Combination of government financial strength ($_n$*ECOSTR*, $_C$*INSSTR*, $_n$*FISSTR*) and susceptibility to event risk ($_n$*SUSRIS*).

Restatement of the translated agencies' data

Restated numerically translated ratings, RNTR, of key factors and combinations of factors are obtained, as indicated in expression E7.2, by computing the weighted average of the translated numerical factors that compose any combination of factors r_nY_i. An "r" preceding any translated key factor or combination of factors, indicates its restatement.

$$r_nY_i = \sum_{i=1}^{n} w_i \, {}_nX_i \qquad \text{(E7.2)}$$

where:

$_nX_i$ represents the translated value of a key factor or combination of factors i (i = 1,. . ., n) expressed in ranking numbers 1 to 15; and
w_i represents the weight assigned by agencies to the value of any key factor or combination of factors expressed in ranking numbers (translated) (i = 1,. . ., n, and Σw_i = 100%).

For example, the restatement of economic resiliency for a given sovereign that has been allocated a VH+ rating for its economic strength ($_n$*ECOSTR*) and VL− for its institutional strength ($_n$*INSSTR*) will be reached in two steps: first by converting agencies alphabetical rating (VH+) for economic strength into 1, and VL−, the institutional strength, into 15 and then by computing the weighted average in the following way: [(0.5 × 1) + (0.5 × 15) = 8], when agencies' weights are 50/50. The results of the restatement of translated alphabetical scale are presented in *B* appendixes:

(i) Appendix *B1*: (r_n*ECORES*), numerically restated economic resiliency: Combination of Economic Strength (E7*COSTR*) and Institutional Strength (*INSSTR*)
(ii) Appendix *B2*: (r_n*FINSTR*), numerically restated government financial strength: Combination of economic resiliency (E7*CORES*) and Fiscal Strength (*FISSTR*)
(iii) Appendix *B3*: (r_n*RATRAN*), numerically restated rating range: Combination of country financial strength (*FINSTR*) and country sensitivity to event risk (*SUSRIS*)

Comparing data in *A* appendixes to those in *B* appendixes may allow measuring the level of accuracy of agencies approach in assessing sovereign solvency, and this can be done through regression analysis (intercept and residual analysis) and gap analysis. The model that fits the data best will be considered as better performing and gaps will help assess the extent of divergences.

Since we should not expect regression $_nY_i$ in numerical numbers, NTR and regression r_nY_i, in restated numbers, RNTR, to diverge significantly by the levels of their significance, as both regressions are based on the same original data and only the weights used to form combinations are expected to distinguish them. We believe that the way agencies allocate weights to factors and combinations is not clear and does not seem to obey any rational rule, therefore we suggest a way of getting around the problem, by using equal weighting at every step of the process – except for combination 2, where agencies' weightings are clear, although still not rational. Note that other weighting systems are also possible and can also be considered by the suggested theoretical model. We therefore expect the two models to diverge significantly at the level of both their constants and residuals and not much at the level of their R2. Consequently, in order to identify which approach is more accurate (agencies' approach $_nY_i$ in NTR or the restatement approach r_nY_i in RNTR, we will be using three different analyses:

(i) Constant analysis
(ii) Residual analysis
(iii) Gap analysis.

Constant analysis

As explained in Chapter 2, the constant term of the regression will be used to make sure that agencies' approach does not omit certain important information. In such case, constant in agencies' model $_nY_i$ and in the restatement model r_nY_i are expected to equate zero. A set of two regressions for each of the three steps composing agencies' approach (see Chapter 6) will be run towards this purpose:

(i) The step of assessing sovereign economic resiliency
(ii) The step of assessing sovereign financial strength
(iii) The step of assessing government bond rating range.

$$_{n}Y_{i} = b0 + b1 *_{n}X1 + b2 *_{n}X2 + \varepsilon_{i} \tag{E7.3}$$

$$r_{n}Y_{i} = b0 + b1 * r_{n}X1 + b2 * r_{n}X2 + \varepsilon_{i} \tag{E7.4}$$

where:
$_{n}Y_{i}$ and $r_{n}Y_{i}$ successively represent NTR and RNTR combination;
$_{n}X1$ represents any factor or combination of factors, expressed in translated numerical ranking, NTR;
$r_{n}X2$ represents any factor or combination of factors expressed in restated numerical ranking, RNTR;
b0, b1 and b2 are the intercept and independent variable coefficients, respectively; and
ε_{I} represents the residuals.

Residuals analysis

Further, in ordinary regression analysis, the model can be validated by analysing residual behaviour. Indeed, randomness and irregularity are crucial components of any regression model and are required for its validity. The regression model can be broken down into several basic components [Y = Constant + Prediction + Error]. The prediction portion is the part of Y that is explained by the prediction variables in the model. All of the explanatory/predictive information of the model should therefore be included in this part. While the error portion is the difference between the expected value and the observed value and the prediction portion of the model should be so good at explaining the response that only the inherent randomness of any real-world phenomenon remains left over for the error portion. One way to make sure the residuals are consistent with random error is by assuring the residuals to be neither systematically high nor systematically low. Further, in the OLS context, random errors are assumed to produce residuals that are normally distributed. Therefore, the residuals should fall in a symmetrical pattern and have a constant spread throughout the range. The non-random pattern in the residuals indicates that the prediction variables portion of the model is not capturing some explanatory information that is "leaking" into the residuals. When explanatory or predictive power in the error are observed, it means that the model's predictors are missing some of the predictive information (Frost, 2012).

Gap analysis

Further, for each of the three steps included in agencies' approach, gaps $_{n}g_{i}$ between any translated factor and combination of factors ($_{n}Y_{i}$) (as published by agencies) and as restated in ranks (r_nY_i), are unearthed, by subtracting $_nY_i$ values from their corresponding values r_nY_i, in the following way:

$$_ng_i = [r_nX_i - {}_nX_i] \qquad \text{(E7. 5)}$$

where:
r_nX_i represents the restated value for any factor/combination of factors, NTR;
$_nX_i$ represents the translated value of any factor/combination of factors, RNTR;
w_i is the weight assigned to each factor.

The analysis results

The use of numerical ranking "1 to 15" instead of alphabetical "VH− to VL+" or alphabetical interval "Aaa to Caa" introduces flexibility to sovereigns' default assessment. Indeed, factors with equal or of different weights can now be combined, once expressed in numerical ranking. Alphabetical scale will always exclude any precise operation of addition/subtraction, division or combination among and within alphabetical ratings. The use of any alphabetical scale will always render combinations of this kind only approximate. Further, the use of numerical scale allows also the use of regression analysis. As explained in the previous section, intercept analysis is used to assess how agencies' model fit the data. Although the value of the constant is generally considered meaningless, in the present case it makes sense to determine whether the intercept value is significantly different from zero – because the closer the intercept to zero, the more fitted the model is to the data. In our case, since each inaccurate sovereign rating can have a devastating effect on the concerned sovereign, it is not enough to require residuals to be centred on zero throughout the range of fitted values to conclude to the fairness of the model. It is also necessary that individual residuals (residual for each sovereign) be near 0. Therefore, the following regression was run, each set of two regressions assesses the accuracy of agencies' approach of a given step of their process.

Regression set 1:

$$_n\mathit{ECORES}_i = b0 + b1 {*} {}_n\mathit{ECOSTR}_i + b2 {*} {}_n\mathit{INSSTR}_i \qquad \text{(E7. 6)}$$
$$r_n\mathit{ECORES}_i = b0 + b1 {*} r_n\mathit{ECOSTR}_i + b2 {*} r_n\mathit{INSSTR}_i \qquad \text{(E7. 7)}$$

Regression set 2:

$$_n\mathit{FINSTR}_i = b0 + b1 {*} {}_n\mathit{ECORES}_i + b2 {*} {}_n\mathit{FISSTR}_i \qquad \text{(E7. 8)}$$
$$r_n\mathit{FINSTR}_i = b0 + b1 {*} r_n\mathit{ECORES}_i + b2 {*} r_n\mathit{FISSTR}_i \qquad \text{(E7. 9)}$$

Regression set 3:

$$_n\mathit{RATRAN}_i = b0 + b1 {*} {}_n\mathit{FINSTR}_i + b2 {*} {}_n\mathit{SUSRIS}_i \qquad \text{(E7. 10)}$$
$$r_n\mathit{RATRAN}_i = b0 + b1 {*} r_n\mathit{FINSTR}_i + b2 {*} r_n\mathit{SUSRIS}_i \qquad \text{(E7. 11)}$$

where:
$_{n}ECORES_{i}$ represents country economic resiliency translated in numerical ranking of a country i;
$r_{n}ECORES_{i}$ represents country economic resiliency in restated numerical ranking of a country i;
$_{n}FINSTR_{i}$ represents financial strength translated in numerical ranking of a country i;
$r_{n}FINSTR_{i}$ represents financial strength in restated numerical ranking of a country i;
$_{n}RATRAN$ represents government bond rating range in translated numerical ranking of a country i;
$r_{n}RATRAN$ represents government bond rating range in restated numerical ranking of a country i;
$_{n}ECOSTR_{i}$ represents economic strength translated in numerical ranking of a country i;
$r_{n}ECOSTR_{i}$ represents economic strength in restated numerical ranking of a country i;
$_{n}INSSTR_{i}$ represents institutional strength translated in numerical ranking of a country i;
$r_{n}INSSTR_{i}$ represents institutional strength in restated numerical ranking of a country i;
$_{n}FISSTR_{i}$ represents country fiscal strength in translated numerical ranking of a country i;
$r_{n}FISSTR_{I}$ represents country fiscal strength in restated numerical ranking of a country i;
$_{n}SUSRIS_{i}$ represents susceptibility to event risk in in translated numerical ranking of a country i;
$r_{n}SUSRIS_{i}$ represents susceptibility to event risk in in restated numerical ranking of a country i;
b0, b1 and b2 are the intercept and independent variables coefficients, respectively of a country i.

Expressions 6 and 7 (set 1) assess the accuracy of agencies' approach in measuring sovereign economic resiliency (ECORES), while expressions 8 and 9 (set 2) assess the accuracy of agencies' approach in measuring sovereign financial strength (*FINSTR*), and expressions 10 and 11 (set 3) assess the accuracy of agencies' approach in measuring the government bond rating range (*RATRAN*).

As regressions data come from agencies' figures, regressions 1, 3 and 5, for instance, are based on numerically translated agencies' data, NTR, while and regressions 2, 4 and 6 are based on the same numerical translated data but restated, using appropriate weightings, RNTR. Therefore, the only expected difference between regressions 1, 3 and 5 (based on numerically translated agencies data) and regressions 2, 4 and 6 (based on restated numerically translated agencies data), is the one that has to do with the divergence in the weightings used. As we know, agencies use much approximation in building their combinations of factors, and the restatement process is intended to correct such approximation. Although the significance of all the regressions is expected to be very high, the comparison of regressions 1, 3 and 5 to their corresponding 2, 4 and 6 is expected to show how agencies approximation is impacting the accuracy of the ratings, and this eventual shortcoming should be added to whatever agencies approach may contain as limits and already decried in the literature (Afonso et al., 2007, Gande and Parsley, 2005, IMF, 2013, Nielsen et al., 2014, Vernazza et al., 2014, etc.).

Regression analysis results

Table 7.2 gives a recapitulation of the regressions used to this end.

The high R2 for all the regressions is due to the fact that these regressions are based on the same data – as it happens, agencies' data themselves. Any missing significance should therefore be considered as an expression of one kind of weakness or another. For this reason the higher R2 for the restated models (except for regression 3 compared with regression 4) can be considered as a sign of a shortcoming in agencies' process of assessing sovereign creditworthiness. Further, although the overall significance of all models is high (around one on average), we should keep in mind that macro-level sovereign under-grades are eventually balanced by over-grades, as evident from standard error estimates. At the individual level, however, under-graded sovereigns will suffer a lot from any unfair assessments. Intercept analysis and residual analysis can help testing the significance of agencies' approach, not on average, but rather based on effects on sovereigns taken individually.

Table 7. 2 Models' recapitulation

No	*Regression*	*R*	*R-square*	*Adjusted R-square*	*Standard error*
1	${}_{n}ECORES_{i} = b0 + b1{*}{}_{n}ECOSTR_{i} + b2{*}{}_{n}INSSTR_{i}$	.993	.985	.985	.40122
2	$r_{n}ECORES_{i} = b0 + b1{*}r_{n}ECOSTR_{i} + b2{*}r_{n}INSSTR_{i}$	1.000	1.000	1.000	.00000
3	${}_{n}FINSTR_{i} = b0 + b1{*}{}_{n}ECORES_{i} + b2{*}{}_{n}FISSTR_{i}$	.982	.963	.963	.982a
4	$r_{n}FINSTR_{i} = b0 + b1{*}r_{n}ECORES_{i} + b2{*}r_{n}FISSTR_{i}$	.915	.837	.836	1.56347
5	${}_{n}RATRAN_{i} = b0 + b1{*}{}_{n}FINSTR_{i} + b2{*}{}_{n}SUSRIS_{i}$	.991	.982	.982	.68226
6	$r_{n}RATRAN_{i} = b0 + b1{*}r_{n}FINSTR_{i} + b2{*}r_{n}SUSRIS_{i}$	.998	.996	.996	.19014

Constant analysis results

The larger the intercept coefficient (in absolute value), the greater the chances of encountering approximation in agencies' approach. Table 7.3 shows that intercepts of regressions 1, 3 and 5 (corresponding to expressions E.6, E.8 and E.10), e.g. intercepts based on agencies' data translated in corresponding numerical ranking NTR are more important than those of their counterparts regressions 2, 4 and 6 (corresponding to expressions E.7, E.9 and E.11), e.g. intercepts based on restated numerical data, RNTR. Meaning that regressions 1, 3 and 5 fit less well the data. They can therefore be considered as less accurate in representing the sovereign creditworthiness than their counterpart regressions 2, 4 and 6.

Constant terms of agencies' models are, in absolute values, two times out of three, higher than those of the corresponding three restated models, −0.693 versus −0.084. −0.791 versus −0.417 and −1.575 versus −0.084. for regression sets 1, 2 and 3 respectively. Therefore regression results confirm the superiority of restated models over the translated only, in fitting the data. Large t-values and consequently the smaller p-value confirm the significance of the results. Consequently restated modes will be used as a benchmark over which gaps will be measured.

Residual analysis results

The superiority of the restated model over agencies' model can also be tested through a residual analysis. Since residual can be set to equate [Observed – Predicted], positive value for the residual means the prediction was too low, and negative values mean the prediction was too high; 0 means the bet was exactly correct. Table 7.4 presents the residuals in notches and shows that although all models seem to show 0 residual mean, as expected given the shared origin of data, they actually diverge regarding residual dispersion, e.g. the squared sum of residuals, their minimum, maximum and standard deviation. For regression 1 (corresponding to E.6), for instance, has as minimum, maximum and standard deviation 35.737, −0.75000, 1.12333 and 0.39942 respectively; translated figures

Table 7.3 Financial strength in numerical ratings and restated ranking: intercept coefficients

	Regression set 1: Economic resiliency (ECORES)		*Regression set 2: Government financial strength (FINSTR)*		*Regression set 3: Government bond rating range (RATRAN)*	
Regression	Regression 1 (E. 6)	Regression 2 (E. 7)	Regression 3 (E. 8)	Regression 4 (E. 9)	Regression 5 (E. 10)	Regression 6 (E. 11)
B coefficient of the Constant	−0.693	−0.084	−0.791	−0.417	−1.575	−0.084
t	−12.35	−2.368	−5.576	−1.427	−12.35	−2.368
p-value Sig	.000	.000	.000	.000	.000	.000

Table 7.4 Comparison of the regressions residuals, in notches

	Model	*Squared residual of residuals*	*Minimum*	*Maximum*	*Mean*	*Standard deviation*	*N*
1	${}_{n}ECORES_{i} = b0 + b1*{}_{n}ECOSTR_{i} + b2*{}_{n}INSSTR_{i}$	35.737	−.75000	1.12333	0.0000	0.39942	225
2	$r_{n}ECORES_{i} = b0 + b1*r_{n}ECOSTR_{i} + b2*r_{n}INSSTR_{i}$	0.00000	0.00000	0.00000	0.0000	0.00000	225
3	${}_{n}FINSTR_{i} = b0 + b1*{}_{n}ECORES_{i} + b2*{}_{n}FISSTR_{i}$	127.963	−2.19484	2.64944	0.0000	0.75582	225
4	$r_{n}FINSTR_{i} = b0 + b1*r_{n}ECORES_{i} + b2*r_{n}FISSTR_{i}$	542.663	−2.58011	7.91172	0.0000	1.55647	225
5	${}_{n}RATRAN_{i} = b0 + b1*{}_{n}FINSTR_{i} + b2*{}_{n}SUSRIS_{i}$	103.336	−2.56111	3.14294	0.0000	0.67921	225
6	$r_{n}RATRAN_{i} = b0 + b1*r_{n}FINSTR_{i} + b2*r_{n}SUSRIS_{i}$	8.026	−.45516	0.54127	0.0000	0.18929	225

only demonstrate higher squared sum of residuals and more dispersion than those of their corresponding figures of model 2, where the minimum, maximum and standard deviation are all nil. The same conclusion can be drawn when considering regressions 5 and 6 (set 3); regression 5 has 103.336, −2.56111, 3.14294 and 0.18929, as minimum, maximum and standard deviation, respectively, and regression 6 has 8.026, −0.45516, 0.54127 and 0.18929, respectively.

The comparison of the residuals of regressions 3 and 4 (set 2) appears, however, to convey another sound of the bell, agencies' model with squared sum of residuals, maximum, minimum and standard deviation of 127,963, −2,19484, 2,64944 and, 75582 appears to be more performing than the restated model with residuals squared sum, maximum, minimum standard deviation of 542,663, −2,58011, 7,91172 and 1,55647. The way economic resiliency and fiscal strength are combined may have artificially increased the performance of agencies' model. At this level indeed agencies use different weighting systems, dependent on the level of economic resiliency 80/20 weight, 70/30, 60/40, 75/25 and 10/90, successively for each group of three levels of economic resiliency (VH+, VH and VH−, H+, H and H−, etc.). For further clarification of the method, see next section.

Gap analysis results

In order to assess the overall extent of the gaps arising from CRAs' approach of assessing sovereigns' default, we built a gap matrix for the three combinations used by agencies, by putting into application equation 5 [$_{n}g_{i} = (r_{n}X_{i} - {}_{n}X_{i})$], and computing differences between translated numerical ranking and their corresponding restated values in the following way:

$$gECORES_{i} = r_{n}ECORES_{i} - {}_{n}ECORES_{i} \quad \text{(E7. 12)}$$
$$gFINSTR_{i} = {}_{n}FINSTR_{i} - r_{n}FINSTR_{i}. \quad \text{(E7. 13)}$$
$$gRATRAN_{i} = r_{n}RATRAN_{i} - {}_{n}RATRAN_{i} \quad \text{(E7. 14)}$$

where:
$gECORES_{i}$ represents gaps between translated and restated country's economic resiliency (Appendix *A1*–Appendix *B1*).
$gFINSTR_{i}$ represents gaps between translated and restated country's financial resiliency (Appendix *A2*–Appendix *B2*).
$gRATRAN_{i}$ represents gaps between translated and restated country's final rating, or government bond rating range (Appendix *A3*–Appendix *B3*).
The rest of the variables are as defined in expressions 6 to 11.

Expressions 12 to 14 are used to build three gap matrixes:

(i) The $gECORES_{i}$ matrix
(ii) The $gFINSTR_{i}$ matrix
(iii) The $gRATRAN_{i}$ matrix.

Table 7.5 shows how theses matrixes are built; it reproduces and focuses on a single line of the $gECORES_{i}$ gap matrix. For instance, the 0 economic resiliency gap at the VH+ score is obtained by subtracting the translated economic resiliency score of one from its corresponding restated score of one. Similarly, the 0.5 economic resiliency gap, at the VH score is obtained by subtracting the translated economic resiliency score of 1 from its corresponding restated score of 1.5.

Agencies seem generally to overestimate economic resiliency for countries whose institutional strength is VH+, for different levels of economic strength, except for VH+ and VL−. Actually there are gaps between CRAs data once

Table 7.5 Single line gaps from economic resiliency gap matrix

		VH+	VH	VH−	H+	H	H−	M+	M	M−	L+	L	L−	VL+	VL	VL−
		Country economic resiliency, *ECORES*														
	$_{n}$***INSSTR***	$_{n}$***ECOSTR***														
Restated, $r_{n}ECORES_{i}$	VH+	1	1.5	2	2.5	3	3.5	4	4.5	5	5.5	6	6.5	7	7.5	8
−Translated, $_{n}ECORES_{i}$		1	1	1	2	2	3	3	4	4	5	5	6	6	7	8
= $gECORES_{i}$		0	0.5	1.0	0.5	1	0.5	1	0.5	1	0.5	1	0.5	1	0.5	0

expressed in numerical values ${}_{n}ECORES$ and once restated $r_{n}ECORES$. Overall gap computations are presented in *C* appendixes:

(i) Appendix *C1*: $g_{n}ECORES_{i}$, gives gaps between translated and restated country's economic resiliency
(ii) Appendix *C2*: $g_{n}FINSTR_{i}$, gives gaps between translated and restated country's financial resiliency.
(iii) Appendix *C3*: $g_{n}RATRAN_{i}$, gives gaps between translated and restated country's final rating, or government bond rating range.

The restated values for countries economic resiliency for 50/50-weight, for different levels of economic strength and for different levels of institutional efficiency/strength, are produced in Appendix *A1*. The outcome is however dependent on the weight assigned to each component of the combination. CRAs use equal weight 50/50; if, however, the weight is allowed to vary, the resulting values of economic resiliency will also change. The result, for instance, of combining VL− rate of economic strength with VH+ rate of institutional strength is 8, when 50/50-weight is used, and 2.4 when 90/10-weight is used (Appendix *A1*). As a rule, divergences should be expected when other levels of economic efficiency or institutional strength are opted for, and gaps between numerical combinations and their corresponding restated combinations of factors should be expected to be significantly important. Appendix *C1* produces computed gaps between translated economic resiliency (Appendix *A1*) and its corresponding restated data (Appendix *B1*); it shows that ranking gaps range from *minus* 1 notches to *plus* 1. CRA approach seems to fail 60 per cent of the time (136 times out of 225 (15^2). VH+ values are systematically overestimated, while VL− grades are underestimated.

Further when translated economic resiliency ${}_{n}ECORES$ is combined with fiscal strength ${}_{n}FISSTR$, in aggregation function, they allow computing government financial strength ${}_{n}FINSTR$, as specified before, the weight of fiscal strength is highest for countries with moderate economic resiliency and changing progressively in the following way:

(i) 20 per cent weight fiscal strength, for VH+, VH and VH− levels economic resiliency
(ii) 30 per cent weight fiscal strength, for H+, H and H− levels economic resiliency
(iii) 40 per cent weight fiscal strength, for M+, M, M− levels economic resiliency
(iv) 25 per cent weight fiscal strength, for L+, L, L− levels economic resiliency
(v) 10 per cent weight fiscal strength, for VL+, VL and VL− levels economic resiliency.

Appendix *A2* produces countries' financial resiliency as reported by agencies once translated in numerical scale 1 to 15. Appendix *A2* seems to lack certain consistency in the manner economic resiliency and fiscal strength are combined. It is warned, however, that the creditworthiness of countries with high economic resiliency is less susceptible to changes in their debt metrics, whereas the creditworthiness of countries with moderate economic resiliency is more sensitive to changes in their fiscal strength. In contrast, the creditworthiness of countries with low economic resiliency tends to be weak irrespective of debt metrics (Moody's, 2013a). A gap matrix $g_nFINSTR_i$ (Appendix *C2*) reproduces differences between translated and restated values of countries' financial resiliency. It is constructed by subtracting each restated government financial strength rating, $r_nFINSTR_i$ (Appendix *B2*), from its corresponding translated government financial strength, $_nFINSTR_i$ (Appendix *A2*). Results seem to point to the absence of any concordance between CRAs' alphabetical rankings VH+ to VL− and their restatement in numerical ranking (1 to 15). CRAs seem to get it right only 11 times out of 225 (less than 5 per cent of the time) and to fail 215 times (225–10) out of 225 (15^2) (more than 95 per cent of the time). Ranking gap ranges from minus 7.5 notches to plus 10. These constitute very important gaps if measured against the 15 notches composing the whole scale.

Finally CRAs use countries' susceptibility to event risk *SUSRIS* as a constraint, which can only decrease countries' financial strength, $_nFINSTR_i$ (called the preliminary rating range). CRAs do not give any further clue regarding how event risk is taken into account, except that event risk can be more effective when it is scored as "Very Low", but will move with increasing severity as the risk is assessed from "Low" to "Moderate" to "High" to "Very High". We therefore decide to restate CRAs' interval alphabetical scale "Aaa-Aa2 to B2-Caa" into ranking scale 1 to 15, in order to highlight their rationality. Note that in our computations of Appendixes *A3*, *B3*, *C3* and Table 7.6, susceptibility to event risk *SUSRIS* numbering classification is reversed, in order to respect our previous classifications. "VH+" is scored 15, because it expresses the highest susceptibility to event risk, while VL− is scored 1, because it expresses the lowest susceptibility to event risk. Appendix *A3* produces countries' "government bond rating range" as ranked by agencies, once translated into numerical scale. Appendix *B3*, on the other hand, reproduces the same factor once restated using 50/50 weight, as adopted by agencies.

A look to Appendix *A3*, shows that agencies seem to poorly rank sovereign debt and these results are difficult to interpret; a sovereign, for instance, with a government financial strength scored within the range "Aaa-Aa2", and presenting a susceptibility to event risk considered at the level "VL−", would still be allocated a final grade in the "Aaa-Aa2", range, while another country with the same government financial strength and a susceptibility to event risk of "VH+" would see its final sovereign ranking located in the range "A2-Baa1", i.e. five ranks lower. Appendix *C3* reproducing gaps between translated and restated countries' final rating, or government bond rating range, $g_nRATRAN_i$, underlines differences between agencies' countries' rating range, once translated into numerical scale (Appendix *A3*) and once restated (Appendix *B3*). CRAs approach seems to accurately rank sovereigns only 5 per cent of the time (12 times out of 225) and fail 95 per cent of the time (213 times out of 225). Often three or more levels of susceptibility to event risk would end up inducing the same rating score interval and gaps range from +2.5 to −6.5. Agencies' computation of the rating range combination indeed requires further clarification. Also, we can recall that financial strength is the combination of economic resiliency and fiscal strength, and that both factors are assessed using a scale of 1 to 15, but when used to assess agencies' rating range, $_{n}RATRAN_{i}$, a different scale seem to have been opted for, namely the interval scale "Aaa-Aa2 to B2-Caa". A number of questions comes to mind, for instance what links these two scales? Why while supposed to use a fifteen-rank interval scale in their computation of rating ranges "Aaa-Aa2 to B2-Caa", agencies actually base their assessment on eighteen-rank scale "Aaa1 to Caa3"? Why when for instance computing a rating range for countries, the "B2-Caa" interval includes also Caa1, Caa2 and Caa3? Why are there overlapping of scale intervals; the interval rate Aaa-Aa2, for instance, seems to include the interval "Aa1-Aa3", which is devoted an interval by itself, and this is the case for other scale intervals? How are components of interval scale (Aaa-Aa2, to B2-Caa) combined in the first place and why?

Table 7.6 maps cumulative gaps between agencies' alphabetical scale once translated in numbering scale ($_{n}$) and later restated (r_{n}). It is constructed by adding together all the three gap matrixes (Appendix *C1* + Appendix *C2* + Appendix *C3*).

Several conclusions can be drawn from Table 7.6. First, only at the level of the combination of the strongest government financial strength and the lowest susceptibility to event risk (Aaa-Aa2, VH+) agencies' scale seems to fit its corresponding restated values. More than 99 per cent of the time agencies' scale does not fit its corresponding restated values, and divergences range from +9 notches to −9.6, meaning that, due solely to computational approximations, a country can see its final rating wrongly underestimated by as much as 9.6 notches, i.e. sometimes moving it from investment grade to speculative, while others can see their rating wrongly overestimated by as much as 9.0 notches or 60 per cent of the whole scale, sometimes moving it from speculative to investment status. Such approximations may be presented as trivial if not for the devastating effect a downgrade under investment threshold can have on a country's economy and social stability. Second, rating overestimation seems to happen more frequently in the rating ranges "Aa3-A2" and higher, and underestimation seems to happen in rating ranges of "A1-A3" and lower.

When we concentrate our attention on the speculative threshold of Ba1-Ba3 (Table 7.6, column 11), we can see that the approximation involved can be of great harm, as it may make the difference for a sovereign of being classified as sovereign investment grade or speculative. Figure 7.1 plots the cumulative gaps between agencies' ratings and the theoretical ratings, resulting from the grading of a sovereign whose government financial strength is Ba1, for different levels of its susceptibility to event risk (Figure 7.1, panel 1) and sovereign susceptibility to event risk at H level, for different levels of government financial strength (Figure 7.1, panel 2). Recall that 'Ba1-ba3' and 'H' represent the threshold rating under which a sovereign is considered to be speculative.

Table 7.6 Cumulative gaps between agencies' alphabetical scale translated in numbering scale and restated

			Government financial strength														
R			1	2	3	4	5	6	7	8	9	10	11	12	13	14	15
E			VH+	VH	VH−	H+	H	H−	M+	M	M−	L+	L	L−	VL+	VL	VL−
V			Aaa-Aa2	Aa1-Aa3	Aa2-A1	Aa3-A2	A1-A3	A2-Baa1	A3-Baa2	Baa1-Baa2	Baa2-Ba1	Baa3-Ba2	Ba1-Ba3	Ba2-B1	Ba3-B2	B1-B3	B2-Caa
E	1	VL−	2.3	1.4	1.4	0.4	0.4	−0.6	−1.6	−2.6	−2.5	−5.5	−4.6	−5.6	−4.6	−4.6	−2.6
R	2	VL	1.3	1.3	0.3	0.3	−0.7	−0.7	−2.7	−2.7	−3.7	−3.6	−4.6	−4.6	−4.6	−3.6	−2.6
S	3	VL+	0	0.3	0.6	0.9	1.2	1.5	1.8	2.1	2.4	1.7	2.2	−0.5	2.8	3.1	2.4
E	4	L−	−0.3	−0.8	−1.3	−1.8	−3.3	−3.6	−4.1	−4.6	−5.1	−5.8	−6.1	−9.6	−7.1	−7.6	−8.3
D	5	L	1.2	−0.5	−0.8	−1.3	−1	−2.5	−2.8	−3.3	−3.8	−3.5	−5	−8.3	−5.8	−6.3	−7
S	6	L+	1.1	1	−0.5	−0.7	−1.2	−2	−3.2	−3.7	−5.2	−5.4	−5.2	−5.7	−7.2	−7.4	−8.2
U	7	M−	3.6	2.5	4	3.5	4.3	5.5	4	4.8	6	6.5	6	6.8	8	7.5	9
S	8	M	2.4	0.5	−0.2	0.5	−1.5	−1.2	−2.5	−3.5	−4.2	−5.2	−5.5	−6.5	−7.2	−6.5	−7.5
C	9	M+	2.7	1.1	0.5	−0.5	−0.5	−1.5	−3.1	−2.5	−4.5	−4.1	−6.1	−5.1	−6.1	−7.1	−7.1
E	10	H−	2.1	0.5	0.9	0.5	−0.5	−0.5	−2.5	−3.1	−2.5	−5.5	−4.5	−6.5	−6.1	−6.5	−5.9
P	11	H	3.1	1.1	−0.5	−0.1	−0.5	−1.5	−2.5	−3.5	−4.1	−3.5	−5.5	−4.5	−6.5	−6.1	−6.5
T	12	H+	0.75	−0.25	0.75	−0.25	−1.25	−1.25	−2.25	−2.5	−3.5	−5.25	−4.5	−5.5	−5.75	−6.5	−4.75
I	13	VH−	1.5	0.5	−0.25	−0.25	−0.5	−1.5	−3.25	−3.25	−3.5	−4.5	−5.25	−5.25	−5.5	−6.5	−4.5
B	14	VH	1.5	1.5	0.5	−0.25	−0.25	−0.5	−2.5	−3.25	−3.25	−4.5	−5.5	−6.25	−6.25	−5.5	−4.5
I	15	VH+	2.1	1.2	0.3	0.3	−0.7	−0.7	−2.6	−2.6	−4.6	−3.7	−4.6	−4.6	−5.6	−4.6	−3.5
L																	
I																	
T																	
Y																	

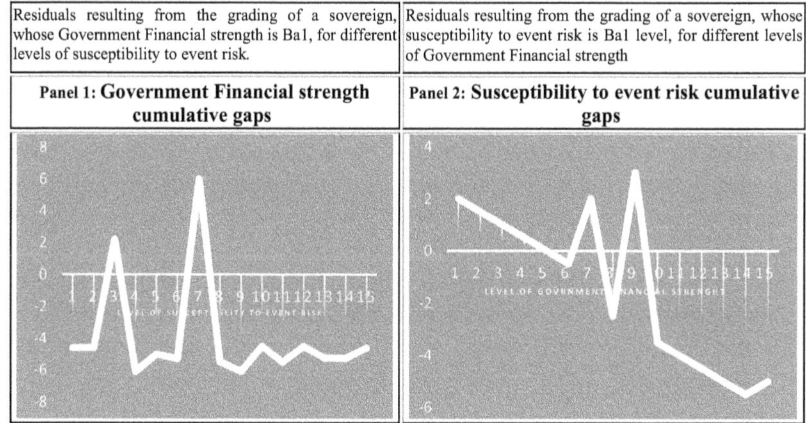

Figure 7.1 Cumulative gaps resulting from the grading of a sovereign whose government financial strength is Ba1, for different level of its susceptibility to event risk (panel 1) and sovereign susceptibility to event risk at Ba1 level, for different levels of government financial strength (panel 2)

The different levels of susceptibility to event risk (Figure 7.1, panel 1) and different levels of government financial strength (panel 2) are represented on the X-axis, and notches on the Y-axis and gaps in notches between agencies ratings and theoretical ratings on the Y-axis. Panel 1 in Figure 7.1 plots gaps resulting from different levels of susceptibility to event risk for the same level of government strength, namely 'Ba1-ba3'. Negative gaps range from −5 to −6, and only twice in fifteen are they positive. Such results can be very disturbing, if we recall that each point corresponds to a one notch and each difference of a single notch can change the final rating. Panel 2 plots gaps resulting from different levels of government financial strength for the same level of susceptibility to event risk, namely 'H' level. Gaps range from 2 to −5.5 and are negative eight times out of fifteen. Figure 7.1 shows that agencies' approach tends to underestimate the quality of sovereign financial strength at Aa1 threshold, for different levels of susceptibility to event risk. Panel 2, on the other hand, indicates that that agencies' approach tends to worsen the risk of default of a sovereign whose susceptibility to event risk is Ba1, for different levels of government financial strength. Starting with the level of government strength of 'Baa3-Ba2'. These two actions combined result in pushing sovereigns at Ba1 level, even further in the speculative zone.

These results can be considered very conservative, given the missed information, namely regarding the choices made by agencies at the level of factors and sub-factors used in determining sovereign ratings, or the specification of their respective weight, that can have impacting effect on the final sovereign score, whenever "changes are made, the distortionary (subjective) tweaking of the 'objective' signals typically have significant impacts on capital flows and asset prices" (Nielsen et al., 2014) and in all cases, wrongly valued sovereign ratings can drain trillions of dollars of assets.

Conclusion

Current degradation of sovereign finances raises very real concerns about how sovereign solvency is measured by credit rating agencies. This chapter specifically focuses on weaknesses of the sovereign rating assessment approach and the results are disturbing. CRAs may defend the idea that their default assessments tend to cluster in the lowest rating grades but it is sometimes argued that anybody with sufficient knowledge of public finance of a defaulting country may perform as good as agencies in classifying it the way CRAs do. It should, however, be recognised that the quality of ratings may depend heavily on sovereign data quality and transparency, and the responsibility for the quality of the information used should not be solely attributed to agencies; it should be concluded that several shortcomings are CRAs' own work. Indeed, "an examination of the analysis accompanying the announcement of each rating action by the Big 3 shows that the drivers were not uniform across types of rating actions or geographic regions" (IMF, 2011). Approximation at every level of agencies' processes seems to be the rule, rather than the exception. This chapter indicates that while common sense cannot be dismissed from agencies' sovereign rating process, it definitely raises the possibility that the door may find itself wide open to eventual actions that can be of great harm to rated sovereigns. One reason of inaccuracy suspected in sovereign ratings has to do with the subjectivity and asymmetry of information within rating processes, as reinforced by the extensive use of rating committees (to be discussed in the next chapter), characterising sovereign ratings and at the very least the chapter advances that CRAs should be expected to be more transparent about their methodologies and the way "they calibrate ratings to default probabilities, loss severities, and stability assumptions" (IMF, 2011).

One can only wonder how agencies can feel confident about their combinations of factors.

8 Subjectivity and asymmetry, why accuracy in sovereign ratings should not be expected

Despite the crucial role sovereign credit ratings may play in the global economy, the process of their determination seems to be surprisingly subjective and marred by secrecy, especially at level of the rating methodologies, as seen in Chapter 7. As a result, investors, issuers and regulators have been looking suspiciously at the role of CRAs in setting sovereign credit ratings and are uncomfortable with the oligopoly they built, over the years, on the global credit market (CAPCO, 2013). The general negative sentiment is that it does not make sense to entrust private companies, whose primary goal is maximising profit, by the mandate of judging the sovereign solvency and to give opinions that are binding for their users (Council of Foreign Relations, 2015). Regulators appear to be disappointed by CRAs' situation and are requiring more transparency from them. Although CRAs have indeed acquiesced to some transparency requirement, it is in the form only and CRAs seem to have been engaged in a new era of asymmetry of information.

This chapter argues that due to subjectivity and information asymmetry, characterising the agency credit assessment process, inaccuracy of the ratings should be expected and raises the possibility that excess of information may prove to be a subtle means of enhancing information asymmetry. This, however, is susceptible of obscuring the real picture of ratings, instead of clarifying it, therefore contributing to increased inaccuracy of the ratings. It indeed gives rating committees more leeway in deciding the ratings. Using agencies' approach of assessing sovereign rating, for example, the chapter shows how the process can be simplified and how very few variables would be better in explaining CRAs' ratings and sovereign failure and concludes that the simpler may prove, here again, to be the better. We present the sample and methodology and study results and focus on what might be wrong with the sovereign credit ratings!

Statutory rules

In 2007, the SEC of the United States adopted its Rules 17g-1 through 17g-6 and Form NRSRO, compelling registered agencies, among other things:

(i) To make certain public disclosures
(ii) To make and retain number of records
(iii) To furnish certain financial reports to the Commission

(iv) To establish and enforce procedures to manage the handling of material non-public information
(v) To disclose and manage conflicts of interest.

The Commission later also amended several of these rules with the objective of further:

(i) Increasing the transparency of rating methodologies
(ii) Strengthening the disclosures of rating performance
(iii) Enhancing record keeping (SEC, 2015).

Agencies have adjusted to these new disclosure requirements and seemingly vow to do their best. It is, however, feared that such additional disclosure requirements may have turned into a system of information asymmetry and instead of clarifying things it may actually have confused, and in all cases they may have acted as market barrier, keeping newcomers from interfering in the rating market. We consider in this chapter a case where excess of disclosure may prove to be equivalent to not enough disclosure. We will concentrate in this chapter on the disclosure requirement for agencies, regarding their approach of assessing sovereign ratings.

Sample and methodology of the chapter

The period covered in this analysis is 2003–2014, and it is based on the data published by Moody's. Agencies' model of assessing sovereign credit rating is built, as presented in Chapter 5, Table 5.2, and it is based on a group of thirty-two fundamentals, segmented in the following way:

(i) 7 fundamentals for expressing sovereign economic strength
(ii) 7 fundamentals for expressing sovereign institutional strength
(iii) 8 fundamentals for expressing sovereign fiscal strength
(iv) 10 fundamentals for expressing sovereign Susceptibility to Event Risk.

Excess of variables in any given model makes the analyst run the risk of losing accuracy of the analysis result, and further some of the fundamentals, included in agencies' model, may prove to be difficult to assess with enough confidence and there seems to be no clear rule for their selection.

The choice of the variables to be included in the model can better be based on mathematical conditions and the Fitch process seems to point to that direction. Once independent variables are selected, their inclusion in the model will depend on their contribution to its improvement. One statistical method that can be used for this purpose is the so-called backward technique, where the initial model may include all the variables thought of, but those with the weakest explanatory contribution will be mechanically removed by SPSS, whenever for instance the variation of R2 is not significant. The procedure can be repeated until all retained variables contribute significantly to the improving of the R2 of the model. The lack of information about the thirty variables used by agencies prevents the use of this method, as it prevents the use of variance analysis for the selection of relevant variables in agencies' model. Given the situation and the objective of this chapter, aiming to show that decreasing significantly the number of fundamentals in agencies' model would not do it any harm, other than improving its accuracy and transparency, we have recourse to a rule of thumb in selecting the most significant variables in agencies' model, based on the parsimony principle that requires any good model to include an optimal number of variables and the presence of a known or suspected theoretical link with the dependent variable. If the results conform with this approach, as limited by the inexistence to us of information, this will mean that any more robust approach will lead to more robust results.

Consequently, and given the correlation that might exist between the thirty-two fundamentals used by agencies, it should be possible to reduce substantially their number without actually affecting the performance of the overall model itself, while at the same time increasing the transparency of the whole process. Note that Fitch uses nineteen variables, S&P only nine. It is indeed currently impossible for anyone to replicate agencies' process and therefore assess the accuracy of the ratings. The rationale for the selected fundamentals included in the suggested simplified model is grounded in finance theory, and for methodological reasons, the choice of variables is limited to the variables already included in actual agencies' analysis. We know the sovereign solvency depends on two distinct facts, the sovereign financial ability to face sovereign debt obligation and the sovereign willingness to pay. Our investigation will therefore be made within agencies' framework and take into account these two considerations.

The capacity of a sovereign to face its debt obligations should, according to finance theory, be strongly linked to both the level of its external sovereign debt and its capacity to face it, in terms of GDP and its stability or low volatility, as the external vulnerability indicator may express it. On the other hand, and to our view, the sovereign willingness to pay should be intimately related to the sovereign effectiveness to manage its public affairs, along with the openness of its economy. Consequently six variables were selected as summary fundamentals, namely, the GDP per capita in PPP, the World Bank government effectiveness index, the sovereign openness of the economy ratio, debt service ratio, external debt/GDP and the external vulnerability indicator. Table 8.1 explains the process of agencies thirty fundamentals, reduced in six summary variables.

Table 8.1 Reduction of the number of fundamentals per strength area and risk, used by Moody's

Economic strength 7 fundamentals are replaced by:	*Institutional Strength 7 fundamentals are replaced by*	*Fiscal Strength 8 fundamentals are replaced by*	*Susceptibility to Event Risk 10 fundamentals are replaced by*
↓	↓	↓	↓
X1. GDP per capita in PPP	X2. World Bank Government Effectiveness Index X3. Sovereign openness of the Economy ratio	X4. Debt service ratio: X5. External Debt/GDP	X6. External Vulnerability Indicator

Table 8.2 indicates, for instance, that sovereign economic strength is built on seven fundamentals, namely the Average Real GDP Growth, the Volatility in Real GDP Growth, the WEF Global Competitiveness index, the Nominal GDP (US$), the GDP per Capita in PPP and the Diversification and Credit Boom, and it can be expressed by a single fundamental, namely the GDP per capita, on a

Table 8.2 Sovereign willingness and financial capacity to pay, as expressed by fundamental means, for the period 2003–2014

	X1: GDP per capita (PPP basis US$)	*X2: Government effectiveness 2003–2011*	*X3: Openness of the Economy 2003–2014*	*X4: Debt service ratio: (Interest + Current-Year Repayment of Principal/ Current Account Receipts) (%)*	*X5: External Vulnerability Indicator*	*X6: External Debt/GDP*
Advanced Industrial Countries		1.57	121.58			
Developing Countries with Aaa to Aa3 ratings	19163	0.77	102.74	7.32	85.89	34.78
Developing Countries with Baa1 to Baa3 ratings	11844	0.24	82.56	19.45	143.67	54.30
Developing Countries with Ba1 to Ba3 ratings	6267	−0.12	90.84	11.06	88.86	48.52
Developing Countries with B1 to C ratings	5536	−0.49	90.80	12.63	119.53	48.53
All developing countries	9393,27	81.04	0.04	11.52	95.64	41.87

Source: Adapted from Moody's Investors service (2013a), Moody's Statistical Handbook Country Credit May 2013. At: http://alleuropalux.org/fileserver/2013/78/153213.pdf. Accessed January 24, 2016.

purchasing-power-parity basis. Indeed, such fundamentals attempt to better capture the relative standard of living of a country's population. It adjusts national income by cost-of-living differences (Moody's Statistical Handbook).

Similarly, the sovereign institutional strength is based on fundamentals such as the World Bank government effectiveness index, the World Bank rule of law index, the World Bank control of corruption index, the inflation level, the inflation volatility and the sovereign track record of default, and can best be expressed through two different fundamentals, namely the World Bank government effectiveness index, and the sovereign openness of the economy ratio. The World Bank government effectiveness index is a fundamental that combines responses on the quality of public services and the bureaucracy that provides them the competence and political independence of civil servants, and the credibility of the government's commitment to its policies. This index is a composite one that is based on as many as fifteen measures of government effectiveness drawn from polls and surveys published by a variety of official and private sources. With higher values this indicator suggests greater government effectiveness and "provides a useful, albeit partial measure of the maturity and responsiveness of government institutions" (Moody's Statistical Handbook). The sovereign openness of the economy ratio, on the other hand, expresses sovereign integration with the world economy through trade and investment; it constitutes an important channel for the transfer of technology and other managerial skills, as well as a powerful force for greater competition in local markets. "This indicator is one of the most widely used measures of openness, focusing on the trade channel" (Moody's Statistical Handbook).

The sovereign fiscal strength is based on fundamentals like the general government debt/GDP, the $_{\text{general}}$ government debt/revenue, the genral government interest payments/revenue, the general government Interest payments/GDP, the debt trend, the general government foreign currency debt/general government debt, other public sector debt/GDP and the public sector financial assets or sovereign wealth funds/GDP. This element may significantly be grasped through two fundamentals, namely the debt service ratio and the external debt/GDP. The debt service ratio (Interest + Current-Year Repayment of Principal/Current Account Receipts) (%) takes account of interest cost, maturity structure, debt stock and foreign-exchange receipts. It does not, however, take into account problems associated with a high level of debt with less than one-year maturity. However, "in a confidence crisis, short-term debt may not be renewed and the debt service ratio may understate the degree of pressure being exerted on the country's reserve position" (Moody's, 2013a). On the other hand, the external debt/GDP ratio expresses external debt as a proportion of the gross domestic product, as published by the IMF; it specifies that countries of different sizes should naturally be expected to have debt of different sizes, consequently, the classification by GDP allows for consistency in international comparisons. This ratio is considered one causal factor of the future flow of interest payments that the residents of the country will have to pay over time to non-residents, relative to the capacity of the country to generate income (Moody's Statistical Handbook).

Finally, the sovereign susceptibility to event risk is based on variables such as the domestic political, geopolitical risk, fundamental metrics, market funding stress, strength of banking system, its size, funding vulnerabilities, current account balance + FDI/GDP, external vulnerability indicator and net international investment position/GDP. The sovereign susceptibility to event risk can be identified by a single element, namely the sovereign external vulnerability indicator (Moody's, 2013a). This is a ratio that expresses, in percentage of official foreign exchange reserves, the sum of short-term external debt, added to currently maturing long-term external debt and total non-resident deposits over one year, and indicates whether a country's immediately available foreign exchange resources are sufficient to allow it to make all external debt payments, even if there is a complete refusal of creditors to roll over debt due within a given year. It actually measures the sovereign capacity to endure a sudden loss of investor confidence, resulting from heightened risk perception. A high ratio may signal a high level of vulnerability or may originate either from excessive short-term debt or from a serious delay of repayments on long-term debt, possibly exacerbated by insufficient reserves (Moody's, 2013a). The rationale for these fundamentals chosen is grounded in economic theory and are variables CRAs themselves have chosen for use in their model.

A regression analysis will be conducted to assess the relationship between sovereign defaults and the sovereign ratings assigned by agencies to defaulted countries for the period 2003–2014. If the simplified model shows high level of significance, this means a higher fit to the data, and consequently, it can be considered as a proof of excess use of variables by agencies, eventually for the purpose of less transparency. Expression 8.1 will be used for assessing the overall significance of the overall simplified model and 8.2 and 8.3 for assessing its significance in case of default and non-default respectively:

$$rating_i = \alpha_i + \beta' X_i + D_i + \varepsilon_i \quad i = 1, \ldots, n \qquad \text{(E8.1)}$$
$$rating_d = \alpha_i + \beta' X_{di} + D_i + \varepsilon_i \quad i = 1, \ldots, n \qquad \text{(E8.2)}$$
$$rating_{nd} = \alpha_i + \beta' X_{ndi} + D_i + \varepsilon_i \quad i = 1, \ldots, n \qquad \text{(E8.3)}$$

where:

$rating_i$ is a numeric value for the alphanumerical long-term foreign currency rating of country i during the period 2003–2014;

X_i is the vector of measurable fundamentals;

X_1: GDP per capita in PPP basis US$;

X_2: Sovereign government effectiveness ratio (Index ranging from about −2.50 to 2.50), given by the composite index with values from about −2.50 to 2.50. Higher values suggest greater maturity and responsiveness of government institutions;

X_3: Sovereign openness of the Economy ratio (Sum of Exports and Imports of Goods and Services/GDP %), given by the sum of Exports and Imports of Goods and Services/GDP;

X_4: Debt service ratio: (Interest + Current-Year Repayment of Principal/Current Account Receipts) (%);
X_5: External Vulnerability Indicator;
X_6: External Debt/GDP;
X_{di} and X_{ndi} represent fundamentals X_1 to X_6, for defaulting ($_{di}$) and non-defaulting ($_{ndi}$) sovereign, respectively;
D_i: a dummy variable, with a value of 0 in case of non-default and 1 in case of default;
β is a vector of coefficients to be estimated;
α_i is a country specific fixed effect; and
εi is an error term.

Expression 8.1, representing the sovereign credit rating, can be divided into two distinct components, as discussed in Chapter 2: an objective component, Ob, and a subjective component, Sub. The objective component, e.g. the part the sovereign rating assessed through the fundamentals, is simply the weighted sum of these fundamentals or the fitted value. The subjective part of the sovereign rating is the part that is formed of supplementary adjustment factors used by rating committees. It can be computed as the difference between the actual rating and the objective component, e.g. the residual (Vernazza et al., 2014). As a rule, the more fundamentals used, the more latitude rating committees will enjoy in deciding the ratings. We will therefore be analysing the selected fundamental to assess the rationality of agencies' choices of the quantitative factors used for sovereign rating determination, as well as analysing residuals to assess the rationality of agencies' subjective intervention.

To proceed, however, with the formal estimation of the agencies' sovereign ratings, we must first convert their alphanumerical ratings into numerical ones, NTR. We use toward this end, as in previous chapters, a linear mapping where the higher the rating, the lower the number assigned. More specifically, the top rating Aaa is assigned the value 1, the next rating below Aa1 is assigned the value 2, and so on, till Ccc, which is assigned the value of 15. We therefore have recourse to a method of replacing each alphabetical value of a factor, by its corresponding numerical rank using a fifteen-point numerical scale, from the strongest to the weakest. The quantitative (objective) component of the sovereign rating is given by the weighted sum of the fundamentals in Expressions 8.1, 8.2 and 8.3. The subjective component is expressed as the difference between the actual rating and its corresponding objective component.

Table 8.2 gives mean values for the six variables used in this chapter, as defined previously, and for the period 2003–2014, except for government effectiveness, whose mean was computed for the period 2003–2011. It is expected that the sovereign willingness to pay will be impacted by the sovereign capacity to generate revenue, to be effective and to open its economy. Therefore, the willingness to pay can be expressed by the variables X_1, X_2 and X_3, in Table 8.2. Similarly, the sovereign capacity to pay should be dependent on the sufficiency of the sovereign foreign currency revenue to pay sovereign foreign currency debt obligations. Variables X_4, X_5 and X_6 can be used for this purpose. Table 8.2 therefore allows the assessment of the impact on sovereign rating of sovereign's willingness to service debt (columns 2, 3 and 4) and the financial capacity to do so (columns 5, 6 and 7).

Overall, Table 8.3 reveals a certain linear relation between both sovereign willingness and capacity to service debt and sovereign rating. Regarding sovereign willingness to pay, high GDP per capita tends to decrease, with the decrease of sovereign solvency, as well as the government effectiveness ratio scores, and openness of the economy, with less precision for Developing Countries with Ba1 to Ba3, B1 to C ratings. On average and on the scale −2.50 to 2.50, the government effectiveness ratio scores ranges from 1.57 for Advanced Industrial Countries, 0.77 for Developing Countries within the class Aaa to Aa3 rating grades, to −0.49 for sovereign Developing Countries within the class B1 to C rating grades. The Openness of the Economy ratio, as expressed by the sum of Exports and Imports of Goods and Services/GDP, ranges from 102.74 on average for Developing Countries with Aaa to Aa3 ratings, to 90.80 for sovereign Developing Countries with B1 to C. Advanced economies have scored 121.58. It appears that both effectiveness and economic openness of sovereigns affect their ratings, with effectiveness impacting more (0.77 to −0.49 vs 102.74 to 90.80).

Variables of sovereign solvency express more erratic relation with sovereign ability to pay; the sovereign external debt/GDP ratio, for instance, is on average vacillating between 34.78 for Aaa to Aa3 class of sovereign rating, and 48.53 for B1 to C class of sovereign ratings. Debt Service ratio is ranging from 7.32 to 12.63 and the External Vulnerability Indicator from 85.89 to 119.69 for Aaa to Aa3 sovereign rating class and for B1 to C sovereign rating class, respectively. All the three variables of financial capacity to pay register degradation as we advance in the rating scale from Aaa to C. Note however, a certain discontinuity at the level of the B1 to C class of sovereigns.

Table 8.3 presents means and standard deviations of the six fundamental variables used in regression analysis, for defaulting and non-defaulting sovereigns

Table 8.3 Fundamentals for sovereign defaulters and non-defaulters

	Default		*Non-default*	
	Mean	Std. dev.	Mean	Std. dev.
X1 GDP per capita (PPP basis US$)	8078 US $	5470 US $	11160 US $	11835 US $
X2 Openness of the Economy	289.69	59.25	94.38	35.05
X3 Government Effectiveness	213.82	51.95	0.13	0.67
X4 Debt Service Ratio	228.48	53.62	11.78	10.93
X5 External Vulnerability Indicator	208.99	157.68	98.34	120.48
X6 External Debt/GDP	50.00	25.21	47.30	39.75

and shows that although non-defaulting sovereigns are expected to perform better than the defaulting, the regression results in 8.4 do not always confirm such rule. Although this may point to some inaccuracy in the data, the quality control of some data may, however, prove to be beyond agencies' reach. If we take, for instance, the "openness of economy" fundamental, it appears to show more economic liberalisation for defaulted sovereigns than for non-defaulted (289.69 compared with 94.38). Although in certain circumstances this should not be a surprise for large economies such as the United States, Brazil, and India, which, given their large scale, may show a lower degree of openness (Moody's, 2013a). Further, defaulted sovereign governments seem to show more effectiveness, as expressed by the government effectiveness fundamental, with 213.82 for defaulted sovereign compared with 0.13 for non-defaulted sovereign. Greater government effectiveness should indeed be an expression of the maturity and responsiveness of government institutions. Although these figures are averages for the period 2003–2014, they don't exclude the possibility that some sovereign may mingle with the system and raise the possibility of balance of payment fraud. This issue will be discussed in Chapter 9.

The rest of the fundamentals appear to be in line with what is expected, sovereign defaulters appear, for instance, to show 27.61 per cent lower GDP per capita in PPP basis (8078/11160), capturing the relative lower standard of living. This is also the case of the debt service ratio, which shows how fundamentals like interest cost, maturity structure, debt stock, and foreign-exchange receipts have strong effect on sovereign capacities to face external debt obligations, and defaulters seem to be impacted even more in this regard. The external vulnerability indicator of defaulters appears to be 2.1 times (208.99/98.34) more important. This is the expression of whether a sovereign's immediately available foreign exchange resources are sufficient to allow it to make all the necessary external debt payments, even if there is a complete refusal of creditors to roll over debt due within a given year. Finally, external debt to GDP of defaulters is 1 per cent (50/47.30) higher than the corresponding indicator for the non-defaulters. This ratio indicates whether a sovereign is more likely to face a disruption of its capacity to service debt when faced with adverse external or internal shocks. Further, correlation coefficient analysis indicates small correlation between the variables used in the model.

Regression results

Coefficient estimates from Equation 8.1 regarding the general sample composed of eighty-nine sovereign defaulting and non-defaulting countries are presented in Table 8.4. The model controls for X_1, the GDP per capita in PPP basis (US$); X_2, the Openness of the Economy; X_3, the Government Effectiveness; X_4, the Debt Service Ratio; X_5, the External Vulnerability Indicator; X_6, the External Debt/GDP; and X7, a dummy variable with 0 for non-defaulted and 1 for defaulted sovereigns. The overall fit of the model including only six

Table 8.4 Estimates of regression 1, overall sample: $rating_i = \alpha_i + \beta' X_i + \varepsilon_i$

Model	*R*	*R-square*	*Adjusted R-square*	*Standard deviation*	*Non standardised coefficient*		*Standardised coefficient*	*t*	*Sig.*
1	.783a	.613	.580	2.69043	B	Standard deviation	Beta		
(Constant)					9.221***	.950		9.706	.000
X1 GDP per capita (PPP basis US$)					.000***	.000	−.332	−3.896	.000
X2 Openness of the Economy					.004	.009	.035	.441	.660
X3 Government Effectiveness					−2.833***	.528	−.458	−5.368	.000
X4 Debt Service Ratio					−.032	.038	−.089	−.834	.407
X5 External Vulnerability Indicator					.001	.004	.031	.280	.780
X6 External Debt/GDP					.029**	.012	.266	2.532	.013
X7 Dummy variable					3.139***	.816	.291	3.845	.000
Number of sovereigns					89				

Significance levels: * 10%; ** 5%; *** 1%.

fundamentals, instead of the thirty included in agencies' model, is fairly good, with an R^2 of 61.3 per cent. The percentage of the cross sovereign variation of ratings that is explained by the objective fundamentals is over 61 per cent, leaving the remaining 39 per cent to be explained by the judgement of the rating committees. This result means that six fundamentals out of thirty explain at least 61 per cent (if we assume 0 residual and the intervention of rating committees) of the sovereign rating.

Most variables are statistically highly significant and have the expected sign, with the exception of government effectiveness and the GDP per capita. The high level of the constant points to the high level of subjectivity exercised by rating committees. This result does not express the accuracy of the rating but seems rather to indicate that adding extra fundamentals to the model would not improve its significance.

Table 8.5 presents the coefficient estimates from Equation 8.3 regarding the non-default sample, composed of seventy-three sovereigns. The percentage of the cross sovereign variation of ratings that is explained by the objective fundamentals has improved slightly, to register 62.5 per cent, leaving the remaining 37.5 per cent to be explained by the subjective judgement of the rating committees.

The GDP per capita in PPP and the external vulnerability indicator seem to have no impact on sovereign ratings of non-defaulting countries. Government effectiveness, on the other hand, appears to be the most impacting factor of non-default.

Ultimately the usefulness of credit ratings depends on their ability to predict actual default events. The second test concerns a defaulting sovereign. The main sample is consequently split into two sub-samples, the sub-sample of sovereign countries that have actually defaulted and the sub-sample of those that have not. The default sub-sample includes Argentina, Belize, Dominican Republic, Ecuador, Grenada, Greece, Jamaica, Moldova, Nicaragua, Pakistan, Russia, Suriname, Uruguay, Ukraine and Venezuela. Means and standard deviations for the measurable fundamentals of creditworthiness of defaulted sovereigns are presented in Table 8.6. This figure presents the coefficient estimates from Equation 8.2 regarding the default sample and composed of the fifteen sovereigns. Unsurprisingly, default events tend to be associated with low GDP in PPP per capita, openness of the economy, government effectiveness, debt service ratio, external debt/GDP and external vulnerability. Most variables are not, however, statistically significant, with an overall R^2 of only 21 per cent.

This result can be considered highly important, since it may suggest that when rating non-defaulting sovereigns, agencies tend to make more use of fundamentals, and when rating defaulting sovereigns, to make more use of subjectivity. Indeed, the constant and the R^2 for the general sample are 9.221 and 0.580, respectively; 8.886 and 0.591 when defaulting sovereigns are excluded and 12.861 +−0.317 when non-defaulting are excluded. Note, however, the small size of the default sample.

Table 8.5 Estimates of regression 3, non-default sample: $rating_{nd} = \alpha_i + \beta' X_{ndi} + \varepsilon_i$

Model	*R*	*R-square*	*Adjusted R-square*	*Standard deviation*	*Non standardised coefficients*		*Standardised coefficients*	*t*	*Sig.*
3	.790a	.625	.591	2.47414	B	Standard deviation	Beta		
(Constant)					8.886***	.924		9.614	.000
X1 GDP per capita (PPP basis US$)					.000***	.000	−.385	−4.084	.000
X2 Openness of the Economy					.007	.009	.063	.736	.464
X3 Government Effectiveness					−3.249***	.509	−.565	−6.384	.000
X4 Debt Service Ratio					−.024	.040	−.068	−.602	.549
X5 External Vulnerability Indicator					.000	.004	−.016	−.113	.911
X6 External Debt/GDP					.034**	.014	.347	2.380	.020
Number of sovereigns					73				

Significance levels: * 10%; ** 5%; *** 1%.

Table 8.6 Estimates of regression 2, default sample: $rating_d = \alpha_i + \beta' X_{di} + \varepsilon_i$

Model	*R*	*R-square*	*Adjusted R-square*	*Standard deviation*	*Non standardised coefficient*		*Standardised coefficient*	*t*	*Sig.*
2	.458a	.210	−.317	3.59738	B	Standard deviation	Beta		
(Constant)					12.861	5.448		2.361	.043
X1 GDP per capita (PPP basis US$)					−4.193E-5	.000	−.076	−.168	.871
X2 Openness of the Economy					.002	.043	.014	.035	.973
X3 Government Effectiveness					.852	2.643	.133	.322	.755
X4 Debt Service Ratio					−.122	.139	−.504	−.873	.405
X5 External Vulnerability Indicator					.011	.010	.554	1.053	.320
X6 External Debt/GDP					.043	.049	.359	.881	.401
Number of sovereigns					15				

Significance levels: * 10%; ** 5%; *** 1%.

Discussion: something seems to be wrong with the sovereign credit ratings!

Away from the quasi-impossible rational choice between the unlimited number of variables that can be included in the assessment of sovereign credit ratings, let's stick to the ratings objective and recall that sovereign credit ratings are supposed to signify to investors the level of sovereign issuers' capacity to pay them in due time. Ratings are therefore intended to help investors to assess the long-term solvency of sovereign issuers. Logically and in accordance of the finance theory, for a sovereign country to gain investor favour, it must show its capacity to generate enough cash flow to face its sovereign debt obligations, namely the payment of interest charges on the contracted debt and the yearly repayments of the principal. If there is a single fundamental within the thirty-one used by agencies, to express such capacity of servicing sovereign debt, it should be a composite ratio called sovereign debt service, SDS ratio. Of course such ratio is seen as the final consequence of a number of other micro, macro economic and policy factors, and other ratios may partially do the same job. SDS is chosen as proxy for other ratios in its category, with the advantage of being the most representative; it can be expressed as followed:

$$\text{SDS} = \text{primary budget balance} / [\text{Interest} + \text{Current-Year Repayment of Principal}] \quad (\text{E8.4})$$

SDS compares interest and current repayment of principal with current account balance before debt payments. The interest and current repayment of principal represent the flows of payments due on debt stock and indicate the resources, as external receipts, existing reserves, or new borrowing, and that are required to service debt fully and timely. For its part, the primary budget balance is simply the difference between total sovereign revenues and total sovereign expenditures, excluding interest payments on debt. It expresses sovereign capacity to face its debt obligation and therefore plays a key role in the dynamics of debt growth or reduction. Although data on primary budget balance were not directly available to us, we compute primary budget balance figures, using the ratio primary budget balance/GDP, and setting primary budget balance = PBB × GDP. Expression E.4 can therefore be rewritten as:

$$\text{SDS} = (\text{PBB x GDP}) / [\text{Interest} + \text{Current-Year Repayment of Principal}] \quad (\text{E8.5})$$

The SDS states the number of times sovereign government primary budget balance can cover its current-year interest and repayment of principal of long term-debt. Consequently, the lower the SDS ratio is, the higher the risk that the sovereign issuer be expected to fail in the eyes of investors, with default starting at SDS > 1. Further, an optimal level of the SDS ratio should be looked for, and should correspond to the average SDS for the whole sovereign population. Our assumption is that SDS should account significantly in agencies' sovereign creditworthiness assessment. We therefore ran a regression with rating as dependent variable and SDS as independent variable:

$$rating_i = \alpha_i + \beta' \text{ SDS}_i + \varepsilon_i \qquad \text{(E8.6)}$$

where:
SDS_i is the debt service ratio;
β is a vector of coefficients to be estimated;
α_i is a country specific fixed effect; and
εi is an error term.

The data come from the IMF publications as reported in Moody's (2013a) for the period 2003–2014 and concerned a sample of 87 developing countries:

(i) 17 developing countries with credit rating in the range of Aaa to A3
(ii) 25 developing countries with credit rating in the range of Baa to Baa3
(iii) 15 developing countries with credit rating in the range of Ba1 to Ba3
(iv) 27 developing countries with credit rating in the range of B1 to C.

Table 8.7 states means of sovereign debt service ratios for all developing sovereign countries by rating class, for the period 2003–2014.

Data in Table 8.7 seem erratic, even if they show a certain progressive decrease in sovereign SDS, therefore a progressive increase in risk. The class Aaa to A3 of sovereign ratings presents on average, for the period 2003–2014, a debt service ratio (DSR) 34 times higher than the one of the rating class Baa to Baa3, 9.8 times higher than the one of the class Ba1 to Ba3, and only 3.17 times the one of the class B1 to C. Although there seems to be a relation between the classes of ratings and the debt service ratio values, such relationship is somehow surprisingly missing for the class Baa to Baa3.

Table 8.8 gives the results of the regression : $rating_i = \alpha_i + \beta' \text{ SDS}_i + \varepsilon_i$. With an R^2 of 0.002, the regression result talks for itself and shows a very weak explanation power of the ratings by the DSR, and this is very surprising and might mean one of two things: either the data is not faithful, or agencies process is majority subjective. Indeed the proportion of ratings that is not explained by the solvency of sovereigns tops 99.8 per cent.

Such weak relation between sovereign credit ratings and sovereigns' capacity to pay their long-term obligations, as expressed by the DSR is also encountered when other measures of sovereign financial capacity are used, such as the external debt/current account receipts ratio, for instance. This result may also raise the question of the appropriateness of the variables used by agencies in determining sovereign credit ratings, if not of the whole process.

Table 8.7 Mean sovereign debt service ratios, for different developing countries rating classes

Rating class of sovereign	*2003*	*2004*	*2005*	*2006*	*2007*	*2008*	*2009*	*2010*	*2011*	*2012*	*2013*	*2014*	*2003–2014*
Aaa to A3 (17)	188.32	136.03	123.66	172.76	180.75	162.40	150.40	73.14	89.86	133.87	47.06	32.53	25.82
Baa to Baa3 (25)	−76.98	−61.39	24.38	49.90	−24.72	−10.05	14.65	−11.48	7.13	−48.15	22.02	7.94	−8.89
Ba1 to Ba3 (18)	16.66	−23.87	32.61	−33.08	72.59	−27.08	3.06	59.02	14.13	72.72	−23.84	29.31	16.02
B1 to C (27)	12.37	17.58	33.89	200.52	5.59	3.76	−41.87	−33.73	−13.92	25.28	34.81	27.52	22.65

Table 8.8 Estimates of regression $rating_i = \alpha_i + \beta' \text{SDS}_i + \varepsilon_i$

Model	*R*	*R-square*	*Adjusted R-square*	*Standard deviation*
1	.043[a]	.002	−.010	4.14219

Model	*Non standardised coefficients*		*Standardised coefficients*	*t*	*Sig.*
	B	Standard deviation	Beta		
(Constant)	8.760	.445		19.684	.000
VAR00002	−.002	.006	−.043	−.404	.687

Conclusion

Agencies seem to use more fundamentals than necessary in their sovereign creditworthiness assessment and, as we know, any excess of variables in any model runs the risk of decreasing its accuracy and increasing its opacity. Our result shows that it should be possible to reduce substantially the number of fundamentals used by agencies without affecting the performance of their model, while increasing the transparency of the whole process. It is indeed feared that excess may be used as a means of increasing subjectivity in the rating process, as for reinforcing asymmetry of information within rating activity. It is currently impossible for anyone to replicate agencies' process and therefore assess the accuracy of their ratings. Surprisingly, agencies' process seems to neglect some classical measures of financial capacity of honouring debt obligations. Either the figure (coming from agencies) are not free from errors, or subjectivity is dominating the process, and the rating committees are always aware of more than the numbers can say. Over all it seems that agencies tend to trust fundamentals more significantly for rating non-defaulting countries and to trust more rating committees' subjective judgement, when rating sovereign defaulting countries. Although this chapter analysis focuses on the results for Moody's, the results for all the Big 3 are expected to be highly correlated and located between 97 and 98 per cent (Bloomberg). This chapter result may raise the question of the rationality of the choice made by agencies regarding fundamentals included in their model, to be discussed in the next chapter, and suspects that possibility that excess of information may actually allow more extensive use of subjectivity in rating assessment, through rating committees, and therefore the enhancement of information asymmetry.

9 Disclosure and transparency, the quest of accuracy in the sovereign ratings

One solution for agencies to dissipate part of the criticism they are subjected to is by being more transparent. Transparency of the sovereign credit rating system is the way to foster a culture of trust between sovereign issuers and CRAs. When kept in the loop and understanding how their ratings are produced, sovereign issuers are more likely to put their trust in agencies. Conversely, those kept in the dark may feel suspicious about agencies and their ratings and will find it difficult to trust them, as a lack of transparency is likely to lead to a lack of trust. Previous chapters have shown a number of limitations in agencies' process of assessing sovereign creditworthiness.

This chapter adds a milestone to the inaccuracy construct of sovereign ratings, by underlying transparency weaknesses of the rating system disclosure. The next section deals with the principles-based and the rules-based approaches to disclosure, then proceeds to: show how disclosure does not necessarily match transparency and may even reinforce information asymmetry; underline the damaging effect of sovereign ratings approximation; *introduce the sovereign rating "accordion"* and underline the risk of rating manipulation due to weak disclosure; the chapter concludes.

The principles-based and the rules-based approaches to disclosure

As discussed previously, an important shift has occurred within credit ratings, particularly during the period 1985–2014: investment grades have shown tremendous decrease, while speculative grades have registered important increase. The shift in sovereign issuers rating distribution has concerned all levels of investment grade ratings and not everyone was happy about it. Consequently more transparency was required from agencies. It was hoped the searched transparency would allow the replication of the ratings, for the sake of their validation. Many governments, for instance, particularly in response to recent sovereign scandals, have reacted strongly by adopting a number of regulatory changes to their credit rating frameworks, mainly by requiring from agencies a substantial improvement within their disclosure practices. The Dodd-Frank Act, for instance, as already underlined, directed the US Securities and Exchange Commission to adopt rules to implement a number of provisions related to registered agencies. In addition, the SEC has since also proposed new rules to implement certain provisions of the Dodd-Frank Act, with the specific aim of improving disclosure and transparency. Similarly the European market authority, ESMA, carries out policy work in the area of credit rating agencies, in its role as the single supervisor of CRAs within the European Union. We can mention the EU regulation No 462/2013 of the European Parliament and of the Council of 21 May 2013 amending Regulation (EC) No 1060/2009 on credit rating agencies.

Academic discussions of agencies' disclosure and transparency, for its part, commonly focused on the benefit of transparency, in the sense that it reduces asymmetric information, and hence lowers subjectivity in the rating process and also allows decreases in the cost of the capital for issuers, consequently leading to the improvement of market efficiency. To offset such benefits, some academicians typically focus on the direct costs of disclosure. Others, like Hermalin and Weisbach (2007), concentrate on the role of transparency in corporate governance and provide a framework for understanding such role. It is believed, following their reasoning, that agencies disclosure can have an impacting effect on the contractual and monitoring tripartite relationship between agencies, issuers and the rule-makers. Agencies disclosure can be seen as a choice variable that affects agencies' contractual arrangement and/or monitoring frameworks. Higher quality disclosure provides benefits but also imposes costs and in the case of rating agencies and the like, it may also entail stricter monitoring and surveillance. While cost factor can undoubtedly be an important consideration in agencies' disclosure decisions, it should not specifically constitute a constraint to the betterness of their governance systems. There are, however, different forms of disclosure, notably the rules-based approach to disclosure, also called the disclosure for compliance, and the principles-based approach, we name the disclosure for transparency and replication.

The rules-based approach to disclosure or "disclosure for compliance" is the kind of disclosure where an agency concedes to disclosure just to free itself from legal requirements – limiting, therefore, its disclosure actions to their strict minimum expression, aiming a minimum conformity accepted for rules and laws. Regulatory disclosure for compliance describes the goal that organisations aspire to achieve in their efforts to ensure that they are aware of and take the required steps to comply with relevant disclosure laws and regulations. Due to the increasing number of regulations requiring operational transparency, organisations are increasingly adopting and using sets of consolidated and harmonised disclosure compliance control, the IPMR approach. They usually put in place a compliance department whose main functions are:

1 To identify the risks that an organisation may face and advises them (**I**dentification)
2 To design and implement controls to protect an organisation from those risks (**P**revention)
3 To monitor and report on the effectiveness of such controls within the management of risk exposure of an organisation (**M**onitoring and detection)
4 To resolve compliance difficulties as they occur (**R**esolution)

The IPMR approach to compliance disclosure's main objective is ensuring that all legal disclosure requirements are obeyed and met; it is far, however, from guaranty transparency in the sense of replication.

The principles-based approach to compliance or the "disclosure for transparency and replication", on the other hand, describes the situation where organisations will disclose all the necessary information for the purpose of allowing users to gain a real understanding of the rating process, and to be insured of the accuracy of the sovereign ratings and consequently to be in a position of trusting rating agencies. As seen in previous chapters, any undue impediment introduced to the rating process may present a real obstacle to its understanding and therefore an impediment toward disclosure for transparency. The dramatic escalation and expansion of risk over the recent decades has further complicated, and in unprecedented terms, the global financial environments where both the speed of transactions transformation and the new categories of risk have emerged and ended up threatening the durability of most global institutions. To remain useful and even just to survive in this complex and uncertain environment, pioneer thinking and innovation must indeed go beyond disclosure for compliance.

Agencies' reading and understanding of recent transparency requirements seems to be partially limited to the rules-based approach. Hermalin and Weisbach (2007), for instance, underline three ways in which agencies could potentially diverge from the principles-based approach to disclosure and hence distort their ratings signals:

(i) First, agencies can take actions that increase the signal without changing issuers' fundamentals. This is referred to as "exaggerating effort".
(ii) Second, agencies can take actions that affect signal noise. This is referred to as "obscuring effort".
(iii) Finally, agencies can, all together, conceal information.

Authors also evaluate the implications of penalties that potentially might discourage agencies from distorting the information disclosed. In their view, measures that punish distortion of information can be effective only when they are sufficiently severe, and relatively minor penalties can even be counterproductive. It is therefore hoped that agencies would adhere to the principles-based approach to disclosure, but this is a hope. This chapter only deals with "exaggerating effort" and "obscuring effort" situations in agencies' disclosure.

When disclosure does not necessarily match transparency

Agencies seem to base their measurement of sovereign credit rating on a large number of variables, thirty-one variables for Moody's. As shown in Chapter 8, excess of variables runs the risk of obscuring the whole picture of the rating process and may present a real threat to transparency. Agencies can of course argue that they are, on the one hand, required more disclosure, while at the same time they are criticised for excess of such disclosure.[1] What exactly agencies are blamed for is not so much their volume of disclosure, but rather its quality and especially its pertinence for decision making. Chapters 6 to 8 have concluded that there is undue complexity of the approach adopted by agencies for their sovereign creditworthiness assessment. We call this overflow of information the "new wave of information asymmetry", where excess information is disclosed not so much for the sake of informing, but rather for the sake of complicating the task of its understanding.

This section discusses an example of how excess of information may render impossible its understanding. Table 9.1 gives an overview of the process of assessing factors and sub-factors used by CRAs, in determining the sovereign ratings, along with their respective weight and indicators. The definitions of factors and sub-factors can be found in Table 6.2 of Chapter 6.

It can be recalled from Chapter 6 that factors *F1* and *F2* are used by agencies to form the combination 1 (Economic resiliency); *F1, F2* and *F3* are used to form the combination 2 (Government financial strength); and *F1, F2, F3* and *F4* are used form the combination 3 (Government bond range). Besides the excessive number of sub-factors used to be discussed in a coming section, a number of basic remarks come to mind.

Basically, the rationale behind the choice of factors and sub-factors does not seem to be theoretically or empirically justified. Although some agencies do try to back up their choices in their own way, they don't seem to be clear, as they may lack solid theoretical or empirical thinking. Moody's, for instance, refers to the model in Table 9.2 for a detailed description of how weights may vary.

Table 9.1 Factors and sub-factors used in determining sovereign ratings, their respective weight and indicators

Broad rating factors	*Rating sub-factor*	*Sub-factor indicators*	*Sub-factor weighting (toward factor)*	*Broad rating factors*	*Rating sub-factor*	*Sub-factor indicators*	*Sub-factor weighting (toward factor)*
	F1.1	F1.1			F3.1	F3.1.1	50%
F1		F1.2	50%	F3		F3.2.1	
		F1.3			F3.2	F3.2.2	50%
	F1.2	F1.2.1	25%			F3.2.3	
	F1.3	F1.3.1	25%			F3.3.1	
	F1.4	F1.4.1	1–6 scores		F3.3	F3.3.2	1 to 6 scores
		F1.4.2				F3.3.3	
						F3.3.4	
		F2.1.1			F4.1	F4.1.1	Max. Function
F2	F2.1	F2.1.2	75%	F4		F4.1.2	
		F2.1.3			F4.2	F4.2.1	Max. Function
	F2.2	F2.2.1	25%			F4.2.2	
		F2.2.2				F4.3.1	Max. Function
	F2.3	F2.3.1	1–6 scores		F4.3	F4.3.2	
						F4.3.4	
					F4.4	F4.4.1	Max. Function
						F4.4.2	
						F4.4.3	

Table 9.2 Moody's detailed description of how weights may vary

Broad rating factor	*Rating Sub-Factor*	*Sub-Factor Weighting (Toward Factor)*	*Sub-Factor indicators*	*Indicators weight (Toward Factor)*	*VH+*	*VH*	*VH–*	*H+*	*H*	*H–*	*M+*	*M*	*M–*	*L+*	*L*	*L–*	*VL+*	*VL*	*VL–*
	F3.1	50%	F3.1.1	50%	<30.1	30.1; 35	35.1; 40	40.1; 45	45.1; 50	50.1; 55	55.1; 60	60.1; 65	65.1; 70	70.1; 80	80.1; 90	90.1; 100	100.1; 120	120.1; 140	>140
F3			F3.1.2	50%															
	F3.2	50%	F3.2.1	50%															
			F3.2.2	50%															
	F3.3	1 to 6 scores	F3.3.1	N/A															
			F3.3.2	N/A	0.0; 0.5	0.51; 1.0	1.01; 2.0	2.01; 4.0	4.01; 6.0	6.01; 8.0	8.01; 10.0	10.01; 15.0	15.01; 20.0	20.01; 25.0	25.01; 30.0	30.01; 40.0	40.01; 50.0	50.01; 60.0	>60.0
			F3.3.3	N/A															
			F3.3.4	N/A															

Table 9.3 Rating ranges based on mean and standard deviation

	Caa	*B*	*Ba*	*Baa*	*A*	*Aa*	*Aaa*
Factor X	$\mu_F - 3\sigma_F$	$\mu_F - 2\sigma_F$	$\mu_F - 1\sigma_F$	μ_F	$\mu_F + 1\sigma_F$	$\mu_F + 2\sigma_F$	$\mu_F + 3\sigma_F$

Close examination of Table 9.2 rather raises more questions than answers. It does not, for instance, clarify how factor and sub-factor weightings toward factors are determined; similarly it does not explain how for any given factor, scores 1 to 6 are allocated or combined to weight. It is also not clear how maximisation function results are combined to weights. All we know is that "the aggregation of political risk, government liquidity risk, banking sector risk, and external vulnerability risk follows a maximum function, e.g. as soon as one area of risk warrants an assessment of elevated risk, the country's overall susceptibility to event risk is scored at that specific, elevated level" (Moody's, 2015). Agencies use the scale VH+ to VL− to rate sub-factors, as indicated in Table 9.2. Once translated into quantitative values, this scale loses linearity starting L+, for some sub-factors, starting L− for others etc. There seems to be no homogeneity in the process.

The use of an industry average for a given factor and its standard deviation may prove to be less subject to individual judgment in defining distribution. For instance, in the following example, for a given factor F, μ_F represents the sector mean and σ_F, represents its standard deviation. Ratings ranges can be defined based on how many standard deviations a given class is from the factors' mean rating, as in Table 9.3. For instance, for the factor "GDP per capita", any observation with a rank which is higher by three standard deviations from the mean will fall on the score Aaa; and inversely, any observation with a ranking is lower by three standard deviations from its mean will fall on the score Caa. Of course, other sub-classifications are possible, but the suggested corrective process remains the same.

The risk of rating manipulation

In order to get the real extent of the multiple threats facing the sovereign rating process, let us express combinations C1 to C3, used by agencies to assess in a mathematical form sovereign credit ratings. Let's set up:

Combination C1, sovereign economic resiliency (*ECORES*) that combines F1 (*ECOSTR*) and F2 (*INSSTR*):

$$C1 = \omega_{F1}F1 + \omega_{F2}F2 \quad \text{(E9.1)}$$

Combination C2 sovereign financial strength (*FINSTR*) combining F1 (*ECOSTR*) and F2 (*INSSTR*). And F3, fiscal strength (*FISSTR*):

$$C2 = \omega_{C1}C1 + \omega_{F3}F3 = \omega_{c1}(\omega_{F1}F1 + \omega_{F2}F2) + \omega_{F3}F3 \quad \text{(E9.2)}$$

And,

Combination C3, sovereign bond rating range (*RATRAN*) combining F1, economic strength (*ECOSTR*) and F2, institutional strength (*INSSTR*), F3, fiscal strength (*FISSTR*) and F4, sustainability to risk (*SUSRIS*):

$$C3 = \omega_{C2}C2 + \omega_{F4}F4 = \omega_{C2}\,[\omega_{c1}\,(\omega_{F1}F1 + \omega_{F2}F2) + \omega_{F3}F3] + \omega_{F4}F4 = [\omega_{C2}\omega_{c1}\,(\omega_{C2}\omega_{F1}F1 + \omega_{C2}\,\omega_{F2}F2) + \omega_{C2}\omega_{F3}F3] + \omega_{F4}F4 \qquad \text{(E9.3)}$$

where:
F1 (*ECOSTR*);
F2 (*INSSTR*);
F3 (*FISSTR*);
F4 (*SUSRIS*);
ω_i represents the weight assigned by agencies to factors and combination of factors.

In their process of credit risk assessment, credit agencies use a flat weight of 50 per cent, except for combination C2, where different weights are used, as explained before (80/20, 70/30, 40/60, 75/25 and 10/90). For the sake of clarification we use the weighting 50/50, even for combination 2. Expression E9.3, representing the final ranking, can therefore be rewritten in the following way:

$$ranking_i = [(0.0625F1 + 0.0625F2) + 0.125F3] + 0.5F4 \qquad \text{(E9.4)}$$

Table 9.2 shows the composition and weight of sub-factors. F1, for instance, is composed of seven sub-factors, and the same for factors, F2, F3 and F4. Table 9.4 gives the result for the simulation of sovereign rating, for different levels of input and that are sensitive to the choice of sub-factor weighting. In this simulation and in order to respect agencies' ranking, we will use a numerical scale composed of seventeen notches, starting with Aaa, with a rank of 0 notches, to Caa, with a rank of sixteen notches. Ranks Aaa to Baa3 describe investment grades, while ranks Ba1 and lower describe speculative grades.

Using expression E9.4 we can determine the overall sovereign actual rating on the alphanumerical scale of any given sovereign, whose economic strength, *ECOSTR* (*F1*), is Ba1, its institutional strength, *INSSTR* (*F2*) is Baa3, its fiscal strength, *FISSTR* (*F3*) is Ba2, and its susceptibility to event risk, *SUSRIS* (*F4*) is Ba3. We should, however, first translate alphanumerical ranking into numerical

Table 9.4 Alphanumerical ranking and their numerical correspondents

Aaa	*Aa1*	*Aa2*	*Aa3*	*A1*	*A2*	*A3*	*Baa1*	*Baa2*	*Baa3*	*Ba1*	*Ba2*	*Ba3*	*B1*	*B2*	*B3*	*Caa*
0	1	2	3	4	5	6	7	8	9	10	11	12	13	14	15	16
INVESTMENT GRADES											SPECULATIVE GRADES					

scale. For instance, as indicated in Table 9.4, the Ba1 attributed to F1 will be translated into 10, the Baa3 of attributed to F2 will be translated into 9, Ba2 attributed to F3 will be translated to 11, and finally the Ba3 attributed to F4 will be translated into 12.

The final rating corresponding to the current situation, using expression E9.4, is:

$$Ranking_l = (0.0625 \times 10 + 0.0625 \times 9) + 0.125 \times 11 + 0.5 \times 11 = 0.625 + 0.5625 + 1.375 + 5.5 = 8.06$$

In Table 9.4, the 8.06 numerical scale corresponds to an alphanumerical scale of Baa2. Let's now assume that F1, F2 and F3 original alphanumerical scales stay unchanged (their sub-factor weights stay changed), but because of some minor error in the weighting of one of the sub-factors of F4, the appropriate alphabetical grading should have been Caa, corresponding to a numerical scale of 16. In such case, the final rating should have been:

$$Ranking_l = (0.0625 \times 10 + 0.0625 \times 9) + 0.125 \times 11 + 0.5 \times 16 = 0.625 + 0.5625 + 1.375 + 8.00 = 10.56$$

In Table 9.4, the 10.56 numerical scale corresponds to Ba1 alphanumerical, which actually comes to moving the sovereign issuer from the status of investment grade to the one of junk bond status. Even a much smaller correction/error would have been as devastating.

The damaging effect of sovereign ratings approximation

Although small errors are expected to be the common fate of most analysis and studies, this fact should not, however, keep CRAs from reevaluating the performance of their risk assessment model. Errors at this level, given their damaging impact, can only be unforgivable. Sovereign downgrades and even more, those not justified by the sovereign fundamentals, can have a devastating effect on sovereigns. It is indeed generally admitted that sovereign downgrade has an impacting effect on sovereign cost of debt, investment and leverage. In case of a downgrade, credit risk can become significantly problematic for downgraded sovereign countries and even so a shift from investment to speculative grades. Unfortunately, it seems impossible to precisely identify the causal impact of sovereign downgrades or their precise effect on sovereign economic development policy and output. The main reason resides in the fact that changes in sovereign credit risk are supposed to be correlated with changes in sovereign numerous fundamentals. Consequently, credit ratings seem to be among sovereigns' major concerns, mainly due to their discrete costs and benefits associated with their diverse levels. As a general rule, sovereign downgrades can have, among others, the following consequences:

(i) A decline in credit rating and more so a downgrade to speculative status; can have an effect on sovereign access to the debt market, because of regulation on institutional investors. Some investors such as pension funds often follow guidelines that restrict investments to investment-grade bonds (Alderman et al., 2012; Boot et al., 2006).

(ii) Sovereign financial relationships are sometimes so complex and intricate, and the potential damage of downgrades can be amplified enormously and can make a sovereign crisis much worse. Meaning "that deteriorating credit ratings are not simply recording things that have happened after the fact. They are actually part of a self-reinforcing matrix that is making any sovereign crisis worse" (Sivy, 2011).

(iii) The worse the sovereign credit rating, the higher the interest on a loan is likely to be. Further, the uncertainty caused by shaky credit ratings creates another type of financing problem. And this may lead to a so-called money market freeze.[2] An invisible form of financial deterioration is also occurring because private-sector investors "are steadily sloughing off potentially risky sovereign bonds, and government institutions have to soak up the surplus" (Sivy, 2011).

(iv) Credit ratings can convey information to the market about a sovereign's credit quality, and a downgrade can increase the total cortication cost supported by borrowers, who see their access to the debt market reduced and are therefore unable to raise more debt financing (Faulkender et al., 2006).

(v) Downgrades may trigger market disorganising events such as bond covenant violations, increases in bond coupon rates or loan interest rates and forced bond repurchases. Baum et al. (2014), for example, assert that "CRAs downgrade announcements on the value of the Euro during the culmination of the Eurozone debt crisis in 2011–2012, has negatively affected the value of the Euro currency and also increased its volatility".

CRAs are also suspected of having tried to intervene in sovereign political decision making. S&P, for instance, is believed to have threatened to downgrade the seventeen nations that share the euro, largely because it said European politicians were moving too slowly to strengthen the monetary union, a move that was criticised by the European politicians, who describe it as simply stoking a sense of crisis. "Credit-rating agencies have long had a reputation for locking the barn door after the horse is gone", argues Sivy (2011).

The sovereign rating "accordion"

A quick look at Table 9.5, presenting factor F1 and its sub-factors, used in determining sovereign ratings, and their respective weight and indicators, for a given year 20xx shows, for instance, that there are many possibilities of affecting the overall ranking of the F1 final ranking.

First, at the level of F3 Sub-Factor Indicators choice, where the included subfactors are of the number of three: (i) the average real GDP Growth, (ii) the volatility in real GDP growth and (iii) the World Economic Forum, WEF global

Table 9.5 Sovereign's factor F1 and sub-factors used in determining sovereign ratings, and respective weight and indicators, for the year 20xx

Broad rating factors	*Rating sub-factor*	*Sub-factor indicators*	*Ranking*	*Sub-factor ranking*	*Sub-factor weighting (toward factor)*
(1)	(2)	(3)	(4)	(5)	(6)
F1: *ECOSTR* (Economic strength)	***F1.1****:* *ECOSTR*#1 (Growth dynamic)	*F1.1.1:* Average Real GDP Growth t−4 $_{\text{to t+5}}$	VH+	VH−	50%
		F1.1.2: Volatility in Real GDP Growth, 9 $_{\text{to t}}$	VH−		
		F1.1.3: WEF Global Competitiveness index	H		
	F1.2: *ECOSTR*#2 (Scale of the Economy)	*F1.2.1:* al GDP (US$) t−1	H	H	25%
	F1.3 *ECOSTR*#3 (National Income)	*F1.3.1:* GDP per capita (PPP, US$) t−1	Hs+	H+	25%
	F1.4 *ECOSTR*# 4 (Adjustment Factors)	*F1.4.1:* Diversification	H−	2	1–6 scores
		F1.4.2: Credit Boom	H-		

competitiveness index. Different choices of sub-factor indicators can completely change the picture of the overall rating of the factor. Indicators excess, as shown in Chapter 8, may also obscure the rating final result.

Second, at the level of ranking weight of F1 sub-factor indicators, where 50 per cent, 25 per cent and 25 per cent were attributed to sub-factor indicators: F1.1, F1.2 and F1.3, respectively. Any variation in weights can indeed affect the final factor ranking, as shown before.

Third, at the level of the ranking of F1 sub-factor indicators, where ranking varies between VH+ and H, on the scale VH+ to VL−, VH+ having the rank of 1 and VL− having the rank of 15, as explained in Chapter 7. VH+ to H is actually an interval of five notches on the scale of fifteen, and any estimation error can have an impacting effect on the sub-factor ranking. More importantly, when measuring variables, agencies usually justify their choice in one way or another, but the process remains seemingly subjective to a certain extent. Empirical observation is necessary to determine the appropriate mapping.

Obviously, the previous simulation exercise and elements reported in Table 9.5 can be replicated almost indefinitely by varying sub-factor weights, values or both and individually or in conjunction, and each one of the four factors used in the process presents the same risks of error and manipulation, and this short simulation shows how minor error in reporting, computing or even an imperceptible fraudulent manoeuver can transform any tangent sovereign debt into a junk security. Agencies pretend sovereign ratings to fall, in most cases, within one notch of the indicative rating level and often argued that the fact that sovereign ratings are determined by rating committees may prevent the discussed approximation risk. Subjective appreciation on the part of any group of people as knowledgeable as a rating committee can be may not, however, insure accuracy to sovereign ratings (Vernazza et al., 2014). CRAs also usually invoke the historical performance of their ratings in predicting actual default, to dissipate the fear of errors in ratings. They usually highlight the capacity of their ratings to accurately rank-order sovereign default risk, meaning that higher-rated sovereigns are less likely to default than lower-rated sovereigns, over a certain horizon. This can hardly constitute a sufficient consolation/criteria for individual sovereigns that might have been wrongly misstated. More importantly, this may distort the predictive power of the 'objective' and 'subjective' components of ratings. Further, following Nielsen et al. (2014) it was additionally shown "that while the 'objective' component of ratings is informative of future default, the 'subjective' component of ratings has no predictive power at all for default one or more years ahead and, hence, is distortionary at the individual country level".

Global rating agencies should engage in engineering and designing compliance systems that can grow organically. Essentially, they must adopt a culture that takes root, defined by integrity and moved by trust. This seems to be the only way that may ensure them survival in the dynamic risk environment strongly characterised by suspicion. The principles-based approach to compliance may help integrate this new behavioural environment successfully into rating agencies' structures. This is a comprehensive compliance objective that may combine law and integrity, that has to be put into place and that extends beyond legal compliance. The benefits of the principles-based approach to compliance reflect the fact and the hope that more accurate information allows issuers/investors and legislators to make better decisions and insures rating agencies better credibility. There must be, however, costs arising from the adoption of the principles-based approach to disclosure, and disclosing entities will try to be compensated, for the risk increase implicit in higher disclosure levels. But the overall benefit is expected to overcome the overall cost.

Conclusion

This chapter unearths yet another field of sovereign ratings accuracy deterioration, and has demonstrated that the approach used in selecting and using fundamental factors for the assessment of sovereign creditworthiness may allow itself too much approximation, susceptible of casting doubt about the rationality of the whole process.[3] Gains of accuracy are still needed and possible and more conceptual methods should be developed and used. CRA oversight should cover their risk assessment procedures, including their methodologies. "CRAs should be transparent about the quantitative measures they calibrate in the rating process and how they validate their ratings" (IMF, 2010), and their rating should be subjected to the same rigorous calibration conditions that are expected of any finance ranking of risk, otherwise no improvement in accuracy can be measured or expected. One fundamental question persists, however: who can be entrusted with the standardisation process?

Moody's Investors Service ("MIS") European Union Transparency Report

Provided in Accordance with Article 12 and Annex 1 Section E III of Regulation (EC) No 1060/2009 of 16 September 2009 on Credit Rating Agencies, as amended (the "Regulation") in respect of the year ended 31 December 2015.1

Notes

1 The new form of information asymmetry.
2 In an emergency, banks will have to borrow from a Central Bank if no one else will give them overnight money.
3 This chapter has dealt with only a few limits related to agencies risk assessment model, other shortcomings can be encountered and expected, they are certainly worth being discussed, such as how, for instance, sub-factors are determined in the first place.

10 Concluding remarks, sovereign creditworthiness accuracy

Given the suspicion that sovereign credit ratings are met with and the bulk of criticism CRAs are exposed to, the common sentiment is that ratings should not be left to the subjective appreciation of agencies, through their credit rating committees, as knowledgeable as these committees might be. The tests performed in this book have unearthed much inconsistencies and approximations in the rating process, susceptible of jeopardizing its credibility and questioning its fairness. It seems currently that a sovereign country could find itself battling with the hell of the speculative status, due only to vagueness in the process of credit rating assessment. Gains of accuracy are still needed and possible in sovereign credit activity, and CRAs oversight should include improvement and standardisation of procedures and methodologies.

This chapter discusses major limitations discovered in this book and risks some solutions; underlines how a number of limitations in the rating process can present real threat to sovereign rating accuracy; discusses CRAs' sovereign disclosure and transparency, what is called the new form of information asymmetry; and discusses international harmonisation of sovereign credit ratings.

Limitations in the sovereign rating process and threats to accuracy

The book has focused on the fundamental question of whether CRAs, inadvertently (or not), may contribute to sovereign rating inaccuracy and therefore to the acceleration of global financial instability and concluded that there are a number of disturbing limitations in agencies' processes of sovereign rating assessment and capital allocation. Such weaknesses include, among others, the *neglect of the basic risk-return rule;* the dubious use of an alphabetical scale, the weak fitting of the model to the data; the high level of subjectivity in rating assessment; and the sensitivity of the data to creative government accounting. Each one of these limitations in the rating process may alter accuracy of overall ratings.

One major weakness of CRAs approach to credit ratings originates from the neglect by agencies of the now so accepted risk-return rule. Sovereign credit ratings, as we know, affect the sovereign debt market, in both its supply and demand sides, and in case of a downgrade, bond buyers usually require higher interest rates, to be compensated for the greater chance of losing their investment. Potential bond buyers and bond issuers have to worry about legal requirements and internal rules that may require institutional investors or private funds to invest only in bonds with a minimum credit rating (Sivy, 2011). Central Banks, for instance, can only take as collateral bonds that have at least a single A attributed by at least one of the major rating agencies, and institutional investors will only invest in bond portfolio composition taking into account the credit risk perceived via the rating. In what seems to constitute a denial of the risk-return rule, agencies, however, seem to allow ratings to vary only over a specific range, and by specific increments. Consequently, it seems that the only assumed use of ratings, by agencies, resides in solely grouping issuers "ordinally", to assess their level of solvency. Making such assertion to investors is just not enough and does not explain why the crossing from one category of rating to the next is not similar between rating categories – why, for instance, a small downgrade of a given sovereign that is currently assigned a rating in the lower limit of Baa class of risk will prompt it into the suffering of the speculative zone, with all the financial troubles that go with it. Indeed, the transition from a Baa rating to a Ba would be enough to virtually create much risk for that issuer, in the mind of investors, leading to increase in cost, the drying of financing sources and even social unrest (Naciri, 2015).

Linearity in credit rating should not be challenged, since the fundamentals on which ratings are often based and reported are quantitative information, therefore linear by nature, as they are largely rooted in and based on financial statements or statistical data that are linear themselves. Linearity can be introduced to a rating scale by simply assuming that the difference in credit quality between any two subsequent rating classes is a constant. The difference, for instance, in credit quality between an Aaa rated sovereign and another rated Aa1 should be the same as between an A1 and an A rated sovereigns and so on, i.e. the scale should be assumed uniform and each subsequent symbol should see its default increase by the same decrease in credit quality (increase of risk). In other words, rating defaults should follow an arithmetic progression with *d* as the common difference of successive members of the progression.

$$d = 1/16\,(F_{cn}) \qquad \text{(E10.1)}$$

where:
F_{cn} is the default frequency registered that year for the Ccc category (the highest default frequency), assuming n classes scale.

Consequently, we can assign to any rating category for a given year, for the period covered by study a default frequency (F_{cn}), as follows:

$$F_{cn} = F_{c1} + d(n - 1) \qquad \text{(E10.2)}$$

where:
F_{cn} is the default frequency for the rating category n, if linearity in default was assumed;
F_{c1i} is the default frequency for the rating category AA+ i.e. Ccc/C/15;
n is the rank: 1 for Aaa, 2 for Aa1 and so on till n for Ccc;
d is the common difference of successive members of the progression.

Note that *d* is computed by dividing the highest default frequency for Ccc, as given by agencies' average actual default for issuers graded Ccc for the period covered by the study, divided by n, the number of rating categories. Assuming a 15-rank scale and an average of agencies actual default for issuers graded Ccc of 30, and take, for instance, the "Aa" symbol, with a rank of 2, given that *d* the common difference of successive members of the arithmetic progression is 2, i.e. (30/15), its linear default frequency F_{c2} will be 4 [$F_{c2} = F_{c1} + d(2–1) = 2+ 2(2–1)$]. Note that we can introduce acceleration by assuming a uniform acceleration into default distributions, using the uniformly accelerated motion model. See Naciri (2015) for more discussion of the linearity in credit ratings.

The other main weakness in agencies ratings amplifies the negative effect of the neglect of the risk-return rule; it stems from the way CRAs use alphabetical scale in their credit ranking, which may eventually have determinant implications on the final outcome. For the deeper discussion of this issue, the reader is invited to report to Chapter 7. Agencies use three different scales in their assessment of countries default:

(i) First, agencies use the scale VH+ to VL− for assessing sovereign economic resiliency and sovereign financial strength. This is an alphabetically based 15-category scale, where each element receives a score, using a 15-point scale, ranging from VH+ (the strongest) to VL− (the weakest).
(ii) Second, agencies also use an interval scale Aaa-Aa2 to B2-Caa, to assess sovereign bond rating ranks. This scale is also composed of 15-interval categories, the Aaa-Aa2 interval is the strongest and B2-Caa is the weakest.
(iii) Third, although, intervals are translated in the same way, agencies seem however to use a numbering 18-point scale for computing individual rating within rating ranges.

Such multiplication of scales can only be a confusing element and may constitute a peril to transparency. Further, the scales adopted by agencies can neither be summed up nor averaged without hazardous approximation and indeed there are serious risks that the resulting model (based on an alphabetical scale) would not describe the data fully. The high level of imprecision induced by the alphabetical scale may substantially alter part of the information. Consequently, the way combinations of factors are built becomes the subject of criticism, as different issuers with different rankings in fundamentals may still be rated the same by agencies. Finally, agencies' approach does not seem to allow itself to different levels of weighting of the fundamentals used in the different combinations, except for the

50/50 weighting. There is, however, no rational justification for constantly using 50/50 weighting.

Added to the two first mentioned shortages in CRAs' process, the model used by agencies in computing sovereign ratings has its own shortcomings; it does not seem to fit the data and divergences are as substantial as impacting. Actually a number of approximations were uncovered in agencies' approach and they may be presented as trivial, if it is not of devastating effect downgrades may lead to in sovereign economies and the social instability they may end up to, particularly when they are the result of approximation. Indeed, when attention is concentrated on the speculative threshold of Ba1-Ba3, it can be seen that approximation characterising agencies' approach can be very harmful, because it may make the difference for a sovereign between seeing its issued debt classified as investment grade or as speculative. Analysis performed in Chapter 7 shows also that at the individual sovereign level, there are only very few cases where agencies' model seems to fit the data and seems actually to fail more than 99 per cent of the time. Divergences range from +0.3 notches to −8.2, meaning that, due solely to computational approximations, a country can see its final rating wrongly decreased by as much as 8.2 notches, when we know that an error of a single notch is enough to move unfairly a country into the dark side of the speculative zone. Approximation at every level of agencies' processes seems to be the rule, rather than the exception, and these results can be considered very conservative, given the number of variables dismissed for a lack of information reason, such as the unknown choice made by agencies at the level of factors and sub-factors used in determining sovereign ratings, or the non specification of their respective weight, that can have an impacting effect on the final sovereign score. Anyway the situation invites more attention, given that it may leave the door wide open to eventual actions that can be of great harm to rated sovereigns.

Further, it is also feared that the subjectivity currently and intimately involved in the sovereign rating assessment may also jeopardise the whole rating dynamic. Everything rating committees in agencies might be doing can be impacted by subjectivism at every step of the rating process, from the choice of factors/sub-factors to the study of issuer financial position: (i) at the level of the formulation of hypotheses, (ii) the selection of the methodology and (iii) the interpretation of the data. Qualitative variables more than quantitative may lend themselves to more subjectivity. Indeed, subjectivity and or manipulation may easily find their way to the default assessment process in instances like:

(i) When deciding which variable to be included in the framework of default assessment; although agencies usually explain why any given factor/sub-factor is included in the model, they seem to use different frameworks for different industries and there is a need for a certain standardisation in order to overcome some risk of manipulation, as the use of a given factor/sub-factor instead of another can affect the final outcome.
(ii) When assigning ad-hoc weights to factors/sub-factors of the chosen framework. It does not appear clear indeed whether or not such assignment is

based on formal and specific rules. Moody's (2007), for example, asserts that "each sub-factor's numeric value is multiplied by an assigned weight and then summed", without giving any clue about what guides such weight assignment.

(iii) When assigning ad-hoc weights to different countries that seem themselves subjectively determined.

The way agencies seem to assess sovereign credit default may offer several additional challenging threats to sovereign rating accuracy. As previously discussed, credit ratings can be divided into two distinct components: an objective component, and another subjective. Subjective parts of the sovereign rating are the parts that are formed of supplementary adjustment factors used by rating committees. Subjectivity in the rating was expressed by the regression sum of squares of residuals. Analysis of such figures shows that the subjective component of agencies model levels 43.82 per cent for the general sovereign sample that includes both non-defaulting and defaulting countries; as high as 78.99 per cent for defaulting countries; and only 37.52 per cent for non-defaulting countries. These results are very important, since they may indicate a strong negative "a priori" of 35.17 per cent for defaulting sovereigns and a mild positive "a priori" for non-defaulting countries

Added to the previously mentioned limits in the sovereign rating process, creative government accounting may also present a real threat to the accuracy of sovereign ratings. A number of countries around the world are suspected of "lying" about their economy for strategic or political reasons, such as to secure favourable ratings, to attract investors, to obtain cheaper financing to service their debt, to obtain international organisation approvals for financing or to secure a re-election. For instance, as in numerous national cases "in a unanimous vote the US federal accounts court ruled that [. . .] government manipulated its accounts in 2014 to disguise a widening fiscal deficit when campaigning for re-election" (Brandom, 2013). Greece and Italy have also been accused of tinkering with their budget deficit figures prior to joining the Eurozone. Greece was condemned by the European Commission [. . .] for falsifying data about its public finances and allowing political pressures to obstruct the collection of accurate statistics, with also the suggestion that this allowed the Greek government to enjoy lower borrowing rates from investors than would have otherwise been the case (Barber, 2010). The European Commission made it clear in its report that it had next to no faith in Greek statistics. China is believed to embellish its growth figures (Michalski and Stoltz, 2013). Similarly, Argentina has long been suspected of understating its inflation figures to avoid paying high interest rates on government bonds, indexed to inflation. National data are often threatened by what we call "creative government accounting". It is a scourge that seems to spare only few sovereigns. This is the kind of a deliberate misrepresentation, misstatement or omission of information within government accounting for the purpose of misleading the reader and creating a false impression of a sovereign's financial strength. There are actually many ways in which a sovereign can deliberately misreport financial data and these include artificial adjustments, recognising revenues from abolished extra-budgetary accounts and write-offs of all kinds, but the most damaging of all are disclosure frauds. They seem to be commonly based on misrepresenting the sovereign, making false representations in press releases and other sovereign filings and making false statements in the regulatory filings. Some disclosures might be intentionally confusing or obscure and impossible to completely understand. "If corporations keep their books the way governments do, they would all be in jail" goes an anonymous summary of the creative government accounting movement. Although creative government accounting may alter rating accuracy, CRAs can, however, only perform sovereign ratings as efficiently as allowed by the quality of the information made available to them by sovereign issuers, but they should also work to find ways of detecting fraudulent sovereign disclosure.

CRAs disclosure and transparency

Notwithstanding the previously mentioned limitations in the sovereign rating process, CRAs' sovereign disclosure and transparency may constitute the new form of information asymmetry that prevents the deep understanding of sovereign credit rating process and excludes any possibility of testing its accuracy. More than ever before, CRAs are felt to have failed their social duty and are today subjected to much disclosure requirement and monitoring systems, as dictated by the rules-based disclosure approach. Supporters of such approach argue that compliance with such guidance is easier, since the requirements are prescriptive and leave little room for misunderstanding (ICAEW). Furthermore, rules-based approaches are easier to enforce. In order, however, for CRAs' sovereign creditworthiness to be trusted, it should be possible for their users to replicate them. Replication is the fact that a different analyst, using the same data, can reach the same sovereign rating. Agencies may pretend to be harassed by the unceasing public disclosure requirements, the United States Dodd-Frank, The European market authority, etc., all requiring CRAs' additional and better disclosure. And indeed CRAs seem to have significantly adjusted to these new required rules. The respect of the rules or transparency for compliance by agencies may not, however, solve the problem of the opacity of their approach. For instance, information contained in the SEC registration form, provided in accordance with Dodd-Frank and in the European Union Transparency Report provided in accordance with the European Community Regulation on Credit Rating Agencies, despite the very important information they contain, do not insure ratings transparency for replication. Most of the recent disclosure legal frameworks for CRAs seem to have adopted the rules-based disclosure approach, entitling the absence of any strong theoretical basis for guiding the numerous disclosure requirements included in legislations. They mainly require extensive information on multiple issues that do not necessarily help replicating the ratings for the sake of assessing their accuracy. Although these reports present the important advantage of summarizing, often in a single document, diverse information concerning ratings, they also free agencies from additional ethical obligations, for what is not regulated is permitted. On the other hand, results in Chapter 8, for instance, seem to show that agencies may tend to use more information than optimally needed, in their assessment of sovereign creditworthiness. Chapter 8 has shown that a limited number of variables, as low as 6, can have an explanatory power as significant, as the 31 variables used by CRAs and has also suggested one extremely simplified method of assessing sovereign creditworthiness. It is generally felt that a large volume of information required from CRAs may not improve their transparency and most of that information might actually be found elsewhere, whereas some specific body of information, although necessary for replication, is absent from the requirements and it is doubtful CRAs will agree to its disclosure. The situation is making the current disclosure appear as a reinforcing element of asymmetry of information that may even serve as a barrier that keeps away newcomers to the global credit market. More targeted information should be required from agencies, which does not already exist in financial reports and other public documents and helps replicating the ratings.

Far from being a particular behaviour on the part of rating agencies, inception of new strategies of information asymmetry seems to be a common practice nowadays among governments and major modern institutions. In their unwillingness to inform, they simulate effective disclosure, backed up by constant changes in the processes, where new ways of doing things are constantly introduced, mainly for the aim of confusing more than informing the users, and sometimes for the sake of cancelling the effect of the monitoring systems in place. New practices will ultimately call for new rules, although this usually will happen with a certain delay. Additionally to placing organisations ahead of their monitoring systems, innovation in transactions also complicates them to the point where only specialists can meet the respect of requirements. Excessive or unnecessary rules complicate unduly transactions and unfairly treat users and threaten their freedom; it also blows up their cost, to the point where most users are left with no other choice but to give up. Consequently such a system is eliminating all those who cannot afford to pay for services and charging highly those who can. It may pay better to have major institutions working to simplify transactions and governments to ease its various regulations in the name of the common interest. Unless the goal is to create new areas of non-productive activities; there are, however, many areas of productive activities not yet explored. The situation may recall what happens in a developing environment where large administrative rules seem to have been enacted only to provide work for a number of unofficial intermediaries, with office front at the exit of each government office.

The rules-based approach currently followed by credit rating monitoring authorities risk not achieving the sought transparency, but a principles-based disclosure approach can and may prove to be robust and flexible enough to provide guidance that can be applied to the infinite variations in circumstances that arise in practice; it can help coping with rapid changes of the modern global credit environment;

it prevents the development of a mechanistic approach to decision making and the exploitation of legalistic loopholes to avoid compliance with rules; and, more importantly, it focuses on the spirit of the disclosure and enhances responsibility.

International sovereign credit rating harmonisation

Market rule would suggest allowing CRAs to manage their business, the way they think it is best for them, if only not of the monopolistic position, the main three among them exercise cleverly in the whole global credit market, leaving sovereigns, especially those among them from developing countries and the smallest totally helpless under their control and with all the expected damaging consequences. Today's world surely needs a globally well-accepted and trusted credit rating system, and it should always be remembered that today's inequalities are tomorrow's crises. If all countries of the world were seriously convinced of the human common fate and equality of chances, each country should abandon its narrow view of the so called "national interest", in favour of a higher view of "human interest". Global fairness of credit rating and capital allocation faces its main challenge in the diversity of the national sovereignty objectives and the diversity of national systems of monitoring credit rating activities. The harmonisation of the monitoring system seems to be the way forward.

Although agencies, all over the world, seem to use similar scales and symbols to denote credit ratings, the number of the ratings used varies widely. One step toward harmonisation of credit rating activities can be the standardising of credit rating terminology, believed to facilitate comparing credit ratings across rating agencies and expected to result in fewer opportunities for manipulating credit rating scales to give the impression of accuracy (SEC, 2012). Such harmonisation could lead to greater accountability among credit rating agencies. Consequently, harmonisation of credit rating is a major objective for many CRAs monitoring agencies. The SEC, for instance, as required by Section 939(h)(1) of the Dodd-Frank Act, has undertaken a study on the feasibility and desirability of:

- (i) Harmonising credit rating terminology, so that all credit rating agencies issue credit ratings using identical terms
- (ii) Harmonising credit rating terminology across asset classes, so that named ratings correspond to a standard range of default probabilities and expected losses independent of asset class and issuing entity (SEC, 2012)
- (iii) Harmonising the market stress conditions under which ratings are evaluated
- (iv) Quantitative correspondence between credit ratings and a range of default probabilities and loss expectations under standardised conditions of economic stress.

A number of isolated initiatives of monitoring agencies can be encountered, all based on rules-based approaches. Supervision of the CRAs that includes "examinations and inspections conducted on-site and remotely of the books and records" (IOSCO, 2013) has extended since 2006 and an increasing number of governments have established registration and oversight programs for credit rating agencies. The global credit rating monitoring is, however, a field of intense competition. There are mainly three players, disputing its supervision; on the one hand, we have the Securities and Exchange Commission of the United States with its NRSRO registration, on the other hand, the European Union, with its ESMA registration. But there is also the International Organization of Securities Commissions (IOSCO), which believes that although internationally operating CRAs are overseen by multiple national supervisory bodies, the scope of any given oversight varies, however. The dispersion of internationally active CRA affiliates worldwide presents a challenge to national supervisors, as they may only have perspective on the activities of the internationally active CRA conducted in their jurisdiction. Consequently, a number of international supervisors have identified principles relevant to the establishment of supervisory colleges.

IOSCO seeks to tailor existing principles to the CRA business model. "It is suggested that regulators should expand the notion of supervisory cooperation to establish mechanisms to consider and evaluate the global market. Instead of narrowly focusing on entity-specific oversight, regulators should explore opportunities to further collaborate on identifying, assessing and mitigating emerging risks and seek to address and evaluate them on a global basis" (IOSCO, 2010). According to IOSCO, the way to address the challenge of the dispersion of internationally active CRA affiliates worldwide is to form a *college of regulators* to operate as a forum for exchanging information about an internationally active CRA (IOSCO). It was indeed agreed that regulator-to-regulator cooperation through informal mechanisms such as a *college of regulators* might be the best forum to accomplish these goals. A CRA college was viewed as being less likely to raise legal or regulatory issues among the various jurisdictions than the other types of bodies contemplated (see Table 10.1).

CRA colleges should be considered only for internationally active CRAs that have significant cross-border operations and have affiliates and/or branches located in multiple jurisdictions. Some of the most important elements of colleges of supervisors noted in the IOSCO proposal include the following principles (IOSCO, 2010):

Table 10.1 Role of CRA colleges

1	Promotes information sharing among supervisors of an internationally active CRA
2	Conducts collective risk assessment with respect to an internationally active CRA
3	Coordinates supervisory activities (if agreed upon by members)
4	Provides feedback on application of international Cross-Border Principles for CRAs and makes recommendations for updates or clarification
5	Attended by examiners and/or inspectors of CRAs
6	Shares collective risk assessment with other national supervisory agencies

Source: IOSCO (2013).

(i) Authorities should, on the basis of mutual trust, consult, cooperate and be willing to share information to assist each other in fulfilling their respective supervisory and oversight responsibilities for regulated entities operating across borders, such as credit rating agencies.
(ii) Mechanisms for supervisory cooperation should be designed to provide information both for routine supervisory purposes and during periods of crisis.
(iii) As appropriate, authorities should enter into memoranda of understanding (MOUs) to share relevant supervisory information in their possession.
(iv) Authorities must establish and maintain appropriate confidential safeguards to protect all non-public supervisory information obtained from another authority.

Agencies are usually against any harmonisation that may increase efficiency of monitoring systems and, of course, decrease their freedom in assessing ratings; they warn that requiring standardisation may not be feasible given the number and uniqueness of rating scales and differences in credit rating methodologies used. Further, they underline that standardised credit ratings may actually reduce incentives for them to improve their credit rating methodologies and quality control procedures. CRAs seem to have been heard and serious concerns about the feasibility and desirability of standardisation seems, sometimes, to be globally shared, in particular, most did not feel that standardisation would lead to higher levels of accountability, transparency, and competition in the credit rating agency industry (SEC, 2012). Faced and frustrated with such a plea, a number of countries, however, were encouraged to seek the creation of their national credit rating agencies. China, for instance, seem to have trust in its national agencies only. The Chinese rating agency Dagong Global Credit Rating Co. Ltd seems to have been created to counterbalance the Big 3 dominance. Its "value only the truth, creditability and fairness" is iconic. Dagong is materializing many emerging economies, regarding the current global credit market system, and "has established a complete system of credit rating theories, standards development and innovation mechanisms, credit information production and service system".[1]

Having each country with its national rating agencies would be far from solving the problem, and only a fair international collaboration can help. Things, however, may start moving in the right direction and it is becoming clearer now that monitoring of credit rating agencies and standardisation of their procedures should not be left up to CRAs themselves, nor to particular government. Some are even suggesting as a solution the creation of an international monitoring agency for sovereign credit rating, to be placed under the auspices of the IMF or another of the international organisations like the Bank of International Settlement, the International Accounting Standard Board or the International Organization of Securities Commissions. Voices are also requiring that, in the meantime agencies "should be forced to substantially increase transparency, including publishing a separate breakdown of the objective and subjective components of ratings, the minutes of the rating committees, and the voting records" (Vernazza et al., 2014)). CRAs may dismiss these suggestions always on the basis of the same arguments, namely their default assessments only aim to cluster sovereign defaults in the lowest rating grades, or standardisation would not be possible and would not do any good, etc. This, of course, contributes to the increase of dissatisfaction of those who question the usefulness of rating and believe that anybody with sufficient knowledge of defaulting country public finances may perform sovereign ranking as good as agencies classification.

Although everyone seems to agree on stripping the CRAs of their oligopoly powers on the sovereign rating market, nations seem unable to agree on who should take the lead in such endeavour. The reflexion should continue, but one thing is sure, CRAs are so strong in their complete control of the market that only international cooperation can make any perceptible difference. International cooperation should suggest a set of macro indicators agreed on by everybody, to be used by CRAs and whose outcome can be verified and replicated. Only an international legislation that deals with CRAs disclosure on the basis of usefulness for replication can improve the accuracy of the rating and the efficiency of the global credit market. Sovereign ratings are currently substantially determined by rating committees, leaving important room for subjectivity and excluding any chance of replication. One principle should, however, guide the rating process, namely its replication. Replication is important mainly because it may give legitimacy and reliability to the ratings, therefore assuring them confident use. It may not be that important to know if the current system is actually fair; it is more important to know if globally people think it is. Recent events have shown this is not the case, and therefore intelligent rallying reaction is needed.

Conclusion

Each time a sovereign credit rating is reduced, dissatisfaction with agencies increases and quality of rating is questioned, although perceptions about creditworthiness vary incrementally across the spectrum of issuers and users (Sivy, 2011), the weaknesses underlined in this book make one wonder if sovereign credit rating ranking sovereign issuers is any better than flipping a coin. CRAs make themselves generously paid for their creditworthiness assessments and at the same time disclaim any responsibility for their inaccuracy. Moody's, for instance, underlines that although the ratings process involves forming views about the likelihood of plausible scenarios or outcomes, it does not forecast them, but instead it places some weight on their likely occurrence and on the potential credit consequences. No one expects ratings to be 100 per cent reliable in predicting credit failure, but CRAs should at least permit their users to be insured of the rationality of the method of measurement.

In light of the findings of the book, it is suggested that in addition to being stripped of their regulatory powers, it might even be necessary to scrutinise on a continual basis their behaviour. In any case, credit rating agencies should particularly be imposed a standardised methodology of assessing sovereign solvency, one that does not fail the test of replication and is internationally agreed on. CRAs indeed "should be transparent about the quantitative measures they calibrate in the rating process and how they validate their ratings" (IMF, 2010), otherwise no improvement in the accuracy of rating can be expected or such eventual improvement be measured. Although recent legislations may lean towards such objective, it is still like pounding the nail aside.

Note

1 http://en.dagongcredit.com/about/aboutDagong.html.

Bibliography

Afonso, A., D. Furceri and P. Gomes (2011), "Sovereign credit ratings and financial markets linkages application to European data". *Working Paper Series No 1347/JUNE 2011*. European Central Bank.

———, P. Gomes and P. Rother (2007), "What 'hides' behind sovereign debt ratings?" *Working Papers Series No 711/January*. European Central Bank.

———, P. Gomes and P. Rother (2011), "Short and long-run determinants of sovereign debt credit ratings". *International Journal of Finance and Economics*, 16(1), 1–15.

——— and R. Strauch (2007), "Fiscal policy events and interest rate swap spreads: Some evidence from the EU". *Journal of International Financial Markets, Institutions & Money*, 17(3), 261–276.

———, P. Gomes and A. Taamouti (2014), "Sovereign credit ratings, market volatility, and financial gains". European Central Bank. WP No 1654. At: https://www.ecb.europa.eu/pub/pdf/scpwps/ecbwp1654.pdf?642c4eba1f6c93477d000187f03e3ec4

Alderman, L. and R. Donaldio (2012), "Downgrade of debt ratings underscores Europe's woes". *The New York Times*. At: http://www.nytimes.com/2012/01/14/business/global/euro-zone-downgrades-expected.html?_r=0.

Altman, E. I. and D. L. (1992), "The implications of corporate bond rating drift". *New York University Salomon Brothers Center Working Paper, No S-91–51*.

——— and M. L. Heine (2014), "Current Conditions and Outlook for Corporate and Sovereign Credit Markets". *CFA Institute*. Leonard N. Stern School of Business, New York University New York City. At: www.cfapubs.org/doi/pdf/10.2469/cp.v31.n1.3. Accessed December 30, 2015.

Arellano, C. (2008),Default risk and income fluctuations in emerging economies. *American Economic Review*, 98, 690–712.

Arezki, R., B. Candelon and A. N. R. Sy (2011), "Sovereign rating news and financial markets spillovers: evidence from the European debt crisis". World Bank WP /11/68. At:http://citeseerx.ist.psu.edu/viewdoc/download?doi=10.1.1.401.6898&rep=rep1&type=pdf

Bahtia, A. V. (2002), "Sovereign credit ratings methodology: An evaluation". *IMF Working Paper WP/02/170*.

Baklanova, V. (2009), "Regulatory use of credit ratings: How it impacts the behaviour or market constituents". *International Finance Review*, 10, 65–104. SSRN at: http://ssrn.com/abstract=1378627.

Bank of Canada Database of Sovereign Defaults, (2015). At: http://www.bankofcanada.ca/wp-content/uploads/2014/02/tr101.pdf

Barber, T. (2010), "Greece condemned for falsifying data". At: http://www.ft.com/intl/cms/s/0/33b0a48c-ff7e-11de-8f53–00144feabdc0.html#axzz4B1SN86v9.

Bartels, B. (2014), "Why rating agencies disagree on sovereign ratings, Gutenberg school of management and economics & research unit". *Interdisciplinary Public Policy*. Discussion Paper Series.

Baum, C. F., M. Karpava, D. Schäfer and S. Andreas (2014), "Credit rating agency downgrades and the Eurozone sovereign debt crises". *SSRN*. At: http://ssrn.com/abstract=2646513 or http://dx.doi.org/10.2139/ssrn.2646513.

Beers, D. T. and J. Chambers (1999), "Debt indentures to play greater role in sovereign ratings analysis". *Standard & Poor's Credit Week*, April 14.

——— and J.-S. Nadeau (2015), *Database of Sovereign Defaults*. Bank of Canada Technical Report No. 101.

Bloomberg (2015), "Basel restores rating role in overhaul of banks' credit risk". At: http://www.bloomberg.com/news/articles/2015–12–10/basel-restores-rating-role-in-overhaul-of-bank-credit-risk-rules.

Blume, M. E., F. Lim and A. C. MacKinlay (1998), "The declining credit quality of US corporate debt: Myth or reality?" *Journal of Finance*, 53(4), 1389–1413.

Bojesen, L. (2012), "History of defaults: Greece did it first: Spain most often". At: http://www.cnbc.com/id/4781456.

Boot, A. W. A., T. T. Milbourn and A. Schmeits (2006), "Credit ratings as coordination mechanisms". *Review of Financial Studies*, 9, 81–118.

Brandom, R. (2013), "Pentagon guilty of billion-dollar accounting fraud, reveals Reuters investigation". At: http://www.theverge.com/2013/11/18/5117816/pentagon-guilty-of-billion-dollar-accounting-fraud-reveals-reuters.

Broto, C. and L. Molina (2014), "Sovereign ratings and their asymmetric response to fundamentals". *Banco de Espana. Documentos de Trabajo* No. 1428.

Bruner, M. and R. Abdelal (2005), "Sovereign credit ratings, national law, and the world economy". *Christopher Journal of Public Policy*, 25(2), May–August, 191–217.

Cantor, R. and F. Packer (1994), "The credit rating industry". *Federal Reserve Bank of New York Quarterly Review*, Summer–Fall. At: https://www.newyorkfed.org/medialibrary/media/research/quarterly_review/1994v19/v19n2article1.pdf

——— (1996), "Determinants and impact of sovereign credit ratings". *Federal Reserve Bank of New York Economic Policy Review*, 2(1), 37–54.

CAPCO (2013), "The changing role of sovereign credit ratings". February. At: http://www.capco.com/insights/capco-institute/the-changing-role-of-sovereign-credit-ratings.

Cassidy, J. (2013), "The Reinhart and Rogoff controversy: A summing up". *The Economist*, April 26.

CIA (2014), "World Factbook 2014". At: https://www.cia.gov/library/publications/the-world-factbook/fields/2186.html. Accessed January 24, 2016.

Corsetti, G., A. Meier, and G. J. Müller (2012), What determines government spending multipliers?. World Bank WP/12/150. At: https://www.imf.org/external/pubs/ft/wp/2012/wp12150.pdf

Cox, C. (2008), "SEC examinations find shortcomings in credit rating agencies' practices and disclosure to investors". At: https://www.sec.gov/news/press/2008/2008–135.htm.

Council of Foreign Relations (2015), "The credit rating controversy". At :http://www.cfr.org/financial-crises/credit-rating-controversy/p22328

Economictimes (2010), "Issuer-pays model ensures ratings are available to the entire market". At: http://articles.economictimes.indiatimes.com/2010–05–06/news/27585572_1_rating-agencies-downgrades-issuer. Accessed January 23, 2016.

The Economist (2012), "The global debt clock". At: http://www.economist.com/content/global_debt_clock.

——— (2014a), "Usual suspects, Latin American countries are the most likely to default". At: http://www.economist.com/blogs/graphicdetail/2014/07/daily-chart-23.

——— (2014b), "As Argentina ponders its next step, the IMF suggests new rules for broke countries". At: http://www.economist.com/news/finance-and-economics/21605934-argentina-ponders-its-next-step-imf-suggests-new-rules-broke.

——— (2014c), "The Economist explains what happens when a country goes bust". At: http://www.economist.com/blogs/economist-explains.

The Economist (2014d), "Argentina defaults, Eighth time unlucky". At :https://www.google.ca/search?q=Argentina+defaultsEighth+time+unlucky&ie=utf-8&oe=utf-8&client=firefox-b-ab&gfe_rd=cr&ei=Al_oV6u3OYmBqQX85r6oCQ

El Namaki, M. S. S. (2013), "Strategic thinking for turbulent times". *Ivey Business Journal,* 77(1), 1–6.

Faulkender, M. W. and M. A. Petersen (2006), Does the source of capital affect capital structure? *Review of Financial Studies*, 19(4), 45–79.

Ferri, G., L. G. Liu and J. E. Stiglitz (1999), "The procyclical role of rating agencies: Evidence from the East Asian crisis". *Economic Notes by Banca Monte dei Paschi di Siena SpA*, 28(3), 431–432.

Fitch (2010), *Fitch Ratings Global Corporate Finance 2010 Transition and Default Study*. At : https://www.fitchratings.com/jsp/general/login/LoginController.faces

Fitch Ratings (2014), "Sovereign rating criteria". At: https://www.fitchratings.com/credit-desk/reports/report_frame_render.cfm?rpt_id=754428. Accessed January 3, 2016.

Frost, J. (2012), "Why you need to check your residual plots for regression analysis: Or, to err is human, to err randomly is statistically divine". At: http://blog.minitab.com/blog/adventures-in-statistics/why-you-need-to-check-your-residual-plots-for-regression-analysis.

Gaillard, N. (2010), "Les agencies de notation". Repéres Économie Paris.

Gande, A. and D. Parsley (2005), "News spillovers in the sovereign debt market". *Journal of Financial Economics*, 75(3), 691–734.

Gennaioli, N., A. Martin and S. Rossi (2014), "Sovereign default, domestic banks, and financial institutions". *The Journal of Finance*. LXIX, 819–866.

——— Martin and S. Rossi (2015), "Sovereign default, domestic banks, and financial institutions". At: https://www.unibocconi.eu/wps/wcm/connect/4f7066cc-47d6–4d9d-aae6-cd26dacab650/gmr_jf.pdf?MOD=AJPERES.

Gianviti, F., A. O. Kruger, J. Pisani-Ferry, A. Sapir and J. Von (2010), "A European mechanism for sovereign debt crisis resolution: A proposal". *Hagen Bruegel Blueprint Series*.

Grene, S. (2014), "Big 3 credit rating agencies under fire". *Financial Times*. At: http://www.ft.com/intl/cms/s/0/4140e388-cfc1–11e3–9b2b-00144feabdc0.html#axzz3zQBxGmN9.

Hermalin, B. H. and M. S. Weisbach (2007), "Transparency and corporate governance". *NBR Working Papers Series*.

Herndon, T., M. Ash and R. Pollin (2013), "Does high public debt consistently increase economic growth?" *A Critique of Reinhart and Rogo, WP No 322*, University of Massachusetts Amherst, April 15. At: http://www.peri.umass.edu/fileadmin/pdf/working_papers/working_papers_301–350/WP322.pdf. Accessed January 15, 2016.

International Monetary Fund, IMF (2000), "Guidelines for public debt management". *Prepared by the Staffs of IMF and the World Bank*. At: www.imf.org/external/np/mae/pdebt/2000/eng/.

——— (2010), "Global financial stability report: Sovereigns, funding, and systemic liquidity". At: https://www.imf.org/external/pubs/ft/gfsr/2010/02/

——— (2011), "World economic outlook, slowing growth, rising risk." At :http://www.imf.org/external/pubs/ft/weo/2011/02/pdf/text.pdf

——— (2012), "Fiscal transparency, fiscal performance and credit ratings". At:https://www.imf.org/external/pubs/cat/longres.aspx?sk=25996

——— (2013), "Global financial stability report old risks, new challenges", April 2013. At:http://www.imf.org/external/pubs/cat/longres.aspx?sk=40202.

The International Organisation of Securities Commissions, IOSCO (2003), "Report on the activities of credit rating agencies". At: https://www.iosco.org/library/pubdocs/pdf/IOSCOPD153.pdf. Accessed January 6, 2016.

——— (2010), "Principles regarding cross-border supervisory cooperation". At: http://www.iosco.org/library/pubdocs/pdf/IOSCOPD322.pdf.

———, S. Nowak and L. Schumacher (2012), "Are rating agencies powerful? An investigation into the impact and accuracy of sovereign ratings". *IMF Working Paper 12/23*. At: https://www.moodys.com/Pages/amr002002.aspx.

Koopman, S. J., R. Krussl, Lucas and A. B. Monteiro (2009), "Credit cycles and macro fundamentals". *Journal of Empirical Finance*, 16, 42–54.

Kraemer, M. (2014), "Chief sovereign rating officer at S&P". As reported by Grene, 2014.

Kräussl R. (2003), "Do credit rating agencies add to the dynamics of emerging market crises?" *CFS Working Paper No. 2003/18*. http://www.ifk-cfs.de.

Kratzmann, H. (1982), Der Staatsbankrott — Begriff, Erscheinungsformen, Regelung". *Juristenzeitung*, 37(2), 319–325.

Lando, D. and T. M. Skodeberg (2002), "Analyzing rating transitions and rating drift with continuous observations". *Journal of Banking and Finance*, 26(2–3), 423–444.

Lucas, D. and J. Lonski (1992), "Changes in corporate credit quality". *Journal of Fixed Income*, 2(1), 32–41.

Michalski, T. and G. Stoltz (2013), "Countries falsifying economic data: How statistics reveal fraudulent figures". At: http://www.hec.edu/Knowledge/Business-Environment/Macro-economics/Countries-falsifying-economic-data-How-statistics-reveal-fraudulent-figures.

Moody's Investor (2007), Updated Summary Guidance for Notching Bonds, Preferred Stocks and Hybrid Securities of Corporate Issuers. At: https://www.moodys.com/sites/products/AboutMoodysRatingsAttachments/2006400000430106.pdf

——— (2011a), "Core principles for the conduct of rating committees". At: https://www.moodys.com/Pages/atc002.aspx

——— (2011b), "Sovereign default and recovery rates, 1983–2010". (Special comment). At : https://www.moodys.com/Pages/atc002.aspx

——— (2013a), "Moody's statistical handbook country credit May 2013". At: http://alleuropalux.org/fileserver/2013/78/153213.pdf. Accessed January 24, 2016

——— (2013b), "Rating methodology". *Sovereign Bond Ratings*. September 12.

——— (2015), "Rating methodology". *Sovereign Bond Ratings Boot*. At : https://www.moodys.com/Pages/atc002.aspx

Naciri, A. (2015), "Credit rating agencies governance, the global credit gatekeepers". Francis Taylor, London, New York: Routledge.

Nielsen, E. F., G. Vasileios and D. Vernazza et al. (2014), "The damaging bias of sovereign ratings". *UniCredit, Global Themes Series -March*. At: http://www.dt.tesoro.it/export/sites/sitodt/modules/documenti_en/analisi_progammazione/brown_bag/GlobalThemesSeries_26Mar14.pdf.

OECD (2010), "Competition and credit rating agencies". At: https://www.oecd.org/competition/sectors/46825342.pdf

Popovych, Z. (2015), "History of accumulation of the Ukrainian sovereign debt, defaults and its effects on the economic development of the country. Committee for the Abolition of Third World Debt". At: http://cadtm.org/History-of-accumulation-of-the. 9 July.

Reinhart, C. M. and K. S. Rogof (2010), "This time is different: Eight centuries of financial folly". Princeton, NJ: Princeton University Press.

Ryan, J. (2012), "The negative impact of credit rating agencies and proposals for better regulation". *Working Paper FG1SWP*, Berlin.

Securities and Exchange Commission (2012), "Report to congress credit rating standardization study". At: https://www.sec.gov/news/studies/2012/939h_credit_rating_standardization.pdf.

——— (2013), "Summary report of commission staff's examinations of each nationally recognized statistical rating organization". At: https://www.sec.gov/news/studies/2013/nrsro-summary-report-2013.pdf.

——— (2014a), "Annual report on nationally recognized, statistical rating organizations". At: https://www.sec.gov/ocr/reportspubs/annual-reports/nrsroannrep1214.pdf.

——— (2014b), 2014 Summary Report of Commission Staff's Examinations Of Each Nationally Recognized Statistical Rating Organization. At :https://www.sec.gov/ocr/reportspubs/special-studies/nrsro-summary-report-2014.pdf

——— (2015), "2015 summary report of the commission staff's examinations of each nationally recognized statistical rating organization". At: https://www.sec.gov/ocr/reportspubs/special-studies/nrsro-summary-report-2015.pdf.

Sivy, M. (2011), "Why Europe's downgrades matter". *Business Time*. At: http://business.time.com/2011/12/19/why-europes-downgrades-matter/.

Standard & Poor's, S&P (2011a), "Sovereign government rating methodology and assumptions". *Global Credit Portal Ratings Direct*.

——— (2014), "Default, Transition, and Recovery: 2014 Annual Sovereign Default Study And Rating Transitions". At :https://www.standardandpoors.com/en_US/web/guest/article/-/view/sourceId/9160087

Sylla, R. (2001), "A historical primer on the business of credit ratings, conference on the role of credit reporting systems in the international economy". World Bank, March 1–2.

Tyler Durden, T. (2014), "Will Spain default?" At: http://www.zerohedge.com/news/2014–06–11/will-spain-default.

Vernazza, D., F. Nielsen and V. Gkionakis (2014), "The damaging bias of sovereign ratings". *UniCredit Global Themes Series*.

Wall Street Journal (2011), "S&P strips U.S. of top credit rating." At :http://www.wsj.com/articles/SB10001424053111903366504576490841235575386

——— (2015), "Justice department investigating Moody's investors service". At: http://www.wsj.com/articles/justice-department-investigating-moodys-investors-service-1422822296.

White, L. J. (2009), "A brief history of credit rating agencies: How financial regulation entrenched this industry's role in the subprime mortgage debacle of 2007–2008". *Mercatus Center George Mason University WP* 9. At: http://mercatus,org/publication/brief-his to ry-credit-rating-agencies-how-financial-regulation-entrenched-industrys-role.

White, L. J. (2010), "Markets :The Credit Rating Agencies". *Journal of Economic Perspectives*, 24, 211–226.

World Bank data site (2016), http://data.worldbank.org/indicator/DT.DOD.DECT.GN.ZS. Accessed January 16, 2016.

Data appendices A–C

1. Raw data

Most data come from:

Moody's Investors Service (2015), Rating methodology: Sovereign bond ratings

Economic Resiliency: Combination of Economic Strength (F1) & Institutional Strength (F2), Exhibit 4, p. 5.

Government Financial Strength: Combination of Economic Resiliency (F1xF2) & Fiscal Strength (F3), Exhibit 5, p. 6

Rating Range: Combination of Government Financial Strength (F1xF2xF3) & Event Risk (F4), Exhibit 6, p. 6

Moody's Investors Service (2013), Moody's Statistical Handbook Country Credit, May 2013

Beers D. T. and J.-S. Nadeau (2015), Database of Sovereign Defaults 2015. Bank of Canada Technical Report No. 101.

Standard & Poor's Rating Services (Excel data).

Fitch

2. Appendices *A*'s: numerically translated alphabetical factors/combinations

Appendix A1 Numerically translated alphabetical ranking country economic resiliency, $_{n}$*ECORES*: (Combination of Economic Strength in numerical scale, $_{n}$*ECOSTR* & Institutional Strength in numerical scale, $_{n}$*INSSTR*, 50/50 weight)

	Economic strength														
INSTITUTIONAL STRENGTH	VH+	VH	VH−	H+	H	H−	M+	M	M−	L+	L	L−	VL+	VL	VL−
1(1) VH+	1	1	1	2	2	3	3	4	4	5	5	6	6	7	8
2(VH)	1	2	2	3	3	4	4	5	5	6	6	7	7	8	9
3(VH−)	1	2	3	3	4	4	5	5	6	6	7	7	8	8	10
4 (H+)	2	3	3	4	4	5	5	6	6	7	7	8	8	9	10
5 (H)	2	3	4	4	5	5	6	6	7	7	8	8	9	9	11
6 (H−)	3	4	4	5	5	6	6	7	7	8	8	9	9	10	11
7 (M+)	3	4	5	5	6	6	7	7	8	8	9	9	10	10	12
8 (M)	4	5	5	6	6	7	7	8	8	9	9	10	10	11	12
9 (M−)	4	5	6	6	7	7	8	8	9	9	10	10	11	11	13
10(L+)	5	6	6	7	7	8	8	9	9	10	10	11	11	12	13
11 (L)	5	6	7	7	8	8	9	9	10	10	11	11	12	12	14
12 (L−)	6	7	7	8	8	9	9	10	10	11	11	12	12	13	14
13(VL+)	6	7	8	8	9	9	10	10	11	11	12	12	13	13	15
14 (VL)	7	8	8	9	9	10	10	11	11	12	12	13	13	14	15
15(VL−)	8	9	10	10	11	11	12	12	13	13	14	14	15	15	15

Appendix A2 Numerically translated alphabetical ranking of agencies' financial strength, $_{n}$*FINSTR*: (Combination of Fiscal Strength, $_{n}$*FISSTR* and of Economic Resiliency, $_{n}$*ECORES*, based on the following weights: 80/20, 70/30, 60/40, 75/25 and 10/90, successively

		Fiscal strength															
		VH+	VH	VH–	H+	H	H–	M+	M	M–	L+	L	L–	VL+	VL	VL–	Weight ER/FS
ECONOMIC RESILIENCY	VH+	1	1	1	1	1	1	1	1	1	2	2	2	2	2	3	80/20
	VH	2	2	2	2	3	3	3	3	3	4	4	4	4	4	5	
	VH–	2	3	3	3	3	4	4	4	4	4	5	5	5	5	6	
	H+	3	3	4	4	4	5	5	5	6	6	6	6	7	7	8	70/30
	H	3	4	4	5	5	5	6	6	6	6	7	7	7	8	8	
	H–	4	5	5	5	6	6	6	7	7	7	7	8	8	8	9	
	M+	4	5	5	6	6	7	7	7	8	8	9	9	9	10	11	60/40
	M	5	6	6	6	7	7	8	8	8	9	9	10	10	10	11	
	M–	5	6	7	7	7	8	8	9	9	9	10	10	11	11	12	
	L+	7	8	8	8	9	9	9	9	10	10	10	10	11	11	12	75/25
	L	8	9	9	9	9	10	10	10	10	11	11	11	11	12	12	
	L–	9	9	10	10	10	10	11	11	11	11	12	12	12	12	13	
	VL+	12	12	12	12	12	12	12	12	13	13	13	13	13	13	13	90/10
	VL	13	13	13	13	13	13	13	13	13	14	14	14	14	14	14	
	VL–	15	15	15	15	15	15	15	15	15	15	15	15	15	15	15	

Appendix A3 Numerically translated alphabetical agencies' rating range, $_nRATRAN_i$ (*Combination of government financial strength* $_nFINSTR_i$ *& reversed susceptibility to event risk,* $_nSUSRIS$)

SUSCEPTIBILITY to EVENT RISK	*Government financial strength*														
	VH+ Aaa-Aa2	VH Aa1-Aa3	VH− Aa2-A1	H+ Aa3-A2	H A1-A3	H− A2-Baa1	M+ A3-Baa2	M Baa1-Baa2	M− Baa2-Ba1	L+ Baa3-Ba2	L Ba1-Ba3	L− Ba2-B1	VL+ Ba3-B2	VL B1-B3	VL− B2-Caa
1	1	2	3	4	5	6	7	8	9	10	11	15	13	14	15
2	1	2	3	4	5	6	7	8	9	10	11	15	13	14	15
3	1	2	3	4	5	6	7	8	9	10	11	15	13	14	15
4	1	2	3	4	5	6	8	9	10	11	12	13	14	15	16
5	1	2	3	4	5	6	8	9	10	11	12	13	14	15	16
6	1	2	3	4	5	6	8	9	10	12	13	14	15	16	17
7	2	3	4	5	6	7	9	10	11	12	13	14	15	16	17
8	2	3	4	5	6	7	9	10	11	13	14	15	16	17	18
9	3	4	5	6	7	8	10	11	12	13	14	15	16	17	18
10	3	4	5	6	7	8	10	11	12	14	15	16	17	18	18
11	4	5	6	7	8	9	11	12	13	14	15	16	17	18	18
12	4	5	6	7	8	9	11	12	13	15	16	17	18	18	18
13	5	6	7	8	9	10	12	13	14	15	16	17	18	18	18
14	5	6	7	8	9	10	12	13	14	16	17	18	18	18	18
15	6	7	8	9	10	11	13	14	15	16	17	18	18	18	18

3. Appendices *B*'s: restated numerically translated factors/combinations

Appendix B1 Restated numerical translated country economic resiliency, $r_n ECORES_i$ (*Combination of Economic Strength, $r_n ECOSTR_i$ & Institutional Strength, $r_n INSSTR_i$, 50/50 weight*)

ECONOMIC EFFICIENCY			*Economomic strength*														
			VH+	*VH*	*VH−*	*H+*	*H*	*H−*	*M+*	*M*	*M−*	*L+*	*L*	*L−*	*VL+*	*VL*	*VL−*
			1	2	3	4	5	6	7	8	9	10	11	12	13	14	15
	VH+	1	1	1.5	2	2.5	3	3.5	4	4.5	5	5.5	6	6.5	7	7.5	8
	VH	2	1.5	2	2.5	3	3.5	4	4.5	5	5.5	6	6.5	7	7.5	8	8.5
	VH−	3	2	2.5	3	3.5	4	4.5	5	5.5	6	6.5	7	7.5	8	8.5	9
	H+	4	2.5	3	3.5	4	4.5	5	5.5	6	6.5	7	7.5	8	8.5	9	9.5
	H	5	3	3.5	4	4.5	5	5.5	6	6.5	7	7.5	8	8.5	9	9.5	10
	H−	6	3.5	4	4.5	5	5.5	6	6.5	7	7.5	8	8.5	9	9.5	10	10.5
	M+	7	4	4.5	5	5.5	6	6.5	7	7.5	8	8.5	9	9.5	10	10.5	11
	M	8	4.5	5	5.5	6	6.5	7	7.5	8	8.5	9	9.5	10	10.5	11	11.5
	M−	9	5	5.5	6	6.5	7	7.5	8	8.5	9	9.5	10	10.5	11	11.5	12
	L+	10	5.5	6	6.5	7	7.5	8	8.5	9	9.5	10	10.5	11	11.5	12	12.5
	L	11	6	6.5	7	7.5	8	8.5	9	9.5	10	10.5	11	11.5	12	12.5	13
	L−	12	6.5	7	7.5	8	8.5	9	9.5	10	10.5	11	11.5	12	12.5	13	13.5
	VL+	13	7	7.5	8	8.5	9	9.5	10	10.5	11	11.5	12	12.5	13	13.5	14
	VL	14	7.5	8	8.5	9	9.5	10	10.5	11	11.5	12	12.5	13	13.5	14	14.5
	VL−	15	8	8.5	9	9.5	10	10.5	11	11.5	12	12.5	13	13.5	14	14.5	15

Appendix B2 Restated numerically translated government financial strength. $r_n FINSTR_i$ (Combination of Economic Resiliency. $r_n ECORES_i$ & Fiscal Strength. $r_n FISSTR_i$)

			Fiscal strength (FS)															
ECONOMIC RESILIENCY (ER)			VH+ 1	VH 2	VH− 3	H+ 4	H 5	H− 6	M+ 7	M 8	M− 9	L+ 10	L 11	L− 12	VL+ 13	VL 14	VL− 15	Weigh. ER/FS
	VH+	1	1	1.8	2.6	3.4	4.2	5	5.8	6.6	7.4	8.2	9.2	10	10.8	11.6	12.4	
	VH	2	1.2	1.2	1.2	1.2	1.2	1.4	1.4	1.4	1.4	2.2	2.4	2.4	2.4	2.4	3.2	80/20
	VH−	3	2.2	2	2.2	2.2	3	3	3.2	3.2	3.2	4	4	4.2	4.2	4.2	5	
	H+	4	2.6	3	3	3.3	3.3	4	4.3	4.3	4.3	4.6	5.3	5.3	5.3	5.6	6.3	
	H	5	3.6	3	4	4	4.3	5	5	5.3	6	6	6	6.3	7	7	8	70/30
	H−	6	3.9	4	4.3	5	5	5.3	6	6	6.3	6.3	7	7	7.3	8	8	
	M+	7	5.2	4.6	5	5	6	6	6.4	7	7	7.4	7.4	8.4	8.4	8.4	9.4	
	M	8	5.6	5	5.4	6	6	7	7	7.4	8	8	9	9	9.4	10	10.6	60/40
	M−	9	6.6	5.6	6	6.4	7	7	8	8	8.4	9	9	10	10	10.4	11	
	L+	10	6.25	6.25	7.25	7.25	7.25	8.25	8.25	9	9	9.25	10	10	10.75	11	11.75	
	L	11	8	8	8.25	8.25	9	9	9.25	9.25	10	10	10.25	10.25	11	11	12	75/25
	L−	12	9	9	9	9.25	9.25	10	10	10.25	10.25	11	11	11.25	11.25	12	12	
	VL+	13	12.6	11.7	11.8	11.8	11.8	11.8	11.9	11.9	11.9	12.8	12.9	12.9	12.9	12.9	13	
	VL	14	13.8	12.9	12.9	12.9	12.9	12.9	12.9	12.9	13	13	13.9	13.9	13.9	13.9	13.9	90/10
	VL−	15	14.8	14.8	14.8	14.8	14.8	14.8	14.8	14.8	14.8	14.9	14.9	14.9	14.9	14.9	14.9	

Appendix B3 Restated numerical translated country rating range. $r_n SUSRIS_i$ (*Reversed susceptibility to event risk*)

			Government financial strength														
S			*Aaa-*	*Aa1-*	*Aa2-*	*Aa3-*	*A1-*	*A2-*	*A3-*	*Baa1-*	*Baa2-*	*Baa3-*	*Ba1-*	*Ba2-*	*Ba3-*	*B1-*	*B2-*
U			*Aa2*	*Aa3*	*A1*	*A2*	*A3*	*Baa1*	*Baa2*	*Baa3*	*Ba1*	*Ba2*	*Ba3*	*B1*	*B2*	*B3*	*Caa*
S			1	2	3	4	5	6	7	8	9	10	11	12	13	14	15
C	VL−	1	1.0	1.5	2.0	2.5	3.0	3.5	4.0	4.5	5.0	5.5	6.0	6.5	7.0	7.5	8.0
E	VL	2	1.5	2.0	2.5	3.0	3.5	4.0	4.5	5.0	5.5	6.0	6.5	7.0	7.5	8.0	8.5
P	VL+	3	2.0	2.5	3.0	3.5	4.0	4.5	5.0	5.5	6.0	6.5	7.0	7.5	8.0	8.5	9.0
T	L−	4	2.5	3.0	3.5	4.0	4.5	5.0	5.5	6.0	6.5	7.0	7.5	8.0	8.5	9.0	9.5
I	L	5	3.0	3.5	4.0	4.5	5.0	5.5	6.0	6.5	7.0	7.5	8.0	8.5	9.0	9.5	10
B	L=	6	3.5	4.0	4.5	5.0	5.5	6.0	6.5	7.0	7.5	8.0	8.5	9.0	9.5	10.0	11
I	M−	7	4.0	4.5	5.0	5.5	6.0	6.5	7.0	7.5	8.0	8.5	9.0	9.5	10.0	10.5	11
L	M	8	4.5	5.0	5.5	6.0	6.5	7.0	7.5	8.0	8.5	9.0	9.5	10.0	10.5	11.0	12
I	M+	9	5.0	5.5	6.0	6.5	7.0	7.5	8.0	8.5	9.0	9.5	10.0	10.5	11.0	11.5	12
T	H−	10	5.5	6.0	6.5	7.0	7.5	8.0	8.5	9.0	9.5	10.0	10.5	11.0	11.5	12.0	13
Y	H	11	6.0	6.5	7.0	7.5	8.0	8.5	9.0	9.5	10.0	10.5	11.0	11.5	12.0	12.5	13
to	H+	12	6.5	7.0	7.5	8.0	8.5	9.0	9.5	10.0	10.5	11.0	11.5	12.0	12.5	13.0	14
Event	VH−	13	7.0	7.5	8.0	8.5	9.0	9.5	10.0	10.5	11.0	11.5	12.0	12.5	13.0	13.5	14
risk	VH	14	7.5	8.0	8.5	9.0	9.5	10.0	10.5	11.0	11.5	12.0	12.5	13.0	13.5	14.0	15
	VH+	15	8.0	8.5	9.0	9.5	10.0	10.5	11.0	11.5	12.0	12.5	13.0	13.5	14.0	14.5	15

4. Appendices *C*'s: differences between translated and restated agencies data

Appendix C1 DIFFERENCES BETWEEN CURRENT AND RESTATED ECONOMIC RESILIENCY, 50/50 WEIGHT ($C_1 = A_1 - B_1$) (*ECORES*)

			Economic strength														
E			VH+	VH	VH−	H+	H	H−	M+	M	M−	L+	L	L−	VL+	VL	VL−
C			1	2	3	4	5	6	7	8	9	10	11	12	13	14	15
O	VH+	1	0	0.5	1.0	0.5	1	0.5	1	0.5	1	0.5	1	0.5	1	0.5	0
N	VH	2	0.5	0	0.5	0	0.5	0	0.5	0	0.5	0	0.5	0	0.5	0	−0.5
O	VH−	3	1	0.5	0	0.5	0	0.5	0	0.5	0	0.5	0	0.5	0	0.5	−1
M	H+	4	0.5	0	0.5	0	0.5	0	0.5	0	0.5	0	0.5	0	0.5	0	−0.5
I	H	5	1	0.5	0	0.5	0	0.5	0	0.5	0	0.5	0	0.5	0	0.5	−1
C	H−	6	0.5	0	0.5	0	0.5	0	0.5	0	0.5	0	0.5	0	0.5	0	−0.5
E	M+	7	1	0.5	0	0.5	0	0.5	0	0.5	0	0.5	0	0.5	0	0.5	−1
F	M	8	0.5	0	0.5	0	0.5	0	0.5	0	0.5	0	0.5	0	0.5	0	−0.5
F	M−	9	1	0.5	0	0.5	0	0.5	0	0.5	0	0.5	0	0.5	0	0.5	−1
I	L+	10	0.5	0	0.5	0	0.5	0	0.5	0	0.5	0	0.5	0	0.5	0	−0.5
C	L	11	1	0.5	0	0.5	0	0.5	0	0.5	0	0.5	0	0.5	0	0.5	−1
I	L−	12	0.5	0	0.5	0	0.5	0	0.5	0	0.5	0	0.5	0	0.5	0	−0.5
E	VL+	13	1	0.5	0	0.5	0	0.5	0	0.5	0	0.5	0	0.5	0	0.5	−1
N	VL	14	0.5	0	0.5	0	0.5	0	0.5	0	0.5	0	0.5	0	0.5	0	−0.5
C	VL−	15	0	−0.5	−1	−0.5	−1	−0.5	−1	−0.5	−1	−0.5	−1	−0.5	−1	−0.5	0
Y																	

Appendix C2 DIFFERENCES BETWEEN CURRENT AND RESTATED GOVERNMENT FINANCIAL STRENGTH ($C_2 = A_2 - B_2$) (*FINSTR*)

			Financial srength															
			VH+	VH	VH−	H+	H	H−	M+	M	M−	L+	L	L−	VL+	VL	VL−	Weigh. ER/FS
E			1	2	3	4	5	6	7	8	9	10	11	12	13	14	15	
C	VH+	1	0	0.8	1.6	2.4	3.2	4	4.8	5.6	6.4	6.2	7.2	8	8.8	9.6	9.4	80/20
O	VH	2	−0.8	−0.8	−0.8	−0.8	−1.8	−1.6	−1.6	−1.6	−1.6	−1.8	−1.6	−1.6	−1.6	−1.6	−1.8	
N	VH−	3	0.2	−1	−0.8	−0.8	4.44089E-	−1	−0.8	−0.8	−0.8	0	−1	−0.8	−0.8	−0.8	−1	
O							16											
M	H+	4	−0.4	−4.44089E-	−1	−0.7	−0.7	−1	−0.7	−0.7	−1.7	−1.4	−0.7	−0.7	−1.7	−1.4	−1.7	
I				16														70/30
C	H	5	0.6	−1	0	−1	−0.7	0	−1	−0.7	−8.88178E-	−8.88178E-	−1	−0.7	0	−1	0	
R											16	16						
E	H−	6	−0.1	−1	−0.7	0	−1	−0.7	−8.88178E-	−1	−0.7	−0.7	0	−1	−0.7	0	−1	
S									16									
I	M+	7	1.2	−0.4	0	−1	0	−1	−0.6	0	−1	−0.6	−1.6	−0.6	−0.6	−1.6	−1.6	
L	M	8	0.6	−1	−0.6	0	−1	0	−1	−0.6	0	−1	0	−1	−0.6	0	−0.4	60/40
I	M−	9	1.6	−0.4	−1	−0.6	0	−1	0	−1	−0.6	0	−1	0	−1	−0.6	−1	
E	L+	10	−0.75	−1.75	−0.75	−0.75	−1.75	−0.75	−0.75	0	−1	−0.75	0	0	−0.25	0	−0.25	
N	L	11	0	−1	−0.75	−0.75	0	−1	−0.75	−0.75	0	−1	−0.75	−0.75	0	−1	0	75/25
C	L−	12	0	0	−1	−0.75	−0.75	0	−1	−0.75	−0.75	0	−1	−0.75	−0.75	0	−1	
Y	VH+	1	0	0.8	1.6	2.4	3.2	4	4.8	5.6	6.4	6.2	7.2	8	8.8	9.6	9.4	
	VH	2	−0.8	−0.8	−0.8	−0.8	−1.8	−1.6	−1.6	−1.6	−1.6	−1.8	−1.6	−1.6	−1.6	−1.6	−1.8	
	VH−	3	0.2	−1	−0.8	−0.8	4.44089E-	−1	−0.8	−0.8	−0.8	0	−1	−0.8	−0.8	−0.8	−1	90/10
							16											

Appendix C3 DIFFERENCES BETWEEN CURRENT AND RESTATED GOVERNMENT BOND RATING RANGE ($C_3 = A_3 - B_3$) (*RATRAN*)

			Government financial strength														
S			Aaa-	Aa1-	Aa2-	Aa3-	A1-	A2-	A3-	Baa1-	Baa2-	Baa3-	Ba1-	Ba2-	Ba3-	B1-	B2-
U			Aa2	Aa3	A1	A2	A3	Baa1	Baa2	Baa3	Ba1	Ba2	Ba3	B1	B2	B3	Caa
S			1	2	3	4	5	6	7	8	9	10	11	12	13	14	15
C	VL−	1	0	−0.5	−1	−1.5	−2	−2.5	−3	−3.5	−4	−4.5	−5	−8.5	−6	−6.5	−7
E	VL	2	0.5	0	−0.5	−1	−1.5	−2	−2.5	−3	−3.5	−4	−4.5	−8	−5.5	−6	−6.5
P	VL+	3	1	0.5	0	−0.5	−1	−1.5	−2	−2.5	−3	−3.5	−4	−7.5	−5	−5.5	−6
T	L−	4	1.5	1	0.5	0	−0.5	−1	−2.5	−3	−3.5	−4	−4.5	−5	−5.5	−6	−6.5
I	L	5	2	1.5	1	0.5	0	−0.5	−2	−2.5	−3	−3.5	−4	−4.5	−5	−5.5	−6
B	L=	6	2.5	2	1.5	1	0.5	0	−1.5	−2	−2.5	−4	−4.5	−5	−5.5	−6	−6.5
I	M−	7	2	1.5	1	0.5	0	−0.5	−2	−2.5	−3	−3.5	−4	−4.5	−5	−5.5	−6
L	M	8	2.5	2	1.5	1	0.5	0	−1.5	−2	−2.5	−4	−4.5	−5	−5.5	−6	−6.5
I	M+	9	2	1.5	1	0.5	0	−0.5	−2	−2.5	−3	−3.5	−4	−4.5	−5	−5.5	−6
T	H−	10	2.5	2	1.5	1	0.5	0	−1.5	−2	−2.5	−4	−4.5	−5	−5.5	−6	−5.5
Y	H	11	2	1.5	1	0.5	0	−0.5	−2	−2.5	−3	−3.5	−4	−4.5	−5	−5.5	−5
to	H+	12	2.5	2	1.5	1	0.5	0	−1.5	−2	−2.5	−4	−4.5	−5	−5.5	−5	−4.5
E	VH−	13	2	1.5	1	0.5	0	−0.5	−2	−2.5	−3	−3.5	−4	−4.5	−5	−4.5	−4
V	VH	14	2.5	2	1.5	1	0.5	0	−1.5	−2	−2.5	−4	−4.5	−5	−4.5	−4	−3.5
E	VH−	15	−2	−1.5	−1	−0.5	0	0.5	2	2.5	3	3.5	4	4.5	4	3.5	3
N																	
T																	
Risk																	

Figure ??

Index

For Product Safety Concerns and Information please contact our EU representative GPSR@taylorandfrancis.com
Taylor & Francis Verlag GmbH, Kaufingerstraße 24, 80331 München, Germany

www.ingramcontent.com/pod-product-compliance
Ingram Content Group UK Ltd.
Pitfield, Milton Keynes, MK11 3LW, UK
UKHW020951180425
457613UK00019B/617

* 9 7 8 0 3 6 7 8 7 8 8 4 9 *